48

The Future of Gender

'Gender' is used to classify humans and to explain their behaviour in predominantly social rather than biological terms. But how useful is the concept of gender in social analysis? To what degree does gender relate to sex? How does gender feature in shifts in familial structures and demography? How should gender be conceived in terms of contemporary inequality and injustice, and what is gender's function in the design and pursuit of political objectives? In this volume a collection of international experts from the fields of political philosophy, political theory, sociology, economics, law, psychoanalysis and evolutionary psychology scrutinise the conceptual effectiveness of gender both as a mode of analysis and as a basis for envisioning the transformation of society. Each contributor considers how gender might be conceived in contemporary terms, offering a variety of (often conflicting) interpretations of the concept's usefulness for the future.

Jude Browne is a Nuffield Foundation Fellow at the Centre for Research in the Arts, Social Sciences and Humanities, a Director of the Cambridge University Centre for Gender Studies and a Fellow in Social and Political Sciences at Downing College, University of Cambridge.

The Future of Gender

Edited by

JUDE BROWNE

CAMBRIDGE
UNIVERSITY PRESS

CAMBRIDGE UNIVERSITY PRESS
Cambridge, New York, Melbourne, Madrid, Cape Town, Singapore, São Paulo

Cambridge University Press
The Edinburgh Building, Cambridge CB2 8RU, UK

Published in the United States of America by Cambridge University Press, New York

www.cambridge.org
Information on this title: www.cambridge.org/9780521697255

© Cambridge University Press 2007

This publication is in copyright. Subject to statutory exception
and to the provisions of relevant collective licensing agreements,
no reproduction of any part may take place without
the written permission of Cambridge University Press.

First published 2007

Printed in the United Kingdom at the University Press, Cambridge

A catalogue record for this publication is available from the British Library

Library of Congress Cataloguing in Publication data

Browne, Jude.
  The Future of Gender / edited by Jude Browne.
      p.   cm.
  Includes bibliographical references and index.

    ISBN 13: 978-0-521-87441-0 (hardback)
    ISBN 13: 978-0-521-69725-5 (paperback)

1. Sex role. 2. Gender identity 3. Equality. 4. Social justice.
5. Feminist theory. I. Title

HQ1075.B77 2007
305.4201–dc22   2007003514

    ISBN 978-0-521-87441-0 hardback
    ISBN 978-0-521-69725-5 paperback

Cambridge University Press has no responsibility for the persistence or
accuracy of URLs for external or third-party internet websites referred to
in this publication, and does not guarantee that any content on such
websites is, or will remain, accurate or appropriate.

Contents

Figure

Tables

Contributors

Simon Baron-Cohen, Professor of Developmental Psychopathology, University of Cambridge, and Fellow, Trinity College

Jude Browne, Nuffield Fellow, Centre for Research in Arts, Social Sciences and Humanities, University of Cambridge, and Fellow, Downing College

Valerie Bryson, Professor of Politics, University of Huddersfield

Terrell Carver, Professor of Political Theory, University of Bristol

Rosemary Crompton, Professor of Sociology, City University

Nancy Fraser, Henry A. and Louise Loeb Professor of Politics and Philosophy, New School University

Catherine Hakim, Senior Research Fellow in Sociology, London School of Economics

Susan Hurley, Professor of Philosophy, Bristol University, and Fellow, All Souls College, Oxford

Tony Lawson, Reader in Economics, University of Cambridge

Juliet Mitchell, Professor of Psychoanalysis and Gender Studies, University of Cambridge, and Fellow, Jesus College

Ingrid Robeyns, Research Fellow in Political Theory, University of Amsterdam

Acknowledgements

I thank the Nuffield Foundation for funding my research and Bob Hepple, my academic mentor during the period I put this book together. I am particularly grateful to Marc Stears with whom I worked on the original ideas for this edition and who put in a great deal of time and effort at the early stages of its development. I am also indebted to Daniel Beer for helping me to craft the final version and to Umar Salam for commenting on several drafts. I would also like to thank John Haslam and Richard Fisher at Cambridge University Press for being incredibly supportive and giving invaluable guidance.

Introduction

THIS BOOK offers an analysis of the conceptual efficacy of 'gender', both as a mode of analysis and as a basis for envisioning the emancipatory transformation of society. It should be pointed out at once, however, that whilst its title suggests that 'gender' has a future, not all the volume's contributors are persuaded that this is the case.

Today, the terms 'gender' and 'sex' are deployed indiscriminately – or, to be more precise, 'gender' is increasingly being used to cover both terms. It is, then, worth re-establishing the traditional difference between the two concepts. As proselytized from the late 1960s, 'sex' is deemed a category of analysis which relates to the identification of an individual by biological endowments and functions. 'Gender' is concerned with the ascription of social characteristics such as 'womanly', 'manly', 'feminine' and 'masculine', all of which can be seen as culturally variable and not necessarily associated with the sex of an individual. Whilst this distinction is admittedly rough around the edges, its general acceptance since the 1970s has heralded a rare, albeit minimal, consensus across mainstream academia: that the concept of sex is inadequate for the description of social identities. Previously, 'sex' invoked an analysis of men and women based upon an a priori set of assumptions about how each sex behaves. In an attempt to overcome what was seen as cultural bias, the term 'gender' was introduced as a way of classifying individuals socially rather than just biologically. The ramifications of this ostensibly obvious point have been profound and have remained the object of fierce intellectual and ideological conflict.

Post-modern theories of subjectivity and identity have attacked early theorizing and interpretations of 'gender' for relying on a binary account of either 'male' or 'female'. Instead, the post-modernists sought to destabilize the notion of gender by insisting upon a spectrum of fluid identities. This view has in turn been hugely complicated by the development of radical new technologies in sex reassignment and reproduction techniques. Moreover, in a related attack on the universalizing claims of the gender binary, many have criticized the concept for its homogenization of female experience pitted against a singular understanding of oppression, discrimination and patriarchy. Such descriptions and analyses of gender have largely been generated by white, liberal, relatively wealthy women whose range of experience is inadequate to appreciate the multiple faces of subjugation. Consequently there have been many challenges to the imposition of predominantly western norms on a wide variety of multicultural, racial, ethnic, religious and socio-economic groups and their various social relations, roles, living conditions, beliefs and practices.

However, these principally cultural analyses, which quickly embraced methodologies from across the social sciences and humanities, have themselves recently been challenged by what we might term a rein-vigoration of 'the biology of gender'. New theories from the natural sciences and the field of evolutionary psychology are emerging to confront the standard late twentieth-century view of how 'gender' and 'sex' relate, demanding instead that we revisit the possibility that 'gendered behaviour' is biologically derived.

At the core of 'gender analysis' is a concern with unjust inequalities between men and women. One only needs to scan the mission statements of major international bodies such as the United Nations and the European Union to find 'gender equality' stated as a principal political objective. Of course, enormous progress has been made regarding the situation of women who profit from the highly sophisticated legal and political structures of western democracies. Under the individualist liberal doctrine of equal rights, men and women alike are, in principle at least, protected from prejudicial treatment. However, whilst the fruits of this hegemonic construc-tion have been hailed by some as emancipatory, to others they serve to obfuscate patterns of injustice and group discrimination. Even within such progressive environments, substantive equality remains elusive in everyday life as men and women fail to enjoy equal rights and privileges in practice: unrelenting pay gaps between men and women in employment; persistent institutional stereotyping and bigotry; the under-representation of women in decision-making and authoritative positions; the difficulties faced in seeking to reconcile professional and family responsibilities. All these, as features of modern society, show that a multitude of systemic inequalities and injustices between men and women remain deeply entrenched.

In the advent of new technological, methodological, theoretical and social advances then, we return to vital questions for gender analysis. One primary challenge is to decide whether any innate differences between men and women should be accepted as legitimately causing naturally unequal social outcomes. If so, should these outcomes be celebrated or compensated for through social engineering? If, however, various differences between the sexes are considered negligible and not justifying substantially different social outcomes for each, then we are faced with what must be institutional prejudices and discriminatory traditions as the causes of inequality, and ought to orientate our political practices accordingly.

To what degree does 'gender' in fact relate to sex? How useful is the concept of 'gender' in social analysis? How does 'gender' feature in shifts in familial structures and demography? How should we conceive of 'gender' in terms of contemporary inequality and injustice? What is 'gender's' function in the design and pursuit of political objectives? These are the essential questions to which ten thinkers, who together span the disciplines of evolutionary psychology, psychoanalysis, sociology, socio-economics, socio-legal studies, social theory, political theory and political philosophy, apply themselves and offer their interventions.

Structure of the book

Part I of the book, 'Reorienting the feminist imagination', contains three essays, by Nancy Fraser, Valerie Bryson and Ingrid Robeyns, which consider the failings of previous feminist imaginations and consequently offer quite contrasting future theoretical orientations for the pursuit of 'gender justice'. The authors in Part II, 'Variations on the theme of gender', Simon Baron-Cohen, Susan Hurley, Terrell Carver, Tony Lawson and Juliet Mitchell, offer provocative and conflicting perspectives on the challenges which face traditional understandings of 'sex' and 'gender'. Finally, Part III, 'Gender and political practice', consists of essays by Catherine Hakim, Rosemary Crompton and Jude Browne, who examine the various implications for public policy of different understandings of 'gender' and offer some radically divergent views on why men and women experience such dissimilar social outcomes.

Part I: Reorienting the feminist imagination

The book begins with Nancy Fraser's assertion that there has been a 'major shift in the geography of feminist energies'. Her claim that the cutting edge of gender analysis has migrated from the USA to Europe has considerable implications for how we conceive of the whole topic and how we might reinvent some of the core elements of feminism in order to secure 'gender equality' and justice in the contemporary age of globalization. Fraser introduces us to a new 'practical mapping' for how to proceed. In setting the context, she divides the post-war feminist imaginations into three major phases. The first is that of the New Social Movements of the 1960s in which feminism joined the various collectives of marginalized social categories demanding inclusion in the egalitarian objectives of welfare stateism. The second is that of identity politics, pioneered in the USA, which dominated the intellectual hub of feminism for two decades from the end of the 1980s. The final phase, to which Fraser commits her own allegiance and designs of future 'gender justice', is that of 'trans-national politics', which emerged post 9/11. This phase, she argues, is the only possible site of substantive progress in that it has the actual capacity to transcend and overturn habitual biases within modern territorial state traditions entrenched in gendered stereotypes and unaccommo-dating historical legacies. Throughout the chapter, Fraser charts how feminists turned away from redistribution-centred economic reform, which she identifies as an 'indispensable dimension of a feminist politics', and instead concentrated on recognition and identity politics. This approach waned, however, in the shadow of increasing capitalistic atomization, continued economic retrenchment policies and a revival of conservative family values (as typified in the recent spread of evangelicalism in the USA). According to Fraser, only a vision which encompasses the renovation and synthesizing of both redistribution and recognition together with a new form of representation at the trans-national level can provide the necessary mechanisms and objectives for 'gender justice' in what she terms the contemporary 'post-socialist' order.

Valerie Bryson's chapter provides a critique of hegemonic western liberal movements which, she argues, have firmly cast individual equal rights as the response to issues of inequality. Claiming such rights as fundamentally androcentric, she insists that nothing less than a resuscitation of specific elements of radical feminism, in particular the concept of 'patriarchy', can provide an effective view of present-day gender relations. Bryson suggests that this approach, in combination with a return to socialist and Marxist analyses of societal relations, is, albeit unsavoury to some, the only route to securing 'gender equality'. If we are to take equality as a serious and genuine societal goal, she argues, we must accept that current liberal strategies will unequivocally fail to secure the necessary steps towards it. Bryson recognizes that the concept of patriarchy has become rather unfashionable, but in reconceptualizing it, not as a conscious collective project on the part of men to subordinate women, but rather as a descriptive device which enables an accurate explanation of the status quo, she reintroduces 'patriarchy' to the centre stage of 'gender equality analysis'. She describes how the largely unchallenged focus on liberal rights discourse has obscured patriarchy and the discriminatory repercussions it harbours. Without conceiving of liberal societal workings through the lens of patriarchy, she asserts that we cannot help but be seduced by the idea that any unequal outcomes apparent between the sexes are a consequence of choice, merit or luck. Inevitably then, we are likely to conclude that such outcomes, set against a backdrop of equal rights, must be justified. This doctrine is what Bryson refers to with irony as 'common sense', which she asserts is by far the dominant thinking in liberal democracies. In a Marxist vein, Bryson argues that 'common sense' renders people incapable of recognizing societal inequality and discrimination which are not in fact, as 'common sense' would lead us to believe, merely a sequence of unfortunate individual experiences, but are rather instantiations of systematic 'gender injustice'. Bryson not only calls for an alternative analysis of 'gender equality' through a reinterpreted notion of patriarchy, but also demands that certain activities which cause gendered divisions, such as responsibility for domestic work, be redefined as social responsibilities and not purely as the consequences of private choices. Despite emphasizing widespread policies of welfare state retrenchment and the common demise of socialist objectives, she concludes by explaining how such a redefinition is not beyond our current and plausible political reach.

Ingrid Robeyns presents an innovative account of 'gender justice', based on Amartya Sen's capability approach. The capability approach is one which prescribes that individuals should be free to pursue certain 'functionings' – this means that one has the freedom to be and to do something one has good reason to consider worth 'being' and 'doing'. Capabilities then are the full sets of functionings one identifies as being the composite parts of the life one has good reason to consider living. As a metric of well-being the capability approach is an equal-opportunity-based approach which is able to focus on the individual in a way that is particular to needs and preferences rather than assuming 'well-being' by extraneous or aggregate measures such as household income, for example, which may not be distributed satisfactorily between individual inhabitants. Similarly, a simple comparison of men's and women's pay does not, in and of itself, tell us anything about an individual's real freedom to live satisfactorily.

Sen's 'conversion factors' are social, personal and environmental factors which affect the way in which one is able to convert one's resources, such as educational degrees and professional or social skills, into desired capabilities. Robeyn identifies 'gender' as such a conversion factor and illustrates its relationship to social norms, stereotypes, identities and social institutions. In so doing, she argues that stereotypes and social norms reinforce gender inequalities and gendered behaviour which in turn render women's position in society structurally weaker than men's. In this way she describes how we should consider 'gender' as morally relevant when constructing political strategies to eradicate injustice.

Robeyns introduces three principles to the capability approach without the fulfilment of which, she argues, a society cannot become 'gender just'. These principles are first, that the capability sets for men and women should be equal except for inequalities that are due to sex differences, not gender differences, and cannot be rectified by human intervention. Second, constraints on individuals' choices from the capability set should not be structured according to 'morally irrelevant characteristics' such as 'gender'. And third, 'pay-offs' of different options in the capability set must not be 'gender biased'.

In applying these principles along the lines of an opportunity-based capability approach to inequality Robeyns asserts that even in progressive democracies we are far from achieving 'gender just' societies, and offers a mechanism by which to proceed in the future.

Part II: Variations on the theme of gender

In the fourth chapter, Simon Baron-Cohen explicates his new theory, based in evolutional psychology, about the essential differences between the average male and female brain. Although his approach is scientific, he presents the empathizing-systemizing theory (E-S) in a highly accessible way to those outside the field of experimental psychology. Writing from the perspective that 'the pendulum has settled sensibly in the middle of the nature–nurture debate', Baron-Cohen emphatically denies claims of crude essentialism. Rather, his aim is to establish that behaviour and psychology are products not *only* of experience but *also* of biology. Based on psycho-physiological research on humans, he proposes that 'the female brain is predominantly hard-wired for empathy and that the male brain is predominantly hard-wired for understanding and building systems'. The proclivity to 'empathize' describes the ability to classify another person's emotions and to respond to them appositely (brain type E). 'Systemizing' is epitomized by the compulsion to explore systems and to deduce their laws, rules and mechanisms (brain type S). Baron-Cohen is adamant that the brain type cannot be assumed merely by the sex of an individual, as not all men possess brain type S, nor all females brain type E. The E-S theory is strictly one of averages which relies upon the premise that 'more males than females have a brain of type S and more females than males have a brain of type E'.

Crucially however, Baron-Cohen infers from his results that unless we are prepared to administer strict interventionist policy mechanisms which would impede a form of natural selection (such as a 50 per cent quota system for each occupation) we should not expect the sex ratio in certain jobs like professional mathematician or physicist ever to be equal. This is a claim from which the social, political and philosophical interpretations of inequality, such as those related to occupational sex segregation and in particular the perennial pay gap between men and women, have long shied away. Within the context of this volume, Baron-Cohen attempts to carve out an analytic space in which the importance of biology in creating different drives in the average male and female mind can be legitimately assessed and compared to other competing views.

Susan Hurley considers how we might address 'gender justice' by turning to the tensions between evolutionary psychology and main-stream feminism. She offers a rare feminist reading of standard views in evolutionary psychology for the purpose of investigating how they might be of use for understanding the nature of sex and consequently the construction of 'gender'.

Particularly in light of dramatic increases in marital instability over recent decades, Hurley asks whether contemporary western familial structures and social policies are currently constructed along the right lines. Hurley claims that feminists, preoccupied with the political deconstruction of patriarchal social orderings, should turn to 'nature' as a source of inspiration for devising innovative policies which would genuinely serve gender equality and justice. In her article she highlights research in the field of evolutionary psychology which shows how the human pattern of social monogamy is extremely rare and unstable in nature and how, in order for it to survive, it must be culturally constructed and supported. Nature, on the other hand, provides a great variety of alternative stable reproductive patterns from which, Hurley argues, feminists can learn a great deal. On contemplating how monogamy enforces sexual equality among materially unequal men in societies that are so inegalitarian in other respects, Hurley questions the widespread institutional endorsement of the monogamous model and calls for a reconsideration of present and future societal ideals. In particular, she asks whether unconventional familial structures might be better suited to our present-day circumstances which have been marked by dramatic increases in marital instability. Her argument has radical implications for policy design; for example, a move towards a polygamous society might herald the separation of the social institu-tion of childrearing from private sexual relations. Ultimately, Hurley argues that evolutionary psychology is not necessarily an enemy of feminism, in the way suggested by a traditional opposition between sex as nature and gender as nurture, and that we should seek to embrace some of its insights in order best to navigate some of the revolutionary social changes of the new century.

Terrell Carver's chapter focuses on the ways in which pioneering scientific developments impact on the future of gender as a category of analysis. Along post-modernist lines, he argues that the emergence of trans-sexual technologies and trans-gender identities has become profoundly troublesome, if not fatal, for the concept of 'gender' altogether.

Carver suggests that, in all modern societies, the standard ethical discourse presupposes and reproduces a particular conception of the individual (the ethical subject) which is essentially deficient. He argues that binary or stable concepts of sexuality, or purported biological certainties about the relationship between individuals and reproduction, or even 'normal' embodiments of the male and female, cannot be assumed. In particular, he asserts, 'gender' can only offer a crude bifurcation of individuals which consequently encourages an all too easy 'slide between masculine and the humanly "normal"' in social and institutional settings. Consequently, Carver argues that there must be a philosophical and legal reconceptualization of the human subject which is able to appreciate a full range of 'complex gradations' and 'hybridities' concerning the self.

His central claim is that the theory and practice of trans-sexuality, together with the technologies of assisted reproduction (including donor and surrogacy combinations) and the politics of same-sex marriage and of 'non-singular individuals', mark an important stage in the deconstruction and resignifying of the human as the ethical subject. 'Physical singularity', for example, should not be assumed of the ethical subject when she is a gestating mother-to-be and the 'heteronormative' model of the ethical subject is but a distant legacy of past legal, political and social practices. Accordingly, Carver argues that the concept of gender is in trouble as it is a central feature of the insufficient traditional frameworks which underpin current conceptualizations of the human subject and one which we might do well to consider obsolete if we are to bring ethical discourses up to speed. Although traditional conceptualizations have permitted some exceptions in the past, it is Carver's claim that these very exceptions are increasingly proving to be the *rule*, and producing significant changes in everyday practice. Numerous individuals and groups have begun to bring forward legal cases, engage in political campaigns and use liberal rights-governed frameworks and democratic institutions to challenge traditional understandings of the self. Carver maps these challenges through an analytical approach to historical and contemporary theorizations and attempts to create a counterpoint between current instabilities in 'fixing' the human person and examples of practical conceptualizations that re-create the ethical subject in increasingly diverse ways.

Tony Lawson sees the commonplace use of 'gender' as highly problematic and, particularly in the wake of post-modernist critiques, he seeks to salvage the concept both as a category of analysis and as a basis for the progressive transformation of society. He suggests that feminists need to engage far more than they have done in a systematic ontological understanding of the concept as the first step on the way to a more coherent and effective prescription of political practice. His principal argument is that we must develop a conception of gender that, on the one hand, absorbs the fact that we are all different and that our experiences and identities are historically, culturally and socially contextual, but that, on the other, is able to act as an emancipatory device which can facilitate the need to organize collectively. Whilst Lawson supports the post-modernist critique of early 'gender theorizing', he maintains that the critique itself obviates the potential for recognizing systematic forces of societal discrimination such as the fact that 'biological females are very often dominated or oppressed by males, and in ways that have little if anything to do with sexual as opposed to social differences'. Drawing on the philosophical insights of 'critical realism', Lawson argues for a conception of gender as a feature of social structure ('something that is irreducible to human practices or experiences'). 'Gender', then, should be regarded as a social system whereby *social* discriminations are made between individuals based on their identified biological sex. Once we have grasped this crucial insight, he argues, it is possible to retain gender as a useful category of analysis, and to see that the project of combating gender discrimination is itself a project of wholesale social transformation. In so doing, he seeks to provide a new way of looking at the relationship between gender and sex.

Juliet Mitchell examines the hypothesis that the rise of second-wave feminism both reflected and spearheaded an aspect of demographic transition to non-replacement populations. She asserts a very different distinction between the terms 'sex' and 'gender' by considering the tension between the formation of 'sexual difference' to enable reproduction and what she calls the 'engendering of gender' in lateral relations which are indifferent to procreation.

In contextualizing this distinction, Mitchell shows how, with the achievements of feminism as a political vanguard and a demographic transition as its socio-economic base, women no longer became defined by 'the family', in that their definition ceased to depend on reproduction. She claims the commonplace use of the term 'gender' entered the political arena to become a key concept of feminism which indicated non-procreative sexuality and sexual relations that were not necessarily aligned with heterosexuality or biological reproductive functions. Mitchell argues that the advent of 'gender' reflects the transition to a new demographic order and thus must be rethought if it is to be a concept of any use to a politics of radical change.

Mitchell goes on to propose that demographic transitions may be bringing the role of 'caring' rather than 'birth' into prominence. She makes critical use of psychoanalysis, to look at the 'gendering of caring' along a lateral, horizontal axis (i.e. non-parental relationships). Central to her argument is the observation that the demographic transition to non-replacement populations as reflected in contemporary birth-rates is a phenomenon of post-industrial wealth (or aspirants thereto). Poor countries and poor people, Mitchell suggests, disproportionately produce babies who die, and the rise of 'child-free gender' belongs only to dominant populations. She concludes with a consideration of 'gender' as potentially indicating sexual 'indifference' in an era where caring takes precedence over procreation. The practices of lateral heterosexuality or homosexuality, conception and pregnancy, could, she claims, be independent of gender neutral parenting/caring altogether and sibling relations (blood and social) offer a key to what Mitchell sees as a likely 'world historical development'.

Part III: Gender and political practice

In the ninth chapter, Catherine Hakim presents her preference theory, which is designed to explain why gender equality appears to have ground to a slow halt since the equal opportunities revolution which began in the 1970s and indeed why it is unlikely to progress much further. Preference theory, both descriptive and predictive, is intended to explain women's choices between paid and unpaid work, currently and in the future. Hakim claims that to look at the pay gap between men and women is no longer appropriate as an indicator of gender inequality because lifestyle preferences are what determine patterns of work and employment over the lifecycle, not gender. Hakim criticizes the policies which became prevalent in the twentieth century, in particular those that aimed to be 'family friendly', and along with them the primary objectives of most feminists today.

She instead identifies five major qualitative changes in the modern state which create a 'new scenario' for women which is unique to the twenty-first century. These are the contraceptive revolution, the equal opportunities revolution, the expansion of white-collar work, the increase in secondary-earner jobs, and a vast swing in social attitudes. Currently, only Britain, the Netherlands and the USA display this 'new scenario'. Born out of these conditions are three major lifestyle preference groups of women, who differ significantly in their value systems and in their life-goals. These three groups are the 'home-centred', the 'adaptives' and the 'work-centred'. The heterogeneity of interests between these three female populations renders them collectively less likely to be represented at higher-status occupations within the workforce to the same degree as men who are more uniform in their social values and life-goals. Hakim therefore concludes that 'gender' is redundant in explaining the pay gap. Instead the dividing line is between mothers and childless women – not between men and women. Hakim calls for us to move beyond 'gender' and 'sex' as vehicles for analysing unequal outcomes and instead to focus on the social roles that men and women *prefer*. Consequently, she suggests, we must come to recognize that feminist theory, as it stands, is out of touch with contemporary reality.

Rosemary Crompton files a particular complaint against preference-based theories as she argues they rely upon an assumption that men and women are inclined towards certain choices according to their differing biological endowments – a logic which can only serve as justification for inequalities between men and women. She focuses in particular on 'Wollstonecraft's dilemma' which highlights that an emphasis on 'difference' can undermine claims to 'gender equality'. Crompton argues that preference-based theories tend to dovetail all too neatly with neoliberal validations of large socio-economic inequalities and for that reason should be called into question. She emphasizes assumptions about 'female behaviour' and in particular she alleges that preference-based explanations of gender inequality under-appreciate the impact of welfare state centred policies on social and economic life. Unlike those who have faith in trans-national sites of politics, however, Crompton thinks that the EU setting may not be as promising a conduit for gender equality. Her forecast is rather that Member State welfare programmes might bow to the weight of increasingly dominant US-style corporate strategies which best serve private employers. For example, she draws attention to how Britain, as one of the most powerful members of the EU, repeatedly navigates its way under EU edicts by implementing EU Directives in a minimalist fashion in order to tally with the interests of UK businesses. As a result, some very significant policies have been rendered ineffective. In a similarly suspicious vein, Crompton, whilst on the one hand welcoming of new flexible working arrangements offered by employers to enable parents better to balance their home and work commitments, is, on the other, wary of the attractions of such policies for the employer. As she points out, 'employment flexibility, which is concentrated amongst women, is not usually associated with individual success in the labour market, and flexible workers often tend to be in lower level positions'. In essence, Crompton calls for us to take stock of what seems to be the neoliberal direction of modern economic systems and to acknowledge that it is straightforwardly incompatible with the needs of men and women both as workers and as family members in modern economies.

Finally, my chapter (Jude Browne) exemplifies the problems of operationalizing normative ideals of equality. In so doing, I reject the concept of 'gender equality' as an appropriate goal of public policy, arguing instead that the eradication of discriminatory stereotypes is better suited to the pursuit of equal treatment between men and women. My primary focus is the translation of the normative principle of 'equal treatment' into legislative practice. Central to the principle is the idea that individuals should be treated equally only in 'relevant respects', and it is with the question of which respects are relevant in the context of equal treatment of men and women that I am primarily concerned. In particular I track the various ways in which the principle of equal treatment has been interpreted and implemented by the European Union's Equal Treatment Principle (EPT) which has become the bedrock of all Member States' equality policies and anti-discrimination legislation. In particular, I present a detailed account of how equal pay and sex discrimination legislation, as well as specific rights such as maternity, parental and paternity leave, are thwarted by anachronistic conceptions of men's and women's social capabilities. Accordingly, I argue it is imperative that what takes place is an interrogation of the assumptions that underpin the purportedly sound interpretations of the principle of equal treatment and the stereotypes which they effectively uphold. On my view, anti-discrimination measures should be prised apart from the pursuit of an inadequately conceived goal of 'gender equality'. This, I assert, would not only crucially afford individuals far more freedom to explore and realize their preferences and needs, but also result in new social norms and institutional procedures which better lend themselves to the principle of equal treatment. A reinterpretation of the 'relevant respects' in which men and women of the twenty-first century should be treated equally is, I argue, well overdue.

PART I

Reorienting the feminist imagination

1 | Mapping the feminist imagination

From redistribution to recognition to representation

NANCY FRASER

F OR MANY YEARS, feminists throughout the world looked to the United States for the most advanced theory and practice. Today, however, US feminism finds itself at an impasse, stymied by the hostile, post 9/11 political climate. Unsure how to pursue gender justice under current conditions, Americans are now returning the favour, by looking to feminists elsewhere for inspiration and guidance. Today, accordingly, the cutting edge of gender struggle has shifted away from the United States, to trans-national spaces, such as 'Europe', where the room for manoeuvre is greater. The consequence is a major shift in the geography of feminist energies.[1]

What lies behind this geographical shift? And what are its political implications for the future of the feminist project? In what follows, I will propose an account of the historical trajectory of the second-wave feminism aimed at illuminating these matters. My strategy will be to relate geographical shifts in feminist energies to shifts of two other kinds. On the one hand, I will identify some major transformations in

---

[1] This chapter originated as a keynote lecture delivered at the conference on 'Gender Equality and Social Change', Cambridge University, March 2004. A later version was delivered at the conference on 'Gender in Motion', University of Basel, March 2005. Thanks to Juliet Mitchell, Andrea Maihofer, and the participants at those conferences who discussed these ideas with me. Thanks, too, to Nancy Naples; although she does not share all of my views, our conversations influenced my thinking greatly, as is clear from our joint project: 'To Interpret the World and To Change It: An Interview with Nancy Fraser', by Nancy Fraser and Nancy A. Naples, *Signs: Journal of Women in Culture and Society* 29, 4 (Summer 2004), 1103–24. Thanks, finally, to Keith Haysom for efficient and cheerful research assistance and to Veronika Rall, whose German translation ('Frauen, denkt ökonomisch!' in *Die Tageszeitung* 7633 (7 April 2005), 4–5) so greatly improved on the original that I incorporated some of her phrasings here.

17

the way feminists have imagined gender justice since the 1970s. On the other hand, I will situate changes in the feminist imaginary in the context of broader shifts in the political *Zeitgeist* and in post-war capitalism. The result will be a historically elaborated *Zeitdiagnose* through which we can assess the political prospects of feminist struggles for the coming period.

In general, then, the point of this exercise is political. By historicizing shifts in the geography of feminist energies, I aim to gain some insight as to how we might reinvigorate the theory and practice of gender equality under current conditions. Likewise, by mapping transformations of the feminist imagination, I aim to determine what should be discarded, and what preserved, for the struggles ahead. By situating those shifts, finally, in the context of changes in post-war capitalism and post-communist geopolitics, I aim to stimulate discussion as to how we might reinvent the project of feminism for a globalizing world.

Historicizing second-wave feminism

How should we understand the history of second-wave feminism? The narrative I propose differs importantly from the standard one told in US academic feminist circles. The standard story is a narrative of progress, according to which we have moved from an exclusionary movement, dominated by white, middle-class, heterosexual women, to a broader, more inclusive movement that better allows for the concerns of lesbians, women of colour, and/or poor and working-class women.[2] Naturally, I support efforts to broaden and diversify feminism, but I do not find this narrative satisfactory. From my perspective, it is too internal to feminism. Preoccupied exclusively with developments inside the movement, it fails to situate interior changes in relation to broader historical developments and the external climate. Thus, I will propose an alternative story, which is more historical and less self-congratulatory.

For my purposes, the history of second-wave feminism divides into three phases. In a first phase, feminism stood in a close relation to the various 'New Social Movements' that emerged from the ferment of the 1960s. In a second phase, it was drawn into the orbit of identity

[2] See, for example, hooks (1981); Rosen (2001); Roth (2004).

politics. In a third phase, finally, feminism is increasingly practised as a trans-national politics, in emerging trans-national spaces. Let me explain.

The history of second-wave feminism presents a striking trajectory. Nourished by the radicalism of the New Left, this wave of feminism began life as one of the new social movements that challenged the normalizing structures of post-World War II social democracy. It originated, in other words, as part of a broad effort to transform an economistic political imaginary that had narrowed political attention to problems of class distribution. In this first (New Social Movements) phase, feminists sought to burst open that imaginary. Exposing a broad range of forms of male dominance, they propounded an expanded view of the political as encompassing 'the personal'. Later, however, as the utopian energies of the New Left declined, feminism's anti-economistic insights were resignified, selectively incorporated into an emerging new political imaginary, which foregrounded cultural issues. Effectively captured by this culturalist imaginary, feminism reinvented itself as politics of recognition. In its second phase, accordingly, feminism became preoccupied with culture and was drawn into the orbit of identity politics. Although it was not often noticed at the time, feminism's identity politics phase coincided with a broader historical development, the fraying of nationally based social democracy under pressure from global neoliberalism. Under these conditions, a cultural-centred politics of recognition could not succeed. To the extent that it neglected political economy and geopolitical developments, this approach could not effectively challenge either the depredations of free-market policies or the rising tide of right-wing chauvinism that emerged in their wake. US feminism especially was unprepared for the dramatic alteration of the political landscape following 9/11. In Europe and elsewhere, however, feminists have discovered, and are skilfully exploiting, new political opportunities in the trans-national political spaces of our globalizing world. Thus, they are reinventing feminism yet again – this time as a project and process of trans-national politics. Although this third phase is still very young, it portends a change in the scale of feminist politics that could make it possible to integrate the best aspects of the previous two phases in a new and more adequate synthesis.

That, in a nutshell, is the story I intend to elaborate here. Before I proceed to unpack it, however, I need to introduce two caveats.

The first concerns the narrative's highly stylized character. In order to clarify the overall trajectory, I am drawing overly sharp lines between phases that in reality overlapped one another in many places and at many points. The risk of distortion will be worth it, however, if the narrative generates some intellectual and political insights for the period ahead.

My second caveat concerns the geography of feminism's three phases. As I understand it, the first (New Social Movements) phase encompassed North American, and Western European feminisms – and possibly currents elsewhere as well. In contrast, the second (identity politics) phase found its fullest expression in the United States, although it was not without resonance in other regions. Finally, the third phase is most developed, as its name suggests, in trans-national political spaces, paradigmatically those associated with 'Europe'.

Engendering social democracy: a critique of economism

To understand phase one, accordingly, let's recall conditions in what could then still be meaningfully called 'the first world'. When second-wave feminism first erupted on the world stage, the advanced capitalist states of Western Europe and North America were still enjoying the unprecedented wave of prosperity that followed World War II. Utilizing new tools of Keynesian economic steering, they had apparently learned to counteract business downturns and to guide national economic development so as to secure near full employment for men. Incorporating once unruly labour movements, they had built extensive welfare states and institutionalized national cross-class solidarity. To be sure, this historic class compromise rested on a series of gender and racial-ethnic exclusions, not to mention external neocolonial exploitation. But those potential fault lines tended in the main to remain latent in a social-democratic imaginary that foregrounded class redistribution. The result was a prosperous North Atlantic belt of mass-consumption societies, which had apparently tamed social conflict.[3]

In the 1960s, however, the relative calm of this Golden Age was suddenly shattered. In an extraordinary international explosion, radical youth took to the streets – at first to oppose racial segregation

---

[3] See Hobsbawm (1995).

in the USA and the Vietnam War. Soon thereafter they began to question core features of capitalist modernity that social democracy had heretofore naturalized: sexual repression, sexism and heteronormativity; materialism, corporate culture and 'the achievement ethic'; consumerism, bureaucracy and 'social control'. Breaking through the normalized political routines of the previous era, new social actors formed new social movements, with second-wave feminism among the most visionary.[4]

Along with their comrades in other movements, the feminists of this era recast the political imaginary. Transgressing a political culture that had privileged actors who cast themselves as nationally bounded and politically tamed classes, they challenged the gender exclusions of social democracy. Problematizing welfare paternalism and the bourgeois family, they exposed the deep androcentrism of capitalist society. Politicizing 'the personal', they expanded the boundaries of contestation beyond socio-economic redistribution – to include housework, sexuality and reproduction.[5]

Radical as it was, the feminism of this first phase stood in an ambivalent relation to social democracy. On the one hand, much of the early second wave rejected the latter's étatism and its tendency, especially in Europe, to marginalize social divisions other than class, and social problems other than those of distribution. On the other hand, most feminists presupposed key features of the socialist imaginary as a basis for more radical designs. Taking for granted the welfare state's solidaristic ethos and prosperity-securing steering capacities, they, too, were committed to taming markets and promoting egalitarianism. Acting from a critique that was at once radical and immanent, early second-wave feminists sought less to dismantle the welfare state than to transform it into a force that could help to remedy male domination.[6]

By 1989, however, history seemed to have bypassed that political project. A decade of Conservative rule in much of Western Europe

---

[4] See Touraine (1988); Melucci, Keane and Mier (1989); Johnston, Larana and Gusfield (1994).

[5] See Evans (1980); Echols (1990); Marx Ferree and Hess (1995).

[6] For some examples of this ambivalence, see the essays collected by Linda Gordon (1990), including my own contribution, Nancy Fraser, 'Struggle over Needs: Outline of a Socialist-Feminist Critical Theory of Late-Capitalist Political Culture', 205–31.

and North America, capped by the fall of communism in the East, miraculously breathed new life into free-market ideologies previously given up for dead. Resurrected from the historical dustbin, 'neoliberalism' authorized a sustained assault on the very idea of egalitarian redistribution. The effect, amplified by accelerating globalization, was to cast doubt on the legitimacy and viability of Keynesian steering. With social democracy on the defensive, efforts to broaden and deepen its promise naturally fell by the wayside. Feminist movements that had earlier taken the welfare state as their point of departure, seeking to extend its egalitarian ethos from class to gender, now found the ground cut out from under their feet. No longer able to assume social democracy as a basis for radicalization, they gravitated to newer grammars of political claims-making, more attuned to the post-socialist *Zeitgeist*.

From redistribution to recognition: the unhappy marriage of culturalism and neoliberalism

Enter the politics of recognition. If the first phase of post-war feminism sought to 'engender' the socialist imaginary, the second phase stressed the need to 'recognize difference'. 'Recognition', accordingly, became the chief grammar of feminist claims-making in the *fin de siècle*. A venerable category of Hegelian philosophy, resuscitated by political theorists, this notion captured the distinctive character of post-socialist struggles, which often took the form of identity politics, aimed more at valorizing difference than at promoting equality. Whether the question was violence against women or gender disparities in political representation, feminists increasingly resorted to the grammar of recognition to press their claims. Unable to make headway against injustices of political economy, they preferred to target harms resulting from androcentric patterns of cultural value or status hierarchies. The result was a major shift in the feminist imaginary: whereas the previous generation pursued an expanded ideal of social equality, this one invested the bulk of its energies in cultural change.[7]

Let me be clear. The project of cultural transformation has been integral to every phase of feminism, including the New Social

---

[7] Fraser (1997).

Movements phase. What distinguished the identity politics phase was the relative autonomization of the cultural project – its decoupling from the project of political-economic transformation and distributive justice.

Unsurprisingly, the effects of phase two were mixed. On the one hand, the new orientation to recognition focused attention on forms of male dominance that were rooted in the status order of capitalist society. Had it been combined with the earlier focus on socio-economic inequalities, our understanding of gender justice would have been deepened. On the other hand, the figure of the struggle for recognition so thoroughly captured the feminist imagination that it served more to displace than to deepen the socialist imaginary. The tendency was to subordinate social struggles to cultural struggles, the politics of redistribution to the politics of recognition. That was not, to be sure, the original intention. It was assumed, rather, by proponents of the cultural turn that a feminist politics of identity and difference would synergize with struggles for social equality. But that assumption fell prey to the larger *Zeitgeist*. In the *fin de siècle* context, the turn to recognition dovetailed all too neatly with a hegemonic neoliberalism that wanted nothing more than to repress all memory of social egalitarianism. The result was a tragic historical irony. Instead of arriving at a broader, richer paradigm that could encompass both redistribution and recognition, we effectively traded one truncated paradigm for another – a truncated economism for a truncated culturalism.

The timing, moreover, could not have been worse. The shift to a culturalized politics of recognition occurred at precisely the moment when neoliberalism was staging its spectacular comeback. Throughout this period, academic feminist theory was largely preoccupied with debates about 'difference'. Pitting 'essentialists' against 'anti-essentialists', these disputes usefully served to reveal hidden exclusionary premises of earlier theories, and they opened gender studies to many new voices. Even at their best, however, they tended to remain on the terrain of recognition, where subordination was construed as a problem of culture and dissociated from political economy. The effect was to leave us defenceless against free-market fundamentalism, which had meanwhile become hegemonic. Effectively mesmerized by the politics of recognition, we unwittingly diverted feminist theory into culturalist channels at precisely the moment when circumstances

required redoubled attention to the politics of redistribution.[8] I shall
return to this point shortly.

Geographies of recognition: post-communism, post-colonialism and the Third Way

First, however, I need to clarify one point. In recounting the shift from
phase one to phase two, I have been describing an epochal shift in the
feminist imaginary. But the shift was not limited to feminism per se.
On the contrary, analogous shifts can be found in virtually every
progressive social movement, as well as in the worldwide decline and/
or co-optation of trade unions and socialist parties, and in the
corresponding rise of identity politics, in both its progressive and
chauvinist forms. Linked to the fall of communism on the one hand,
and to the rise of neoliberalism on the other, this 'shift from
redistribution to recognition' (as I have called it) is part of the larger
historical transformation associated with corporate globalization.[9]

It might be objected that this *Zeitdiagnose* reflects a limited first-
world, American perspective. But I do not believe that is so. On the
contrary, the tendency for recognition claims to eclipse distribution
claims was quite general, even worldwide, even though the content of
such claims differed widely. In Western Europe, the social-democratic
focus on redistribution largely gave way in the 1990s to various
versions of the Third Way. This approach adopted a neoliberal
orientation to labour-market 'flexibility', while seeking to maintain a
progressive political profile. To the extent that it succeeded in the latter
effort, it was by seeking not to mitigate economic inequalities but
rather to overcome status hierarchies – through anti-discrimination
and/or multicultural policies. Thus, in Western Europe too, the
currency of political claims-making shifted from redistribution to
recognition, albeit in a milder form than in the United States.

Analogous shifts also occurred in the former second world.
Communism had enshrined its own version of the economistic
paradigm, which shunted political claims into distributive channels,
effectively muting recognition issues, which were cast as mere

---

[8] Nancy Fraser, 'Multiculturalism, Antiessentialism, and Radical Democracy: A
   Genealogy of the Current Impasse in Feminist Theory', in Fraser (1997: 173–88).
[9] Fraser (2003).

subtexts of 'real' economic problems. Post-communism shattered that paradigm, fuelling the broad delegitimation of economic egalitarianism and unleashing new struggles for recognition – especially around nationality and religion. In that context, the development of feminist politics was retarded by its association, both real and symbolic, with a discredited communism.

Related processes, too, occurred in the so-called 'third world'. On the one hand, the end of bipolar competition between the Soviet Union and the West reduced flows of aid to the periphery. On the other hand, the US-led dismantling of the Bretton Woods financial regime encouraged the new neoliberal policy of structural adjustment, which threatened the post-colonial developmental state. The result was to reduce greatly the scope for egalitarian redistributive projects in the South. And the response was an enormous surge of identity politics in the post-colony, much of it communalist and authoritarian. Thus, post-colonial feminist movements, too, were forced to operate without a background political culture that guides popular aspirations into egalitarian channels. Caught between downsized state capacities on the one hand, and burgeoning communalist chauvinisms on the other, they too felt pressure to recast their claims in forms more in keeping with the post-socialist *Zeitgeist*.

In general, then, the shift in feminism from phase one to phase two occurred within the larger matrix of post-communism and neoliberalism. Insofar as feminists failed to understand this larger matrix, they were slow to develop the resources needed to fight for gender justice under new conditions.

US gender politics, post-9/11

That was especially the case in the United States. There, feminists were surprised to find that, while they had been arguing about essentialism, an unholy alliance of free-marketeers and fundamentalist Christians had taken over the country. Because this development has proved so momentous for the world at large, I want to pause to consider it briefly, before turning to the emergence of phase three.

The decisive issues in the 2004 US election were the so-called 'war on terrorism' on one hand, and (to a lesser extent) the so-called 'family values' issues, especially abortion rights and gay marriage, on the other. In both cases, the strategic manipulation of gender was a crucial instrument of Bush's victory. The winning strategy invoked a gender-coded politics of recognition to hide a regressive politics of redistribution.

Let me explain. The Bush campaign's strategy painted the 'war on terror' as a problem of leadership, which it addressed in explicitly gendered terms. Mobilizing masculinist stereotypes, Bush cultivated the image of a reassuringly steady and determined commander-in-chief, a protector who never doubts and never wavers – in short, a real man. In contrast, the Republicans presented John Kerry as a 'girlie man', to use Arnold Schwarzenegger's memorable phrase, an effeminate 'flip-flopper' who could not be trusted to protect American women and children from the crazed violence of bearded fanatics.[10]

Despite its distance from reality, this gender-coded rhetoric proved immensely powerful – to male and female voters alike. So powerful in fact that it appeared to neutralize what everyone agreed was the Bush campaign's weak point: its regressive politics of redistribution, which was bringing significant hardship to many Americans. Already, in his first term, Bush had engineered an enormous upward redistribution of wealth to corporate interests and the propertied classes. By eliminating inheritance taxes, and lowering the tax rates of the wealthy, he had obliged the working classes to pay a far greater share of the national budget than before. The effect was to turn the politics of redistribution upside down, to promote increased social *injustice*. But none of that seemed to matter in the face of the 'war on terror'. Thus, a gender-coded politics of recognition effectively trumped a regressive politics of redistribution.[11]

A similar dynamic underlay the strategic deployment of 'family values' rhetoric in the election campaign. The decisive issue in Ohio, which turned out to be the crucial state in the election, may have been 'the defence of marriage'. This issue was deliberately chosen by conservatives for a ballot referendum in that state (and others) as a strategy to ensure a high turnout of fundamentalist Christian voters. The theory was that once you got them to the polls to vote against gay marriage, then they would go ahead and also vote for Bush. And it seems to have worked.

---

[10] Rich (2004).
[11] For related (albeit gender-insensitive) analyses, see Frank (2005) and Sennett (2004).

In any case, 'family values' proved to be a powerful electoral campaign theme. But here lies a major irony. The real tendencies that are making family life so difficult for the working and lower-middle classes stem from the neoliberal, corporate capitalist agenda that Bush supports. These policies include reduced taxes on corporations and the wealthy, diminished social welfare and consumer protections, and very low wages and precarious employment. Thanks to these and related trends, it is no longer possible to support a family on one paypacket, and often not even on two. Far from being voluntary or supplemental, then, women's wage work is obligatory, an indispensable pillar of the neoliberal economic order. So too is the practice of 'moonlighting', whereby working- and lower-middle-class family members must work at more than one job in order to make ends meet. Those are the real forces that are threatening family life in the United States.[12] Feminists understand this, but they have not succeeded in convincing many who are harmed by these policies. On the contrary, the Right has managed to persuade them that it is abortion rights and gay rights that threaten their way of life. Here, too, in other words, the Republicans successfully used an anti-feminist politics of recognition to conceal an anti-working-class politics of redistribution.

In this scenario you can see the whole problem of phase two. Although it was not widely understood at the time, US feminists shifted their focus from redistribution to recognition, just as the Right was perfecting its own strategic deployment of a regressive cultural politics to distract attention from its regressive politics of redistribution. The coincidence was truly unfortunate. The relative neglect of political economy by US feminists and other progressive movements ended up playing into the hands of the Right, which reaped the principal benefits of the cultural turn.

Evangelicalism: a neoliberal technology of the self

But why were Americans so easily fooled by this obvious trick? And why were so many American women so susceptible to the Republicans' gender-coded appeals? Many observers have noted that the Right had some success in portraying US feminists as elite

---

[12] Frank (2005) and Sennett (2004).

professionals and secular humanists, who have nothing but contempt for ordinary women, especially religious and working-class women. At one level, that view of feminism as elitist is patently false, of course, but the fact remains that feminism has failed to reach a large stratum of working- and lower-class women who have been attracted over the past decade to evangelical Christianity. Focused too one-sidedly on the politics of recognition, we have failed to understand how their religious orientation responds to their social-class position.

At first sight, the situation of evangelical Christian women in the United States appears contradictory. On the one hand, they subscribe to a conservative ideology of traditional domesticity. On the other hand, these women do not in fact live patriarchal lives; most are active in the labour market and relatively empowered in family life.[13] The mystery is clarified when we understand that evangelicalism responds to the emergence in the United States of new kind of society, which I call 'the insecurity society'. This society is the successor to the 'welfare society' that was associated with social democracy in the previous period. Unlike the latter, the new society institutionalizes increased insecurity in the living conditions of most people. As I noted before, it weakens social welfare protections, even as it institutionalizes more precarious forms of wage labour, including subcontracting, temp work and non-unionized work, which are low-waged and do not carry benefits. The result is a great sense of insecurity, to which evangelical Christianity responds.

Interestingly, evangelicalism does not actually give people security. Rather, it gives them a discourse and a set of practices through which they can manage insecurity. It says to them: 'You are a sinner, you are going to fail, you may lose your job, you may drink too much, you may have an affair, your husband may leave you, your children may use drugs. But that's okay. God still loves you, and your church still accepts you.' The effect is in part to convey acceptance but also to prepare people for trouble in hard times. Constantly invoking the likelihood of trouble, evangelicalism stokes its followers' feelings of

---

[13] For accounts of right-wing Christian women, see Griffith (1997); Gallagher (2003); and Ingersoll (2003). Also useful are two early accounts: the chapter on 'Fundamentalist Sex: Hitting below the Bible Belt' in Ehrenreich, Hess and Jacobs (1987), and Stacey (1987).

insecurity, even as it seems to offer them a way of coping with it. Perhaps one needs the late Foucault to understand this: evangelicalism is a care-of-self technology that is especially suited to neoliberalism, insofar as the latter is always generating insecurity. As I said, many working-class women in the United States are deriving something significant from this ideology, something that confers meaning on their lives. But feminists have not succeeded in understanding what it is and how it works. Nor have we figured out how to talk to them or what feminism can offer them in its place.

I have lingered on this peculiarly American example because I find it emblematic of the larger situation of our historical epoch. All of us are living in an age of declining security, thanks to neoliberal pressures to increase 'flexibility' and curtail welfare protections amid increasingly precarious labour markets. For less integrated strata, including immigrants, these pressures are compounded when class inequalities of distribution are overlaid with status inequalities of recognition; and the latter can easily be blamed on 'secular feminism'. In such cases, it behoves all feminists, in Europe as well as in the United States, to revisit the relationship between the politics of redistribution and the politics of recognition. Today, as we move into a third phase of feminist politics, we need to reintegrate these two indispensable dimensions of feminist politics, which were not adequately balanced in phase two.

Reframing feminism: a trans-national politics of representation

Fortunately, something like this is already beginning to happen in those strands of feminist politics that are now operating in trans-national spaces. Sensitized to the growing power of neoliberalism, these currents are crafting a new and promising synthesis of redistribution and recognition. In addition, they are changing the scale of feminist politics. Aware of women's vulnerability to transnational forces, they find that they cannot adequately challenge gender injustice if they remain within the previously taken-for-granted frame of the modern territorial state. Because that frame limits the scope of justice to intra-state institutions that organize relations among fellow citizens, it systematically obscures trans-border sources of gender injustice that structure trans-national social relations.

The effect is to shield from the reach of justice all those forces shaping gender relations that routinely overflow territorial borders.

Today, accordingly, many trans-national feminists reject the state-territorial frame. They note that decisions taken in one territorial state often impact the lives of women outside it, as do the actions of supra-national and international organizations, both governmental and nongovernmental. They also note the force of trans-national public opinion, which flows with supreme disregard for borders through global mass media and cybertechnology. The result is a new appreciation of the role of trans-national forces in maintaining gender injustice. Faced with global warming, the spread of AIDS, international terrorism and superpower unilateralism, feminists in this phase believe that women's chances for living good lives depend at least as much on processes that trespass the borders of territorial states as on those contained within them.

Under these conditions, important currents of feminism are challenging the state-territorial framing of political claims-making. As they see it, that frame is a major vehicle of injustice, as it partitions political space in ways that block many women from challenging the forces that oppress them. Channelling their claims into the domestic political spaces of relatively powerless, if not wholly failed, states, this frame insulates offshore powers from critique and control. Among those shielded from the reach of justice are more powerful predator states and trans-national private powers, including foreign investors and creditors, international currency speculators, and trans-national corporations. Also protected are the governance structures of the global economy, which set exploitative terms of interaction and then exempt them from democratic control. Finally, the state-territorial frame is self-insulating; the architecture of the interstate system protects the very partitioning of political space that it institutionalizes, effectively excluding trans-national democratic decision-making on issues of gender justice.

Today, accordingly, feminist claims for redistribution and recognition are linked increasingly to struggles to change the frame. Faced with trans-nationalized production, many feminists eschew the assumption of national economies. In Europe, for example, feminists target the economic policies and structures of the European Union, while feminist currents among the WTO protestors are challenging the governance structures of the global economy. Analogously, feminist struggles for recognition increasingly look beyond the territorial state. Under the umbrella slogan 'women's rights are human rights', feminists throughout the world are linking struggles against local patriarchal practices to campaigns to reform international law.[14]

The result is a new phase of feminist politics in which gender justice is being reframed. In this phase, a major concern is to challenge interlinked injustices of maldistribution and misrecognition. Above and beyond those first-order injustices, however, feminists are also targeting a newly visible meta-injustice, which I have called *misframing*.[15] Misframing arises when the state-territorial frame is imposed on trans-national sources of injustice. The effect is to gerrymander political space at the expense of the poor and despised, who are denied the chance to press trans-national claims. In such cases, struggles against maldistribution and misrecognition cannot proceed, let alone succeed, unless they are joined with struggles against misframing. Misframing, accordingly, is emerging as a central target of feminist politics in its trans-national phase.

By confronting misframing, this phase of feminist politics is making visible a third dimension of gender justice, beyond redistribution and recognition. I call this third dimension *representation*. As I understand it, representation is not only a matter of ensuring equal political voice for women in already constituted political communities. In addition, it requires reframing disputes about justice that cannot be properly contained within established polities. In contesting misframing, therefore, trans-national feminism is reconfiguring gender justice as a three-dimensional problem, in which redistribution, recognition and representation must be integrated in a balanced way.[16]

The developing trans-national political space surrounding the European Union promises to be one important site for this third phase of feminist politics. In Europe, the task is somehow to do three things at once. First, feminists must work with other progressive forces to create egalitarian, gender-sensitive social welfare protections at the trans-national level. In addition, they must join with allies to

---

[14] See Ackerly and Moller Okin (2002); Dickenson (1997). For two assessments of the gender politics of the broader anti-corporate globalization movement, see Vargas (2003) and Rebick (2002).

[15] Fraser (forthcoming).   [16] Fraser (forthcoming).

integrate such redistributive policies with egalitarian, gender-sensitive recognition policies that can do justice to European cultural multiplicity. Finally, they must do all that without hardening external borders, ensuring that trans-national Europe does not become fortress Europe, so as not to replicate injustices of misframing on a broader scale.

Europe, however, is by no means the only site for this third phase of feminist politics. Equally important are the trans-national spaces surrounding the various United Nations agencies and the World Social Forum. There, too, feminists are joining other progressive transnational actors, including environmentalists, development activists and indigenous peoples, in challenging linked injustices of maldistribution, misrecognition and misrepresentation. There, too, the task is to develop a three-dimensional politics that appropriately balances and integrates those concerns.

Developing such a three-dimensional politics is by no means easy. Yet it holds out tremendous promise for a third phase of feminist struggle. On the one hand, this approach could overcome the chief weakness of phase two, by rebalancing the politics of recognition and the politics of redistribution. On the other hand, it could overcome the blind spot of both of the previous phases of feminist politics, by explicitly contesting injustices of misframing. Above all, such a politics could permit us to pose, and hopefully to answer, the key political question of our age: how can we integrate claims for redistribution, recognition and representation so as to challenge the full range of gender injustices in a globalizing world?

References

Ackerly, B. A. and Moller Okin, S. (2002) 'Feminist Social Criticism and the International Movement for Women's Rights as Human Rights', in Ian Shapiro and Casiano Hacker-Cordon (eds.), *Democracy's Edges* (Cambridge: Cambridge University Press), 134–62.

Dickenson, D. (1997) 'Counting Women In: Globalization, Democratization, and the Women's Movement', in Anthony McGrew (ed.), *The Transformation of Democracy? Globalization and Territorial Democracy* (Cambridge: Polity Press), 97–120.

Echols, A. (1990) *Daring To Be Bad: Radical Feminism in America, 1967–75* (Minneapolis: University of Minnesota Press).

Ehrenreich, B., Hess, E. and Jacobs, G. (1987) *Re-making Love: The Feminization of Sex* (New York: Anchor Books).

Evans, S. (1980) *Personal Politics: The Roots of Women's Liberation in the Civil Rights Movement and the New Left* (New York: Vintage).

Frank, T. (2005) 'What's the Matter with Liberals?' *The New York Review of Books* 52, 8: 46.

Fraser, N. (1997) *Justice Interruptus: Critical Reflections on the 'Postsocialist' Condition* (New York and London: Routledge).

(2003) 'Social Justice in the Age of Identity Politics', in Fraser and Axel Honneth, *Redistribution or Recognition? A Political–Philosophical Exchange*, trans. Joel Golb, James Ingram and Christiane Wilke (London: Verso), 7–109.

(forthcoming) 'Reframing Justice in a Globalizing World', *New Left Review*.

Gallagher, S. (2003) *Evangelical Identity and Gendered Family Life* (New Brunswick, NJ: Rutgers University Press).

Gordon, L. (ed.) (1990) *Women, the State and Welfare: Historical and Theoretical Perspectives* (Madison: University of Wisconsin Press).

Griffith, R. M. (1997) *God's Daughters: Evangelical Women and the Power of Submission* (Berkeley: University of California Press).

Hobsbawm, E. (1995) *The Age of Extremes: A History of the World, 1914–1991* (London: Abacus), 320–41, 461–518.

hooks, b. (1981) *Feminist Theory: From Margin to Center* (Boston: South End Press; 2nd edn, 2000).

Ingersoll, J. (2003) *Evangelical Christian Women: War Stories in the Gender Battles* (New York: New York University Press).

Johnston, H., Larana, E. and Gusfield J.R. (eds.) (1994) *New Social Movements: From Ideology to Identity* (Philadelphia: Temple University Press).

Marx Ferree, M. and Hess, B. B. (1995) *Controversy and Coalition: The Feminist Movement across Three Decades of Change* (New York: Routledge).

Melucci, A., Keane, J. and Mier P. (eds.) (1989) *Nomads of the Present: Social Movements and Individual Needs in Contemporary Society* (Philadelphia: Temple University Press).

Rebick, J. (2002) 'Lip Service: The Anti-Globalization Movement on Gender Politics', *Horizons* 16, 2: 24–6.

Rich, F. (2004) 'How Kerry Became a Girlie Man', *The New York Times* 153, Issue 52963 (5 September), section 2, p. 1.

Rosen, R. (2001) *The World Split Open: How the Modern Women's Movement Changed America* (New York: Penguin).

Roth, B. (2004) *Separate Roads to Feminism: Black, Chicana, and White Feminist Movements in America's Second Wave* (Cambridge: Cambridge University Press).

Sennett, Richard (2004) 'The Age of Anxiety', *Guardian Saturday*, 23 October, p. 34, available on-line at http://books.guardian.co.uk/print/ 0,3858,5044940–110738,00.html.

Stacey, J. (1987) 'Sexism by a Subtler Name? Postindustrial Conditions and Postfeminist Consciousness in the Silicon Valley', *Socialist Review* 96: 7–28.

Touraine, A. (1988) *Return of the Actor: Social Theory in Postindustrial Society* (Minneapolis: University of Minnesota Press).

Vargas, V. (2003) 'Feminism, Globalization and the Global Justice and Solidarity Movement', *Cultural Studies* 17, 6: 905–20.

2 | Perspectives on gender equality
Challenging the terms of debate

VALERIE BRYSON

TODAY IN THE WEST, it is not only self-proclaimed feminists who say that women should have the same right as men to vote, enter politics, go to university, work outside the home or receive equal pay when they do equal work. This kind of equality is now part of the 'common sense' of our society. These equal rights were, however, not won easily, and they have still not been won in many parts of the world.

Early feminist campaigns for equal rights used a range of arguments, many of which can still be heard today. Some feminists accepted and adapted traditional ideas about women's 'difference' from men to argue that women needed political rights and legal protection in order that their needs as wives and mothers could be met, and/or so that their alleged qualities, such as peace-making and temperance, could raise the quality of public life. Some saw sex equality as a consequence and/or precondition for a more generally equal socialist society, in which human relationships would be free from ownership and control. Many others used the language of liberal democracy to demand rights on the grounds that women were in relevant respects the same as men, and that as rational individuals they should have the same rights and opportunities (for overviews of early feminism, see Evans 1977; Banks 1986; Bryson 2003). While some feminists continued to stress women's different qualities and needs, or the interconnected nature of socialist and feminist goals, such liberal arguments became the primary justification for sex equality legislation in many western nations in the second half of the twentieth century, and they set the parameters for most public debate in the UK and USA today. This means that equality today is generally understood in individualistic terms and in relation to legal and political rights in the public sphere. From this dominant perspective, women in the West have now achieved equality with men; if we lag behind them, this reflects free choice and/or the legitimate results of free competition.

Most feminists today agree that the rights that most women in the West have won are not 'mere formalities', and that they should be campaigned for and defended wherever they are lacking or under threat. However, some feminists have been highly critical of the underlying assumptions of liberal thought, which they see as an inherently male approach that does not encompass women's needs and experiences and therefore cannot provide a basis for substantive gender equality. In this chapter, I argue that, if we are to achieve a more genuinely egalitarian and equitable society, we must move beyond liberal, male assumptions and reintroduce into public debate the ideals and analytical tools associated with radical feminism and with socialist and Marxist thought. In particular, careful use of the radical feminist concept of patriarchy can enable us to see and challenge the interconnected inequalities and values that permeate every aspect of society. This concept also decentres male experiences and assumptions, and this decentring in turn supports the development of an inclusive version of socialism that recognises the significance of experiences and activities associated with women. While conventional socialists can see that the effective pursuit of the kind of sex equality that would benefit more than an elite minority of women runs against the logic of market capitalism, so that feminism cannot be isolated from wider egalitarian goals, a more inclusive approach also sees that while some form of socialism may be a necessary precondition for sex equality, it is certainly not sufficient.

In considering what we mean by equality, it is also essential that privileged white western feminists such as myself do not assume that we can speak for the whole of our sex, and we must take seriously recent black feminist analysis of the dynamically interactive nature of gender, 'race' and class and the centrality of black women's experience for feminist analysis. While this chapter focuses on western societies, it is also important to remember that most of the world's women do not live in the West, and that while there may be some apparent commonalities of experience, there are also wide divergences.

Such arguments are reinforced by related developments in postmodern feminist theory and its analysis of the dangers of essentialism, the shifting and precarious nature of gender identities, and the role of language, logic and culture in sustaining or subverting these. However, while such theorising may produce significant insights, it should not be allowed to become a rarefied end in itself (or a boost to our academic careers): rather, the role of theory should be to help feminists develop effective strategies that can both see beyond the hegemonic paradigms of inegalitarian societies and adapt to the specificities of particular social contexts. As Nancy Fraser argues in this volume, there are also dangers in a 'politics of identity' if this is prioritised over the politics of redistribution and representation.

Equality and inequality today

Although women in many nations now have more or less the same legal rights as men, women and men in general continue to play different roles and to receive different rewards – and in general this works to the disadvantage of women. Documenting these differences and inequalities is in many ways an important first step towards combating them – if people do not know about them, there will be no policies to address them. Demanding that statistics be disaggregated by sex[1] or measuring the time spent by women and men on unpaid work in the home remain important feminist tasks, which make continuing inequalities visible. Partly as a result of such feminist efforts, we now have plenty of evidence about the pay gap, the lack of women in senior positions and the numbers of women living in poverty throughout the world; there is also an increasing amount of information about the unequal division of unpaid work, particularly in subsistence agriculture and within the home. These differences are more stark in some nations than others, but even the Nordic countries, which occupied the first five places in the 2005 United Nations Human Development Report's 'Gender empowerment measure', significant differences in pay and public voice remain and the domestic division of labour falls well short of equality (Nordic Council of Ministers 2005; UNDP 2005). In addition to these measurable inequalities, feminists have also documented and drawn attention to other problems experienced by many women, particularly domestic violence (which remains a serious problem in the Nordic countries), sexual exploitation and lack of reproductive rights.

Other inequalities and problems to do with culture and beliefs are often less easy to pin down, particularly in western societies, where

---

[1] Such analysis does not preclude questioning the basis for binary classification, critiqued by Terrell Carver in his chapter.

most official public rhetoric stresses equality of opportunity rather than approving traditional gender roles. However, it is clear that until recently our history, philosophy and public culture have been almost exclusively man-made, and that despite the success of some individual women, men still dominate decision-making positions in educational and cultural establishments and in the media (on the UK, see Equal Opportunities Commission 2005). Men have decided what is important and what counts as knowledge – and they have drawn on their own experiences, perceptions and priorities to produce a particular view of the world which they present as universal and objective. I am not suggesting that this is some kind of deliberate conspiracy, but I am suggesting that the resulting picture is inevitably partial and incomplete. Although feminists have had an impact in some areas, this man-made view of the world is the framework within which most women as well as men still have to work most of the time. It is 'normal'; it is 'common sense'.

Some feminists have a word to describe these interlocking in-equalities: they use the term 'patriarchy'. I have deep reservations about using this term, which has sometimes been endowed with inappropriate explanatory power or used in very simplistic ways to suggest that all women are in the same situation, or that all women are eternal victims of unchanging oppression and all men are oppressors. Nevertheless, I think that, handled carefully, the term is politically indispensable, and that it makes visible a number of interrelated points. First, inequalities between men and women are patterned, and cannot be reduced to *individual* experiences, behaviour and attitudes, although without the concept they may seem to be. Second, different kinds of inequality are interconnected, part of a wider pattern, in which disadvantage in one area is reinforced by that in another. Third, as I have already said, in a patriarchal society, men, their attributes and their values are the standard against which we are all measured; so that differences between the sexes generally become disadvantages for women and if women want equality they have to be like men (for an elaboration of these points and the debates around the concept of patriarchy, see Bryson 1999). It is in this context that debates around equality are conducted.

My argument in this chapter – and I am not claiming that it is an original one, just one that needs restating – is that to challenge continuing inequalities we need to challenge the framework within which equality is debated, because most public debate on equality between women and men in the West has been conducted on inappropriate terms. These terms reflect the dominant values of our society – that is, they are liberal and they are male. These values have long been critiqued by many feminists, who have developed increasingly sophisticated theories. However, it often seems that we are simply talking amongst ourselves, and that liberal, male values remain the unquestioned 'common sense' of our society, so that if feminists enter public debate we are sucked back into a set of assumptions and a frame of reference that we would never have chosen and that we hoped we had moved beyond.

'Common sense' and feminist critiques

When we are talking about sex equality in western liberal democracies, we are talking about this in the context of societies that are in many ways profoundly unequal in terms of the gap between rich and poor, powerful and powerless, white and black. These inequalities of course exist in the context of an even more dramatically unequal world, in which living standards in the West are often maintained by the exploitation of workers in other nations. In the context of this widespread inequality, the dominant perspective on equality is based on what the ethical socialist Tawney called the 'tadpole principle' – that only a few of us will ever become frogs, but that we should have an equal right to try. In other words, it means equality of opportunity to compete for rewards and positions; it assumes existing hierarchies and inequality of outcomes (for a recent discussion of this concept of equality, see Evans 2005).

According to this 'common-sense' perspective, women in the West now have equality with men, because we have the same rights and opportunities, enshrined in and protected by law. No longer can we be refused employment or promotion just because we are women, no longer can the bank refuse to give us a loan unless we can find a man who can act as guarantor, no longer can schools refuse to let girls study physics or technology. Previous generations fought for these rights and won. The door is now open; all we have to do is to walk through, and we can see many examples of highly successful women who have done just that.

'Common sense' is sometimes forced to admit that there are some members of selection boards who do not understand the new rules and some rogue employers who deliberately break them, but it holds that these matters can be dealt with by stricter enforcement or tightening up of equality legislation. Faced with a wealth of statistical evidence, 'common sense' is also forced to concede that on average women earn less, are more likely to live in poverty and are concentrated in the bottom half of any hierarchy of public power and influence. However, this is seen as women's *choice*: they choose to have children, they choose to work part-time to fit in with their caring responsibilities, and they choose to work in occupations that are not well paid but which may provide other forms of satisfaction or reward. (See Catherine Hakim's chapter in this volume for an elaboration of this argument.) According to 'common sense', if women want to earn more money, they should take up the opportunities that are there and become engineers, plumbers or stockbrokers rather than nursery nurses, hairdressers and social workers. They should also stop whinging and realise that it is a tough old world out there; indeed 'common sense' often finds itself suggesting (although in a rather less confident tone) that perhaps women don't really have the skills and attitudes to succeed: they can't hack the hours, they haven't got the determination, they haven't got the ambition.

From the 'common-sense' perspective, women and men can now expect to be judged equally on their individual qualifications and merits, and feminists should concentrate on ensuring that the rules of equal competition are enforced so that the best people are able to succeed. Increasingly, this perspective also sees the main threat to such fair competition as now coming from obsessive feminists, who have succeeded in discriminating against men by choosing parliamentary candidates from women-only shortlists, passing men over for promotion to reach artificial gender quotas, and insisting on long periods of maternity leave every time they have a baby.

I disagree with such 'common sense'. Confronted with its arguments, it is however difficult to know where to start, because they rest on a whole set of interlocking values and assumptions. As I have already said, many feminists argue that these values and assumptions are liberal and that they reflect male interests in a patriarchal society. As such, they are neither adequate nor always appropriate for women's needs. Here, I will look briefly at just four overlapping points of criticism: that the 'common-sense' approach ignores the gendered context within which equal rights are exercised; that it focuses too narrowly on the public sphere; that it accepts a scale of values biased in favour of men; and that it fails to question the continued existence of steep hierarchies and inequalities of outcome.

Gender equality in context

The focus on individuals' right to compete equally abstracts people from their society and does not consider the gendered starting-point of the competitive marketplace. In contrast, many feminists have claimed that women are disadvantaged by deep-seated cultural assumptions and ascribed gender roles which produce stereotypes that make it difficult for women to succeed. Much of this feminist work originally built on Kate Millett's pioneering work on patriarchy and her claim that gender expectations and roles are learned within the family, and reinforced by education, the media and religion (Millett 1985, first published 1970). From this perspective, gender roles are particularly difficult to change because they are learned and internalised at an early age, so that women seem out of place in positions of public authority, while even the most 'liberated' woman is likely to feel that running the house is her responsibility and that she is 'lucky' if she has a partner who shares this with her. Others have drawn on psychoanalytic theory to argue that the female monopoly of childcare not only has profound effects on gender identity, but also means that we associate female authority with the anxieties, conflicts of will and humiliations of early childhood (see in particular Chodorow 1978 and Dinnerstein 1987).

All this means that, even when equal opportunities recruitment methods are in place, a woman applying for a senior post or seeking to be selected for political office is likely to be judged as a woman as well as an individual, producing a 'lose–lose' situation of a type not experienced by men: if she is attractive and 'feminine' she cannot be taken seriously, but if she is not, there is something wrong with her; if she has children it is expected that she will find it difficult to do the job, but if she has not, or if she has a full-time nanny, she is unnatural or a bad mother; if her management style is based on persuasion and team working then she lacks leadership qualities, but if she is more assertive she is problematically unfeminine, and may trigger deep-seated insecurities about female authority figures – and anyway, the kind of person the selectors want is like that really excellent chap they had before and this woman is not like him at all.

That kind of discrimination is certainly not confined to men, it is often subconscious, and it can be hard to prove. However, recent research about the way prospective parliamentary candidates in the UK are treated provides evidence for its continuation: women hoping to stand in the 2001 general election faced discriminatory comments and questions such as 'Can't have her, she has young children' and 'What would your husband do for sex when you are away during the week?' (Conservative Party) and 'Well you didn't do so bad for a little woman', 'You are the best candidate but we are not yet ready for a woman', 'We do enjoy watching you speak, we always imagine what your knickers are like' (Labour Party) (Shephard-Robinson and Lovenduski 2002). What seems particularly shocking about these examples is not just that some people think like that, but that some of them still think it is acceptable to say it in public. Tightening up the legislation and getting proper job specifications can obviously help, but the underlying mindset is much harder to change.

Inequality in the private sphere

Another important aspect of the gendered context within which competition takes place is men's and women's domestic situation. This leads to the second point of criticism: that liberalism's focus on the public sphere has no way of conceptualising domestic inequalities, and of understanding that these are important both in their own right and because of their impact on women's and men's employment and political opportunities (for related arguments, see Rosemary Crompton's chapter in this volume). From a liberal perspective, the killing of an average of two women a week in the UK by their partners or ex-partners, and the domestic violence experienced by 25 per cent of women at some time in their lives (Women and Equality Unit 2005) is not a political issue; such violence is interpreted as a series of personal tragedies and criminal acts, rather than a reflection of and contributor to broader patterns of inequality or oppression. The unequal domestic division of labour has similarly been largely ignored by liberal political thought, which sees it as a private matter.

Although there have been significant changes in recent years, and there is a widespread perception that many men now play a much greater role in the home than in the recent past, the evidence from time-use studies around the world indicates that domestic and caring work still remain disproportionately the responsibility of women (for an overview, see Gershuny 2000). Some feminists see this continuing domestic inequality as a product of gender role socialisation as discussed above, while others see gender identity as essentially fragile, something that has to be constantly reasserted through appropriate action, so that people are in effect 'doing gender', making statements about their gender identity, at the same time as performing other tasks. From this perspective, men's gender identity is under threat if they take on household or caring roles, while 'Her doing the laundry and his fixing the light switch not only produces clean clothes and a lit room, they also produce a reaffirmation of gender roles' (Blumberg 1991: 20; see also West and Zimmerman 1991). More prosaically, the traditional gender allocation of labour is often a rational allocation of time, given that in most couples women earn less than their partners. Although a minority of women are able to pay others to do their domestic and caring work for them, as Ruth Lister has pointed out such a strategy reinforces traditional roles, leaving men's 'domestic absenteeism' undisturbed (Lister 2003: 134). Men's exemption from these time-consuming responsibilities clearly limits women's opportunities to compete equally with them outside the home; in the UK a report from the Fawcett Society (a long-established feminist organisation) identified this as a key reason for continuing economic inequalities (Bellamy and Rake 2005). However, from a liberal equal rights perspective, this work is invisible; and because it is not seen, it is neither valued nor rewarded.

This failure to see the value of domestic work and its impact on women's opportunities is certainly not confined to liberalism, but is shared with other male theorists, including those theories of citizenship which stress paid employment as a key responsibility which is also a key source of entitlement, and which have influenced New Labour's thinking in the UK. While some early utopian socialists provide an exception (see Taylor 1983), most male socialist and Marxist writers and activists have neither seen the economic importance of this work nor questioned women's responsibility for it. Indeed, many have seemed to think that a fair division of labour is 'You make the tea; I'll

make the revolution'; the effect of this on women's opportunities for
political participation is captured in the complaint of Hannah
Mitchell, an English suffrage campaigner and socialist, who pointed
out nearly 100 years ago that 'No cause can be won between dinner
and tea, and most of us who were married had to fight with one hand
tied behind us, so to speak' (Mitchell 1977: 130).

The partiality of male perspectives

Such issues are tied in with my third point of criticism of 'common-
sense' approaches: that public debate is conducted within the terms
of a scale of values which reflects men's experiences and priorities
and presents these as 'normal', and which marginalises, devalues
or ignores those associated with women. This view treats men as
the 'default setting' for what it is to be human, compared to which
women are 'different'. This means that equality has been granted to
women on terms which have been set by men, and that men are the
standard against which we are measured. And this means that women
can be 'equal' only to the extent that they can be like men (although,
as I suggested above, they may be regarded with suspicion if they do
this too well).

According to these dominant values, the ability to give birth is not
something to be prized and rewarded, but a disadvantage that may
prevent women behaving like men – that is, like proper human beings.
This is connected to a more general under-valuing of activities on
which women are more likely than men to spend their time. To take
the most obvious example: if asked, many people would agree that
one of the most important jobs in any society is the care and
upbringing of the next generation. However, this is not something
that has attracted economic reward or political recognition. Rather,
those who look after their own children suffer economic penalties
and, according to most of the political and academic rhetoric about
citizenship or stakeholding, they are not active citizens, and they do
not have a stake in society – it is paid employment that is the key to
this. At the same time, if this paid employment involves the caring
work traditionally done by women, it is still economically penalised.
In the UK, this under-valuing of caring work is illustrated clearly by
the rates paid to young people starting work after completing modern
apprenticeships, with those qualified in early years childcare and

education (97 per cent of whom are women) recently earning an average of £148 a week, compared with £242 for those qualified in engineering (96 per cent of whom are men), although all qualifications were assessed as being at an equivalent skills level (Wild 2003 and Equal Opportunities Commission 2003). The message for women seems to be that if they want economic independence, if they want to be valued as citizens, they should behave like men. The same message applies to men who might think of taking on traditionally female roles, but who should do so only if they do not mind losing status and economic independence.

However, the paid and unpaid work that women have traditionally done will not go away if they start behaving like men – so this equality on men's terms leaves open the question of who is to do the work that women used to do, and how we are to meet the 'caring deficit' that is likely to result when women enter paid employment. There are a number of possible solutions. One set of solutions involves providing good, affordable childcare, restructuring employment around family needs and encouraging men to play a greater role in the home. Although many argue that there is still much to do and there are distinct national differences, this has been the general approach in the Nordic nations, where men as well as women are able to take extensive leave for family reasons, educational programmes have been deliberately designed to challenge gender stereotypes from the earliest possible age and care workers are relatively well paid. This collectivist approach clearly involves a high level of taxation and state intervention, and is the product of a form of democratic socialism very different from the liberal assumptions which dominate in the United States and, to a lesser extent, in the UK. It also involves a shift in the terms of debate, as equality is premised upon changes in men's behaviour as well as women's. While such change so far falls well short of equality, the principle that enabling people to take time out of paid employment to look after family members is not 'special treatment' but a way of helping them to meet socially important responsibilities is widely articulated.

In contrast, the individualistic assumptions of the United States mean that it is largely up to each woman to find her own solution within a framework of formal equality of opportunity. Within this framework, caring responsibilities are seen as a consequence of private choices which may impede full citizenship and employment opportunities, but which are not a matter of public concern; although some employers and insurance schemes now provide maternity cover, this has in the past been seen by the courts as unlawful discrimination against men, and there is still no statutory right to maternity leave. As discussed in the final section of this chapter, there is now significantly more support for workers with family responsibilities in the UK; however the 'choices' available to individual women are still often highly constrained. Some of course try to juggle work and family. However a long-hours culture makes this extremely difficult. Long hours also make it difficult for male partners to contribute more at home, even if they want to; indeed, fathers in the UK work even longer hours than childless colleagues, with a third spending more than fifty hours a week at work (Cousins and Tang 2003; for good comparative overviews of such policies, see Daly and Rake 2003, and Gornick and Meyers 2003).

A minority of women are able to behave more like men by paying others to perform domestic duties. However, many women who buy such services may also feel guilty at not spending more time with their family, and fall into the 'super-woman' syndrome of frenetic activity during their limited time at home, as described in Allison Pearson's novel *I Don't Know How She Does It* (2002). This kind of 'solution' does not challenge existing patterns, and means that many women in full-time employment are still competing with one hand tied behind them; many have complained that, contrary to the earlier feminist promise that they could 'have it all', they are simply 'doing it all'.

Unsurprisingly, given existing conditions of full-time employment and the lack of good, affordable childcare in the USA and UK, many other women attempt to reconcile employment with their traditional domestic role by working part-time (women are 46 per cent of the UK labour force, and 45 per cent of women employees work part-time). Such work is in general particularly badly paid: while the hourly rate of full-time women workers is now 82 per cent that of full-time men workers, for part-time women workers it is only 59 per cent; in the USA the gap is even larger (Bellamy and Rake 2005). Part-time employment is also frequently insecure, and often offers little opportunity for training or career advancement. A significant number of UK women still leave paid employment in order to meet family commitments. Over a third of mothers, more than one in ten fathers and nearly one in five people with another unpaid caring role have given up or turned down a job because of their caring responsibilities (Equal Opportunities Commission 2005). Lone parents (90 per cent of whom are women) face particular difficulties; only 56 per cent of lone parents are in paid employment, compared with 72 per cent of those with a partner (Bellamy and Rake 2005).

The alternatives for many women in the UK and USA therefore seem to be the stress of trying to combine long hours of full employment with family responsibilities, the 'sticky floor' of badly paid and insecure part-time work which provides only a degree of economic independence and is unlikely to be a route out of poverty, or total financial dependency on a male partner or on means-tested state benefits. Contrary to the arguments of Catherine Hakim in her chapter, this is often experienced not as a set of choices, but as a dilemma. The experience of the Nordic nations suggests both that state policies can provide more meaningful choices and that these policies must challenge the workplace norms that assume men's domestic absenteeism.

Equality in an unequal society

As noted above, in a world in which women are economically penalised for not behaving as men, domestic and caring work is generally either unpaid or poorly paid. This means that while off-loading such work may enable a minority of women to succeed in the competitive employment market, their success is likely to involve the continuing exploitation of others. This is perhaps the logical result of the kind of advice given by the influential American feminist writer and activist Betty Friedan in the 1960s, when she exhorted women to get out of the home and into the workplace – and promised them that it would be worth it in terms of fulfilment and self-realisation, even if they had to spend most of their salary on a cleaning lady (Friedan 1986: 303). Quite how the cleaning lady would be fulfilled was not clear. Today, paying other women can involve exporting the 'care deficit' to places such as Mexico and the Philippines, as women leave their own children to work as nannies in the West (Ehrenreich and Hochschild 2003). Women's low average earnings also mean that most simply cannot afford to pay their childminders a decent wage; even when childcare is provided or subsidised by the state, rates of pay remain extremely low.

This ties in with my final point of criticism, which also takes me back to where I started – the 'tadpole' philosophy which accepts that most people will never have a taste of frog life and that outcomes will continue to be profoundly unequal. The kind of equality that enables a few high-flying women to behave like privileged men is a very limited kind of equality. I am interested in a much more substantive and inclusive kind of equality that addresses overall inequalities and issues of class and 'race' as well as sex. As Nancy Fraser says in her chapter, such a model of equality cannot be achieved within the frame of the modern territorial state, and feminists are increasingly working through trans-national organisations.

A non-patriarchal approach to equality

Criticising is easy; coming up with positive proposals can be more difficult. However, I think that the points I have made so far have some positive implications which could provide the basis for a non-patriarchal approach to equality. By a non-patriarchal approach, I mean one which does not assume that men are the starting point and the measure of worth, and which sees women as 'normal' rather than 'different'.

This means that a non-patriarchal approach to equality would value the activities and qualities traditionally associated with women as much as those associated with men. It would also expose men as 'free riders', benefiting collectively, and often individually, from the caring work of women. This has clear practical implications. Most women have always known that their unpaid work was important; most men have either ignored it, or paid lip-service to it without taking it seriously; from this new perspective, it would be central to economic, social and political analysis and planning. Status and adequate economic reward would no longer be denied to women or men who do this work either inside or outside the home.

Such a model of equality would require a major re-evaluation of what we understand by 'merit', 'worth' and 'importance', and it would assume that the behaviour and situation of men as well as women would have to change. Employment would be organised on the assumption that 'normal' workers – men as well as women – have family responsibilities and a life outside the workplace. Flexible and shorter working hours would be seen as standard, rather than 'special treatment' for women, and long hours working would be actively discouraged as a cause of 'domestic absenteeism'. There would be good support for caring responsibilities, including childcare provision and the care of elderly people. These changes would facilitate a more equitable division of labour within the home. The importance of domestic and caring work would be recognised, and people would no longer have to sacrifice economic independence if they looked after others. Ultimately, we could move to a 'universal caregiver' model of society, in which 'women's current life-patterns [become] the norm for everyone' (Fraser 2000: 25; see also Kershaw 2005 for development of this idea).

All this adds up to some very major changes which are clearly not going to be put into practice in the short term. Although men might benefit from them in many ways, they have a lot to lose: not just the practical advantage of earning more or not being expected to clean the lavatory, but the less tangible benefits of being central and 'normal'. Expecting men to forgo their advantages and displace themselves from the centre of the world is asking a lot. The kind of changes I have suggested are also clearly expensive, particularly in the short run. They are highly unlikely to be achieved in a pure market economy in which services are provided only if they make a profit. Good-quality, affordable childcare with well-paid workers is never going to be profitable.

In contrast to those who say that there is no necessary connection between feminism and socialism, I would therefore argue that the kind of feminism that is relevant to more than an elite few will never be realised without a more collectivist approach and a modification of market capitalism. Because poverty is disproportionately concentrated amongst women, increased substantive equality between men and women would also inevitably involve a redistribution from the rich to the poor. As I have argued elsewhere, my theoretical starting-point is also a product both of an acceptance of the classic Marxist claim that, if we are to understand the history and future potential of human society, we must look at the production and reproduction of material life, and of an insistence that Marxism must be reconceptualised from a perspective which includes women on an equal basis and recognises the importance of their activities. From this more inclusive perspective, if we are to understand how societies have developed and how they might be changed, we must include an analysis of the changing nature and conditions of (re)production, which I define as 'those human activities (physical and emotional) which are more or less directly linked to the generational reproduction and maintenance of the population and the care of those unable to look after themselves' – that is, activities traditionally associated with women (Bryson 2004, 2005).

A non-patriarchal model of equality may appear to be simply a dream. Nevertheless, and despite the continuing 'retreat from socialism' and rise of neoliberalism in the West, there may be a number of encouraging signs. I do not want to overstate these, but they do suggest that, in Britain at least, the terms of debate may at last be beginning to shift.

First of all, workers in most western nations now have some rights to work more flexible hours and to take time off for family reasons. The UK has lagged behind most of Europe, but there is now an acknowledged need for 'family friendly' hours, or 'work–life balance'; and the TUC has put 'work–life balance' at the top of its political agenda; even in the United States, there is a right to two weeks of unpaid parental leave. This is not enough, but it may be the beginnings of a change, a recognition that men have children too, that equality can be reconstructed on different terms, that women do not have to do all the adjusting.

Second, in the UK we now have a national childcare strategy, and Gordon Brown has repeatedly said that childcare needs to be at the heart of economic policy. In practice the provision is inadequate and the funding insecure – but again, it is a step in the right direction, and an important statement that governments are responsible; as such they may be held accountable.

Thirdly, the Platform of Action agreed at the 1995 World Conference on Women in Beijing committed governments to measuring the value of the unpaid work that is primarily done by women. One key way of doing this is to measure the time that is spent on this work, and time-use research has become a major academic growth area: all over the world, people are being surveyed and asked to complete time-use diaries in which they record their activities throughout the day. Time-use diaries assume that time-use can be recorded as a series of discrete events. Critics have suggested that they therefore cannot capture the 'being there' nature of much caring work, or the extent to which this is often a constraining background to other activities (for example, time diaries would record a mother watching television on her own in a house with a sleeping child as enjoying 'free time', even if she would prefer to be in the pub or at a political meeting) (see Everingham 2002; Budig and Folbre 2004). They may therefore over-record women's free time and under-estimate the impact of the domestic division of labour. Nevertheless, they have revealed the economic importance of unpaid productive work (according to initial analyses in the UK, the GNP is at least 40 per cent and possibly 100 per cent bigger if unpaid work is included). They have also confirmed that, despite some evidence of 'gender convergence' in western nations, this important work remains disproportionately the responsibility of women (for overviews and discussion, see Gershuny 2000 and Folbre and Bittman 2004; for recent research see the conference papers on the website of the International Association of Time Use Research (IATUR)).

Together, these three changes – the introduction of more flexible working practices as a standard condition of employment, the acceptance of some collective responsibility for childcare, and the measurement of unpaid work as valuable productive activity – have the potential to transform the political agenda and the terms on which equality is debated. If politicians say that we are entitled to balance our work with the rest of our life, we will start to expect that fathers as well as mothers should be able to do so; if they say that they are developing a national childcare strategy, we will expect them to deliver; if they discover that unpaid work is economically important, we may expect it to be properly rewarded. We may even start exploring the full potential of our legal right to equal pay for work of equal value, extending these claims to work within the home. These changes therefore might be seen as straws in the wind, a sign that thinking just might be beginning to shift, and that we might be able to think about equality in very different terms.

There are other aspects of women's situation that are difficult to conceptualise within an equality framework, although they are clearly relevant to it. I am thinking in particular of women's right to live free from male violence and to make their own reproductive decisions. However, because different aspects of women's situations are interconnected, changes in one area can have a knock-on effect in others. For example, the increase in women in public life, although far short of equality, has led to an increased awareness of the extent and seriousness of violence against women, while greater economic independence would make it easier to leave a violent partner. Once again, it is not enough, and I would not want to suggest that the relationships are simple. Nevertheless, it may suggest some possibility of transforming the vicious circle of inequality and oppression into a virtuous circle of increased equality and progressive change.

References

Banks, O. (1986) *Faces of Feminism* (Oxford: Basil Blackwell).

Bellamy, K. and Rake, K. (2005) *Money, Money, Money. Is It Still a Rich Man's World? An Audit of Women's Economic Welfare in Britain Today* (London: Fawcett Society).

Blumberg, R. (1991) *Gender, Family and Economy: The Triple Overlap* (London: Sage).

Bryson, V. (1999) ' "Patriarchy": A Concept Too Useful to Lose', *Contemporary Politics* 5, 4: 311–24.

(2003) *Feminist Political Theory: An Introduction*, 2nd edn (Basingstoke: Macmillan Palgrave).

(2004) 'Marxism and Feminism: Can the "Unhappy Marriage" Be Saved?' *Journal of Political Ideologies* 9, no. 1: 13–30.

(2005) 'Production and (Re)production', in G. Blakeley and V. Bryson (eds.), *Marx and Other Four-Letter Words* (London: Pluto), 127–42.

Budig, M. and Folbre, N. (2004) 'Activity, Proximity or Responsibility? Measuring Parental Childcare Time', in N. Folbre and M. Bittman (eds.), *Family Time: The Social Organisation of Care* (London and New York: Routledge), 51–68.

Chodorow, N. (1978) *The Reproduction of Mothering: Psychoanalysis and the Sociology of Gender* (Berkeley, Los Angeles and London: University of California Press).

Cousins, C. and Tang, N. (2003) *Working Time: Flexibility and Family Life in the UK, the Netherlands and Sweden* (University of Hertfordshire Business School, Employment Studies Paper 45).

Daly, M. and Rake, K. (2003) *Gender and the Welfare State* (Cambridge: Polity).

Dinnerstein, D. (1987) *The Rocking of the Cradle and the Ruling of the World* (London: Women's Press).

Ehrenreich, B. and Hochschild, A. (eds.) (2003) *Global Women: Nannies, Maids and Sex Workers in the New Economy* (New York: Metropolitan Books).

Equal Opportunities Commission (2003) Press Release 'Minimum Wage for Modern Apprentices Would Help Close Gender Pay Gap' (Manchester: EOC).

(2005) *Sex and Power: Who Runs Britain?* (Manchester: EOC).

Evans, B. (2005) 'Equality', in G. Blakeley and V. Bryson (eds.), *Marx and Other Four-Letter Words* (London: Pluto), 176–91.

Evans, R. (1977) *The Feminists: Women's Emancipation Movements in Europe, America and Australasia* 1840–1920 (London: Croom Helm).

Everingham, C. (2002) 'Engendering Time. Gender Equity and Discourses of Workplace Flexibility', *Time and Society* 11, 2/3: 335–51.

Folbre, N. and Bittman, M. (eds.) (2004) *Family Time: The Social Organisation of Care* (London and New York: Routledge).

Fraser, M. (2000) 'After the Family Wage: A Postindustrial Thought Experiment', in B. Hobson (ed.), *Gender and Citizenship in Transition* (Basingstoke: Macmillan), 1–32.

Friedan, B. (1986[1963]) *The Feminine Mystique* (Harmondsworth: Penguin Books).

Gershuny, J. (2000) *Changing Times: Work and Leisure in Postindustrial Society* (Oxford: Oxford University Press).

Gornick, J. and Meyers, M. (2003) *Families that Work: Policies for Reconciling Parenthood and Employment* (New York: Russell Sage Foundation).

Kershaw, P. (2005) *Carefair. Rethinking the Responsibilities and Rights of Citizenship* (Vancouver: UBG Press).

Lister, R. (2003) *Citizenship: Feminist Perspectives* (Basingstoke: Macmillan).

Millett, K. (1985) *Sexual Politics* (London: Virago).

Mitchell, H. (1977) *The Hard Way Up* (London: Virago).

Nordic Council of Ministers (2005) 'The Nordic Cooperation Programme on Gender Equality 2005', www.norden.org/pub (visited 16/06/06).

Pearson, A. (2002) *I Don't Know How She Does It* (London: Quality Paperbacks Direct).

Shephard-Robinson, L. and Lovenduski, J. (2002) 'Women and Candidate Selection in British Political Parties' (London: Fawcett Society).

Taylor, B. (1983) *Eve and the New Jerusalem: Socialism and Feminism in the Nineteenth Century* (London: Virago).

UNDP (2005) hdr.undp.org/reports/global/2005/ (visited 15 June 2006).

West, C. and Zimmerman, D. (1991) 'Doing Gender', in J. Lorber and S. Farrell (eds.), *The Social Construction of Gender* (London: Sage), 13–37.

Wild, S. (2003) *Equal Pay in Europe: Making women's work pay in the UK* (Manchester: Equal Opportunities Commission).

Women and Equality Unit 2005 http://www.womenandequalityunit.gov.uk/domestic_violence/index.htm (visited 05/05/05).

3 | *When will society be gender just?*

INGRID ROBEYNS

The question of gender justice[1]

In post-industrial liberal-democratic societies, opinions vary dramatically on whether these societies are gender just. Both scholars and the wider public disagree on this question. Newspaper articles, television programmes and other public debates indicate that gender inequality is not only a topical but also a controversial issue, on which many people have strong views. As Deborah Rhode argues, some claim that unjust inequalities between women and men no longer exist, or that women's liberation has achieved more than enough, and these days it is men who are suffering discrimination.[2] Others disagree, and argue that unjust inequalities to the disadvantage of women remain, despite the post-feminist discourse.[3]

One might expect that the literature in inequality studies, and related fields in the social sciences and political philosophy, would be able to assess these conflicting claims, and inform us on the nature and extent of unjust gender inequalities. Unfortunately, this is not really the case: there are very few systematic studies that provide a satisfying answer to this question. The reason for this is that an adequate answer to this question requires both normative theorising and empirical analysis. Normative political philosophers are concerned with the first, while social scientists specialise in empirical research. But most theoretical studies do not engage with empirical analysis, and most empirical studies are not based on a well-elaborated underlying theory of gender justice. At first glance, it seems that the empirical literatures

[1] This chapter benefited from discussions with Jane Humphries, Patrick Loobuyck, Serena Olsaretti, Anne Phillips, Roland Pierik and Amartya Sen. The financial support of the Netherlands Organisation for Scientific Research (NWO) is gratefully acknowledged.
[2] See Rhode (1997).
[3] This is the dominant view in gender studies. See e.g. McMahon (1999) and Kimmel (2000).

54

in the social sciences pointing to specific inequalities would be most illuminating to answer the question how just or unjust the gender constellations in our societies are. These empirical literatures provide evidence of inequalities between men and women, for example inequalities in earnings, wages, unpaid work, labour market participation, or top positions in companies and politics.[4] However, this applied empirical literature offers no conceptual and normative framework for what the *unjust* inequalities are, and is therefore not able to give us much guidance on which of the observed inequalities should bother us from a normative point of view. In other words, these empirical literatures lack a normative conceptualisation of gender justice.

In this chapter, I want to ask what determines whether a society is gender just. In other words, how should we conceive of gender justice? When will we reach a society that is gender just, or is perhaps our current society already gender just? In developing a conceptualisation of gender justice, I will in part rely on Amartya Sen's capability approach, which is a general normative framework that many feminists and gender scholars have found helpful or promising in thinking about gender issues.[5] But the capability approach is *not* a complete theory of justice. For its specification to issues of gender justice, it requires a conceptualisation of gender, and it requires some minimal principles of justice. The conceptualisation of gender that I will develop in the next section is based on both theoretical and empirical insights from political philosophy, social and cognitive psychology, sociology and economics. The following section presents the capability approach as the normative foundation for interpersonal comparisons that underpin assessments of gender justice. The next section proposes and defends three principles of gender justice that can be used to determine whether a society is gender just. The available empirical evidence suggests that these principles of gender justice are not yet met. In other words, we do not yet live in gender just societies, but clearly spelling out an account of gender justice is needed to determine when – if ever – we will reach a gender just society in the future.

[4] For some examples, see Blau (1998); Pilcher (1999); and Rubery, Smith and Fagan (1999).
[5] See e.g. Nussbaum (2000); Agarwal, Humphries and Robeyns (2005); and Lewis and Giullari (2005).

Conceptualising gender

What is gender? The concept of gender can be theorised in many different ways, and the usefulness of any such conceptualisation depends to some extent on which purposes one wants to use the concept for, and in which intellectual traditions one wants to introduce it. In what follows, I will sketch a conceptualisation of gender that aims to be useful for answering rather mainstream questions, such as the one that is central to this chapter. In other intellectual traditions, such as psychoanalysis, post-modernism and post-structuralism, different conceptualisations of gender are used, which are more suited to the different epistemological goals of these fields.

Sally Haslanger's definition of gender provides a good starting point to sketch a brief account of gender.[6] Haslanger defines gender in terms of the social positions that men and women occupy. A person belongs to a gender because she is thought to have certain bodily features that reveal her reproductive capacities. These bodily features function as markers for evaluating individuals as either men or women, and for justifying their respective social positions. Gender is thus a social category, with two modes, man and woman. Observations or imaginations of sexual characteristics serve as markers to classify individuals in different social positions. The social category 'gender' thus becomes projected on the biological category 'sex'. The point about the concept of gender is that women and men are treated according to their social positions (gender) for reasons that have nothing, or only tangentially, to do with their biological position (sex).

This abstract conceptualisation of gender can be fleshed out in many ways. One way to do so is by using four additional concepts: norms, stereotypes, identities and social institutions. Norms can be legal, social or moral, but all have in common that a person violating a norm will be sanctioned, either by a legal punishment, or by the contempt and disgust of others, which will trigger shame in the violator.[7] Many norms are gendered, that is, they apply to women and men (girls and boys) in different ways. Most laws have been made gender neutral over the past decades, but jurisprudence is still gendered.[8] Social and moral norms are probably more important for our understanding of how norms impact on gender inequalities.

---

[6] See Haslanger (2000).   [7] See Elster (1999).   [8] See Kennedy (1992).

These gender norms impose codes of masculinity and femininity and notions of what the appropriate and 'normal' behaviour for a man or a woman is. For example, it is less socially accepted that mothers leave their children in the care of another person when going on a trip away from home than for fathers. The more a mother's friends and colleagues reveal that they do not consider it 'normal' that she leaves her children in someone else's care, the higher the probability that the mother will feel guilty. Fathers are much less likely to receive disapproving comments if they leave their children in care of another person. Gender norms also affect the distribution of wealth and power, because the norms for success in positions of authority collide with norms of femininity. The social norms for positions of authority include that one should show assertive behaviour and decisiveness, whereas norms of femininity put clear limits on how assertive a woman can be before she is considered aggressive and thus evaluated negatively. Identical behaviour in leadership or problem-solving situations is often judged very differently for women than for men, with women judged more negatively than men.[9] These conflicting norms put women in a no-win situation: either they adhere to the social norms regulating leadership positions and the professions, but then they are seen as too aggressive and too 'masculine', or they conform to the social norms which stipulate how a woman should behave, but then they are seen as too passive, sweet, and insufficiently ambitious to be able to succeed in the hard 'male' world.

Many social norms create and reinforce gender inequalities. Lee Badgett and Nancy Folbre have argued that the norm that places the responsibility of caring for children and the elderly on women reinforces their financial dependence and socio-economic vulnerability.[10] As such, gender norms create and reinforce power imbalances between the two genders. The femininity norms make it much harder for women than for men to gain power. As Pierre Bourdieu put it, 'access to power of any kind places women in a "double bind": if they behave like men, they risk losing the obligatory attributes of "femininity" and call into question the natural right of men to the positions of power; if they behave like women, they appear incapable and unfit for the job'.[11] Whereas empirical studies show that both men and women are socially punished if they violate their respective gender

[9] See Valian (1998).   [10] See Badgett and Folbre (1999).   [11] Bourdieu (2001).

norms, conforming to these norms leads to gendered behaviour that puts women in a structurally weaker position than men.

In addition to gender norms, men and women are also subjected to gender stereotypes. There is now a large body of empirical research in social, cognitive and development psychology to help explain why women achieve less than men in the professions, when there is no indication of *overt* discrimination. In such cases, gender stereotypes play a central role in shaping women's and men's professional achievements. Stereotypes are cognitive devices that operate at the non-conscious level, and help us to make sense of the staggering amount of information that our brain constantly has to process. They are hypotheses about sex differences, which affect our expectations of men and women and our evaluations of their work, qualities and abilities. These expectations and evaluations will affect individuals' actual performance, as well as the aspirations they hold. They are shared by members of a society, and are formed as part of socialisation processes. Both men and women form expectations and judge other people with the same gender stereotypes. According to Valian, in white, western middle-class society male stereotypes include 'being capable of independent, autonomous action (agentic, in short), assertive, instrumental, and task-oriented. Men act.' For women, the stereotypes focuses on 'being nurturant, expressive, communal, and concerned about others'.[12] According to Valian, stereotypes are not wholly inaccurate, but they over-generalise and over-simplify, and ignore that the sexes are more alike than that they are different. The main problem therefore is that people are judged not only on their own performance and abilities, but in part on over-simplified stereotypes attributed to their gender. One effect of these stereotypes is that behaviour associated with being a good professional is typically valued negatively for women and positively for men. For instance, taking on the role of a leader is likely to be praised if it is performed by a man, but is often valued negatively when performed by a woman. As a consequence, our evaluations lead to different treatment of men and women in the labour market. And while each of these biases may be small, they accumulate and result in significant gender inequalities in pay, promotion, power, and so forth.

[12] Valian (1998: 13).

It is not difficult to see how gender norms and stereotypes affect a person's notion of herself, or her personal identity. Adopting an identity that conforms with gender norms will avoid the pain of feeling ashamed. One could opt for a gender non-conformist identity, but this will come at the price of disapproval by members of mainstream society, and the risk of lower levels of material well-being. Gender stereotypes also have far-reaching effects on our conceptions of ourselves.[13] Because of gender stereotypes everyone has different expectations of men and women. The expectations of others will influence our behaviour and mould our preferences. For example, in a setting in which neither men nor women are experts, men are more likely to behave as if they are the experts and women as if they are the non-experts.[14] Considering oneself an expert and claiming social power thus becomes part of the masculine identity through the working of the gender stereotypes. These stereotypes are to some extent self-fulfilling prophecies, because they affect individuals' behaviour and beliefs, and they reify the gender hypotheses that make up the stereotype. In addition children are through socialisation moulded in the existing social patterns, thereby forming their gender identity. Individuals might raise their children in certain ways or decide to lead a gender non-conformist life, but if only a few people make this decision it will not change social norms or societal structures and institutions.

Finally, social institutions are also 'gendered' in the sense that they tend to take gender differences which are created by gender inequalities as 'natural', and use these differences as a justification for those inequalities. These institutions include our educational system, the media, families, labour market, workplaces and labour unions. There is a vast literature in the social sciences showing how structures of social institutions themselves produce and sustain existing gender inequalities. For example, in many liberal-democratic societies childcare facilities are inadequate. But the job requirements for most full-time jobs implicitly assume that the worker is free of caring responsibilities. This makes it very difficult for both parents to hold full-time jobs. In the above formulation, this situation sounds gender neutral, and seems to indicate more a problem that *parents* face, instead of it being a gender issue. But this is not the case, owing

[13] Valian (1998: 145–66).   [14] Valian (1998: 150).

to the gender norm that stipulates that children should be taken care of by their mothers, as they are assumed to be far better at nurturing babies and caring for children than fathers. Moreover, despite scientific evidence to the contrary, it is widely believed that children are harmed if they are left in day care,[15] and that it is primarily mothers' responsibility to care for the children. As the organisation of the workplace makes it very hard for parents to have an egalitarian arrangement, the design of this social institution will contribute to gender inequalities (in income, labour market participation, leadership positions, and so forth), thereby relying upon, and reinforcing, gender norms.[16]

Other social institutions are equally gendered. For example, gendered classrooms reinforce gender stereotypes, both in the differential way that teachers respond to boys or girls, and also in the gender stereotypical messages that many textbooks hide. The media also contribute to spreading gender norms, thereby constructing idealised notions of masculinity and femininity. Similarly, families are gendered institutions, as parents teach children what the 'appropriate' behaviour for boys and girls is, and as most families live according to conventional gender norms.

In conclusion, gender is a complex multilayered phenomenon. For analytical purposes it is useful to have an array of tools, but in real life the workings of gender norms, stereotypes, institutions and identity constantly interact. All of them steer men and women into different social positions, and give them different rewards for their (market and non-market) activities.

Gender justice and capabilities

When thinking about gender justice, we always – implicitly or explicitly – rely on a metric of interpersonal comparisons. For example,

---

[15] The empirical evidence mainly suggests that day care can be harmful to children but only when the day care is of very poor quality (which is the case for some day care in the USA) and if the daily time spent in day care is too long. Moreover, for children from deprived groups, day care can be better than being cared for at home. See Singer (1993).

[16] Egalitarian families exist but are rare and have a hard time to negotiate non-egalitarian public values and social institutions. See Lipsitz Bem (1998) and Risman (1998).

some might compare men's and women's material well-being (earnings and wealth), and argue that as long as women as a group are materially worse off than men, society is gender unjust. Or some might endorse a formal or legalistic metric, and argue that as long as women have the same legal rights as men, society is gender just. Still others might argue that as long as women and men do not have the same 'real choice' in life, our societies are not gender just.

In this chapter, I want to propose an account of gender justice that compares inequality between men and women on the dimension of a person's *capabilities*, which is her real freedom to choose the kind of life one has reason to value. This notion of capabilities has some roots in the history of political thought, but is in contemporary philosophy introduced by the economist and philosopher Amartya Sen.[17]

The capability approach makes interpersonal comparisons by focusing on people's real or effective opportunities to do what they want to do, and be whom they want to be. These beings and doings are called a person's functionings, and include such basic functionings as being healthy, being sheltered, not being mentally ill, having valuable social relations, and more complex and specific functionings such as combining a job with family life. Capabilities are the effective opportunities which a person has to realise these activities and these states of being.

Sen has criticised assessments of justice or inequality that focus exclusively on income or material well-being. He argues that income cannot adequately account for inter-individual differences in people's abilities to convert these primary goods into what people are able to be and to do in their lives. For example, disabilities greatly increase the income one needs to reach the same level of capabilities compared with an able-bodied person. Income and other resources broadly defined (such as skills, degrees or assets) are the means to pursue one's life plan. In contrast, so Sen argues, we should focus directly on people's functionings and capabilities.

Both gender and sex are such 'conversion factors' that influence the conversion of income and other resources into capabilities. How can we understand sex to be such a conversion factor? For example, men's

---

[17] Some key references on the capability approach, in particular in relation to social justice are Sen (1990a, 1992, 1995 and 1999). For a theoretical introduction to the capability approach, see Robeyns (2005b).

and women's different reproductive capacities give (most) women the capability to give birth and breastfeed their children. Many women regard this as a valuable life-choice they can make, which is not available for men (and for infertile women). Other sex differences are not categorical, but are human characteristics of which the distribution among men and women are not the same. For example, men tend to have much more upper-body strength than women (though there are some women who are stronger than some men). Given these differences in the distributions among men and women, many more women than men will lack the minimal bodily strength needed to do extremely heavy physical work, and thus will lack that capability in life. These two examples are virtually uncontroversial cases of sex differences, but for many observed differences between men and women heated controversies exist on whether they are purely and exclusively sex differences, whether they are sex differences which are influenced by the gendered natures of societies and cultures, or whether they are genuinely gender differences but are claimed to be sex differences by anti-feminists as this allows them to justify unjust gender arrangements.[18]

Gender too can be theorised as a conversion factor that impacts on what people can do with their resources. Recall that resources should be broadly understood, and may include educational degrees, professional or social skills, or assets. Gender norms and gendered practices and institutions have an effect on the conversion of these resources into capabilities. For example, prejudice and stereotypes give women with similar professional degrees and experience to men fewer opportunities to reach leadership positions on the labour market. Similarly, notions of appropriate masculinity and femininity make it much more likely that a boy is discriminated against if he wants to be a babysitter compared with a girl.

In addition, the capability approach pays much attention to the material and non-material circumstances that shape people's opportunity sets, and the circumstances that influence the choices that people make from the capability set receive a central place in the interpersonal comparisons. For example, social norms and traditions influence women's preferences, aspirations and choices.[19] Thus,

---

[18] On this last point, see e.g. Bourdieu (2001).
[19] Sen (1990b); Nussbaum (2000).

the capability approach is not content with a focus on people's capability sets *only*, but insists that we also need to scrutinise the context in which economic production and social interactions take place, and whether the circumstances in which people choose from their opportunity sets are just.

If we are to use the capability approach for the question of gender justice, we need to make this theoretical framework more specific. As Sen himself has stressed, the capability approach does *not* amount to a theory of justice, but is merely an 'informational space' for interpersonal comparisons that allows for a class of theories of justice.[20]

A first major theoretical lacuna that needs to be filled in is the question of which capabilities will matter for the question of gender justice. Capability theorists have provided two types of answer to the question of which capabilities matter. Martha Nussbaum has developed a list of central human capabilities of which everyone should be entitled to a minimum threshold. She argues that every government should make sure that its citizens can enjoy minimum levels of these capabilities.[21] Nussbaum's list applies to all issues of justice, hence including the question of gender justice in post-industrial societies. Sen, on the other hand, does not want to endorse one specific list of capabilities, and argues that it is not up to the theorist to make such decisions, but rather to a democratic process among the relevant agents.[22] I subscribe to this second line, as I think that Nussbaum's method lacks both political and epistemological legitimacy. The problem lies not in the list of capabilities per se, but with whether the process by which this list is created gives the list sufficient legitimacy. In contrast to Nussbaum's universal list, I have proposed a procedural method for the selection of capabilities, which can be used to generate a context-dependent list of relevant capabilities for the question of gender inequality in western societies.[23] This list contains life and physical health; mental well-being; bodily integrity and safety; social relations and support; political empowerment; education and knowledge; domestic work and non-market care; paid work and other projects; shelter and environment; mobility; leisure; time autonomy; respect; and

[20] Sen (1995: 266–8).   [21] Nussbaum (2000, 2003).   [22] Sen (2004).
[23] Robeyns (2003, 2005a).

religion.[24] But even this list is and will always remain a list-in-progress that is nothing more than a substantiated proposal. Any participant in the debate on gender justice can propose amendments, as long as arguments are provided for why a particular capability should matter when assessing gender justice.

A second major theoretical lacuna in the application of the capability approach for the analysis of gender justice is the question of which principles of justice will need to be met. Sen has presented the capability approach as a general evaluative framework which focuses in particular on the dimensions in which interpersonal comparisons for the purpose of justice need to be made. But arguing for the dimensions in which we can detect justice is not sufficient to be able to answer the question whether a particular society is gender just. For example, imagine a household in which only the man holds a job, while the woman does not. The first thing we need to ask is whether this woman had the real freedom or capability to hold a job. Perhaps she does have the genuine capability, but chooses not to exercise it because she wants to engage in other activities, such as childcare or voluntary work. Perhaps she only has the formal opportunity, as the lack of childcare facilities or refusal by her partner to share the childcare does not create a real opportunity to hold a job. Most people would think that the first scenario would not pose a question of gender justice, while the second would. Or imagine a man and a woman, who both are equally talented, skilled and ambitious. They both hold similar jobs, hence in both cases they have the capability to engage in professional work which they have chosen to use. Imagine now two scenarios, one in which they both earn the same income from their jobs, while in the second the woman earns less. Surely it would be counterintuitive to conclude that in both scenarios the man and the woman have the same capability to work, and therefore this is a case of gender justice.[25] As these two examples illustrate, the capability approach to gender justice needs to specify the principles of justice that need to be satisfied. This is the challenge taken up in the next section.

[24] Robeyns (2003: 71–2).

[25] This echoes a critique by Thomas Pogge on the capability approach, that it would be unable to account for unjust inequalities in income and other resources. See Pogge (2002).

Three principles of gender justice

As outlined in the previous section, Amartya Sen has recognised that the capability approach does not amount to a theory of justice, and that principles need to be added. But Sen himself has not proposed any such principles or theory. Could we develop an outline of a theory of gender justice which recognises the strengths of capabilities as a metric for interpersonal comparisons for the purpose of justice, but which also includes principles which are needed to make complete judgements of justice, for example principles regarding just earning for gender segregated jobs?

In this section, I want to argue that a society can only be considered gender just if, and only if, the following three principles are met.

1 The capability sets for men and women should be the same. The only inequalities between men and women that are justified are those (a) that are (directly or indirectly) due to sex differences that are not gender differences, and (b) which cannot be rectified by human intervention.
2 The constraints on choice from the capability set should not be structured according to morally irrelevant characteristics, such as gender.
3 The 'pay-offs' of the different options in the capability set need to be justified and should not be gender biased.

Let us first look at the first principle: the capability sets for men and women should be equal, except for inequalities that are (directly or indirectly) due to sex differences that are not gender differences, and where the inequality cannot be rectified by human intervention. There are two important aspects to this principle: first, that it is an opportunity- rather than an outcome-based notion of justice, and second, that it tries to account for the fact that men and women differ because of their sex as well as because of their gender. Let us look at these two aspects in turn.

The principle states that the *capability* sets of men and women should be equal, not their achieved functionings sets. In other words, women and men should have the same real opportunities to valuable doings and beings, but we are not steering or forcing men and women into particular life-choices. By defending an opportunity- rather than an outcome-based notion of gender justice, we immediately touch a nerve of the feminist/anti-feminist debate, as anti-feminists have often claimed that women have the same options these days, but simply choose differently from men. Their different choices, which are often argued to be intrinsic to sex differences, would then explain the observed inequalities in outcomes, such as labour market positions, the amount of unpaid work being done, or positions of power and authority. I side with those feminists who claim that it is far too simple to argue that women and men simply make these choices, which does not create an issue of justice but should instead be respected as such, period. But I do not think that the solution is, as large segments of the women's movement have tended to claim, that as long as we don't see equal outcomes there is no gender justice. Unequal outcomes certainly should make us *investigate* their causes, and there is an argument to be made that the burden of proof should fall on those who claim that women systematically choose differently from men, *and* would do so in a world without unjust preferences formation mechanisms and in which the constraints on choice for men and women are the same.[26] But feminists should engage with an open mind with arguments that the biological differences between men and women, even when tiny in themselves, could create accumulated effects that could explain some of the inequalities in outcomes.[27] Given that, in my view, this academic debate is far from settled, we should concentrate on carefully examining the gender inequalities in *opportunities*, as one need not settle for a certain view on the intrinsic nature of the different preferences of men versus women in order to be able to endorse the principle that each should have the same genuine opportunities.

The second important aspect to note in this first principle is the inclusion of both sex and gender. Recall that the principle states that the capability sets for men and women should be equal, except for

---

[26] See Phillips (2004). Phillips is one of the few remaining theorists in contemporary egalitarian analytical political philosophy who argues against equality of opportunity and in defence of equality of outcome.

[27] In my view, there is a lot of prejudice by many mainstream social scientists towards anything labelled 'feminist' which blocks the spread of insights of the best of feminist knowledge into their research, but also results in a too easy dismissal by many feminist scholars of 'traditional' scientific research and the recent advances in fields such as cognitive psychology.

inequalities that are (directly or indirectly) due to sex differences that are not gender differences, and where the inequality cannot be rectified by human intervention. This implies that if a biological fact impacts on gender inequalities in capabilities, then only when no human intervention can diminish this inequality will it count as an acceptable gender inequality.[28] Two examples may clarify this point.

Consider first the example that only mothers can breastfeed children, while fathers cannot. Breastfeeding creates for some women certain benefits and valuable results, such as emotional closeness with the child. But there are also many direct and indirect costs in both material and capability terms, such as possible physical discomfort in the breasts, the loss of one's time autonomy, the tiredness that breastfeeding might cause, the 'work' of feeding the child, and any forgone labour market earnings. The first principle would indicate that these costs are an inequality but not an injustice, as long as facilitating and compensating policies are in place, such as providing mothers the option of bottle feeding, allowing for paid maternity and breastfeeding leave, and giving mothers free access to lactation consultants. However, because gender and sex interact with inequalities between parents and non-parents in different ways for men and women, developing a theory of gender justice requires the simultaneous development of a theory of justice between parents and non-parents. To the best of my knowledge, there does not, as yet, exist such a theory of parental justice in normative political philosophy. Some authors, often feminists, have argued for support for parents and children, though this literature has not reached by any measure the quality of analytical development and critical scrutiny that can be found in other areas of theories of justice, such as global justice, justice on the labour market, and so forth.

The second example to illustrate the sex–gender nexus of the first principle is the inequality in life-expectancy between men and

---

[28] In fact, at least one further qualification is required. There can be (at least in principle) reasonable limits to how much society wants to pay for achieving gender justice. Suppose that in the future it would be technologically possible for men to become pregnant, but only at a very high financial cost. The first principle would then require that we give men this opportunity. However, there may be good reasons, such as an extreme financial cost, for why a political community might decide not to subsidise this option.

women. In all post-industrial societies, women live on average
several years longer than men. Is this a violation of the first principle?
Living is certainly an important capability, hence the capability sets
of men and women should include not dying prematurely. Whether
or not this difference in life-expectancy between men and women is a
case of gender injustice depends on whether the causes of this
inequality are caused by their sex, or rather by their gender. Insofar as
the biological differences between men and women are responsible
for this difference, it does not create an issue of gender justice.
However, if (part of) the inequality is caused by gender mechanisms,
then this requires rectification. One can indeed think of some such
gender mechanisms: for example, it has been argued that some
health care services are skewed in favour of women and children,
and thereby unnecessarily exclude men.[29] Another example is the
killing of women who have violated the honour of (the men of)
their families. Such mechanisms do indeed create gender injustices,
and a gender just society should try to dismantle them as much as
possible.

The second principle requires that the constraints on choice from
the capability set should not be structured according to morally
irrelevant characteristics, such as gender.[30] This implies that gendered
social and moral norms and gendered practices need to be just in
themselves. It is of course a question whether social and moral norms
can be just if they are gender structured. Some of it may be relatively
innocent, for example that women are not supposed to wear a tie. For
the odd woman who really loves ties, it will be unfortunate that if she
does wear a tie to go to work, she will most likely solicit disapproving
comments from her colleagues, and it might hinder her in her
professional advancement. But other gendered social norms do create
significant injustices, such as the norm that mothers, rather than
fathers, are expected to be the primary responsible parent. This
leads to discriminatory practices against women who do not want to
take up this role, and against men who do, and it also leads to a

---

[29] See Banks (2001).
[30] There exists a large literature in several subfields of feminist and gender studies
describing and analysing the gendered nature of these structural constraints.
For a key reference from feminist economics, see Folbre (1994); for feminist
sociology, see e.g. Risman (1998).

disproportionate time deprivation amongst mothers in comparison with fathers.[31] Moreover, research in social and cognitive psychology has also shown that gendered social and moral norms not only impact on how we judge other people, but also impact on our own preference formation and behaviour. If women who are making similar demands as men are judged much more aggressive or demanding, and experience this negative judgement in the responses to their demands and proposals, then they will lower their demands or become less assertive.[32] The bottom line is that if gendered social and moral norms induce men or women systematically to foreclose certain options, then these norms are unjust.

Note also that this principle opens the door to assessing simultaneously other group-based injustices, because race, ethnicity, class, age, and many other factors of human diversity, can and often do function as dimensions along which the constraints on choice are structured. While in this chapter I do not pay attention to the intersection of all these dimensions of injustice, the theoretical structure of the principles of justice should allow for these dimensions to be fully taken on board.

The third principle stipulates that the 'pay-offs' of the different options in the capability set need to be justified and should not be gender biased. Pay-offs is a somewhat technical term used in the analysis of opportunity sets in game theory and related fields, and denotes the net of burdens and benefits of a certain position. For example, the pay-offs of a job include the wage and related benefits, its status, the labour satisfaction it gives, the quality of the professional relationships and the overall effort that is needed for the job. The pay-offs of unpaid childcare include the joys and satisfaction it creates, the respect one obtains for doing this work, and – again – the overall effort that is needed. The third principle requires that jobs or other social positions that are numerically dominated by either women or men should not systematically be rewarded lower pay-offs without any plausible justification.[33] For

---

[31] The inequalities in time deprivation between mothers and fathers, which is greatest between full-time working mothers and their male partners, has been documented by time budget studies. See Gershuny (2000).

[32] Valian (1998).

[33] This principle can thus be interpreted as a generalisation of the principle of 'equal pay for equal value', which in the USA is generally known as the

example, jobs dominated by women tend to be worse paid than jobs dominated by men. If this were because these jobs are much more pleasant, or much less stressful, then this might be a justification for this lower pay. But if, as many studies suggest, these jobs are worse paid because they are culturally labelled 'feminine jobs' or because they are performed predominantly by women, then the third principle is violated.[34] Another example is the pay-offs of unpaid domestic care work, where there is some evidence that these are lower for men than for women. First, one could argue that maternity leave in some European welfare states provides for a longer period than necessary for the mother's recovery from childbirth. If this argument holds, then part of the maternity leave should in fact be parental leave from which fathers are unjustly excluded.[35] Depending on the parental leave arrangements, which differ quite significantly across Europe and North America, fathers are given lower material pay-offs if they choose to spend time with their small children.[36] In addition, there is some anecdotal evidence from fathers at home that they are excluded from the social networks of mothers at home. On the other hand, the increasing involvement of fathers in caring work has led to reactions of praise and respect, which mothers often tend not to receive as it is simply taken for granted that they do this work. As being respected for what one is and does and recognised for one's effort are important capabilities, these aspects need to be taken on board in our accounts of gender justice.

Conclusions

In this chapter I have outlined an account of gender justice, which is based on the capability approach, and some additional principles of justice. The resulting account of gender justice can be understood as

principle of 'comparable worth'. For an introduction to the comparable worth principle and policies, see Jacobsen (1994). The generalisation is both in terms of scope (not just jobs but all social positions) and in terms of the pay-offs (not just pay, but any other dimension of 'pay-offs' such as status).

[34] For some evidence of violation of the third principle in relation to pay-offs on the labour market, see Figart, Mutari and Power (2002).

[35] Foubert (2002).

[36] For comparative research on the arrangements in a number of countries, see Gornick and Meyers (2003).

an equality of opportunity theory, because the focus is on people's real freedom to lead the lives they have reason to value, that is, on their genuine opportunities in life. However, it is also quite different from other equality of opportunity theories. The first difference is that it focuses on capabilities rather than a few key outcomes such as earnings and jobholding, which allows for the inclusion of non-material dimensions such as caring, psychological well-being, respect and social relations. The second difference is that the account presented here takes *all* factors that have a significant effect on people's opportunity sets into account, including those that are often considered more intangible and non-observable, such as social norms, discriminatory practices, and so forth. Third, in contrast to most mainstream accounts of equality of opportunity for gender justice, the second and third principles of justice in my account stress that we must also acknowledge and include in our analysis the different constraints on choices that men and women face, and the fact that it is not enough that they each have the same options. Rather, I argue, they should also receive the same pay-offs for the same options.

The empirical studies that feed into the discussion of the three principles of justice highlight that these principles of gender justice are not yet met. In other words, people in the post-industrial societies do not yet live in gender just societies on the account of gender justice presented here.[37] Most empirical studies point at injustices that are to the disadvantage of women. But there is also evidence for a few injustices that are to the disadvantage of men. This should not come as a surprise if one endorses the account of gender with which this chapter started off, because norms of dominant masculinities 'sanction' men who are choosing to realise capabilities that are culturally labelled 'feminine', such as being in unpaid caring positions. In addition, many social institutions still reinforce gendered norms and practices, which are often working against women but sometimes also working against men.

For those who believe that in this new millennium we are living in a gender just society, these are sobering conclusions. This is not to deny that much progress towards gender justice has been made over recent

---

[37] There is no reason to assume that this conclusion would be different for less prosperous or non-liberal societies.

decades – but not enough to claim that we are living in a gender just society. Given that some manifestations of gender justice are quite subtle and hard to tackle, this should make us pessimistic about reaching a fully gender just society any time soon. However, if we believe that justice is an important social good, we have to strive for a future with less gender injustice. In order to know when – if ever – we will reach a gender just society in the future, we need an account of gender justice. My aim in this chapter has been to present, and briefly defend, such an account of gender justice.

References

Agarwal, A., Humphries, J. and Robeyns, I. (eds.) (2005) *The Work and Ideas of Amartya Sen: A Gender Perspective* (New York: Routledge).

Badgett, L. and Folbre, N. (1999) 'Assigning Care: Gender Norms and Economic Outcomes', *International Labour Review* 138, 3: 311–26.

Banks, I. (2001) 'No Man's Land: Men, Illness and the NHS', *British Medical Journal* 323: 1058–60.

Blau, F. (1998) 'Trends in the Well-being of American Women, 1970–1995', *Journal of Economic Literature* 36: 112–65.

Bourdieu, P. (2001) *Masculine Domination* (Cambridge: Polity Press), 67–8.

Elster, J. (1999) 'Shame and Social Norms', in his *Alchemies of the Mind: Rationality and the Emotions* (Cambridge: Cambridge University Press), 145–64.

Figart, D., Mutari, E. and Power, M. (2002) *Living Wages, Equal Wages: Gender and Labour Market Policy in the United States* (New York: Routledge).

Folbre, N. (1994) *Who Pays for the Kids? Gender and the Structures of Constraints* (New York: Routledge).

Foubert, P. (2002) *The Legal Protection of the Pregnant Worker in the European Community* (The Hague: Kluwer Law International).

Gershuny, J. (2000) *Changing Times: Work and Leisure in Postindustrial Society* (Oxford: Oxford University Press).

Gornick, J. and Meyers, M. (2003) *Families That Work: Policies for Reconciling Parenthood and Employment* (New York: Russell Sage Foundation).

Haslanger, S. (2000), 'Gender and Race: (What) Are They? (What) Do We Want Them To Be?', *NOÛS* 34, 1: 31–55.

Jacobsen, J. (1994), *The Economics of Gender* (Cambridge, MA: Blackwell), 348–65.

Kennedy, H. (1992) *Eve Was Framed: Women and British Justice* (London: Vintage Books).

Kimmel, M. (2000) *The Gendered Society* (New York: Oxford University Press).

Lewis, J. and Giullari, S. (2005) 'The Adult Worker Model Family, Gender Equality and Care: The Search for New Policy Principles and the Possibilities and Problems of a Capabilities Approach', *Economy and Society* 34, 1: 76–104.

Lipsitz Bem, S. (1998) *An Unconventional Family* (New Haven: Yale University Press).

McMahon, A. (1999) *Taking Care of Men: Sexual Politics in the Public Mind* (Cambridge: Cambridge University Press).

Nussbaum, M. (2000) *Women and Human Development* (Cambridge: Cambridge University Press).

(2003) 'Capabilities as Fundamental Entitlements: Sen and Social Justice', *Feminist Economics* 9, 2/3: 33–59.

Phillips, A. (2004) 'Defending Equality of Outcome', *Journal of Political Philosophy* 12, 1: 1–19.

Pilcher, J. (1999) *Women in Contemporary Britain* (London: Routledge).

Pogge, T. (2002) 'Can the Capability Approach Be Justified?' *Philosophical Topics* 30, 2: 167–228.

Rhode, D. (1997) *Speaking of Sex: The Denial of Gender Inequality* (Cambridge, MA: Harvard University Press).

Risman, B. (1998) *Gender Vertigo* (New Haven: Yale University Press).

Robeyns, I. (2003) 'Sen's Capability Approach and Gender Inequality: Selecting Relevant Capabilities', *Feminist Economics* 9, 2/3: 61–92.

(2005a) 'Selecting Capabilities for Quality of Life Measurement', *Social Indicators Research* 74: 191–215.

(2005b) 'The Capability Approach: A Theoretical Survey', *Journal of Human Development* 6, 1: 93–114.

Rubery, J., Smith, M. and Fagan, C. (1999) *Women's Employment in Europe: Trends and Prospects* (London: Routledge).

Sen, A. (1990a) 'Justice: Means versus Freedoms', *Philosophy and Public Affairs* 19: 111–21.

(1990b) 'Gender and Cooperative Conflict', in Irene Tinker (ed.), *Persistent Inequalities* (New York: Oxford University Press), 123–49.

(1992) *Inequality Reexamined* (Oxford: Clarendon Press).

(1995) 'Gender Inequality and Theories of Justice', in Martha Nussbaum and Jonathan Glover (eds.), *Women, Culture, and Development* (Oxford: Clarendon Press), 259–73.

(1999) *Development as Freedom* (New York: Knopf Publishers).

(2004) 'Capabilities, Lists and Public Reason', *Feminist Economics* 10, 3: 77–80.

Singer, E. (1993) *Kinderopvang: Goed of Slecht?* [Childcare: Good or Bad?] (Utrecht: SWP).

Valian, V. (1998) *Why So Slow? The Advancement of Women* (Cambridge, MA: MIT Press).

PART II

Variations on the theme of gender

4 | Does biology play any role in sex differences in the mind?

SIMON BARON-COHEN

THERE ARE INTERESTING DIFFERENCES between the *average* male and female mind. Recognizing these could lead to mutual respect of difference. In using the word 'average' I am from the outset recognizing that such differences may have little to say about individuals. In addition, the differences are subtle, and are to do with the relative proportions of different drives in the typical male and female mind. The field of sex differences in psychology in the 1960s and '70s was so conflict ridden as to make an open-minded debate about any possible role of biology contributing to psychological sex differences impossible. Those who explored the role of biology – even whilst acknowledging the importance of culture – found themselves accused of defending an essentialism that perpetuated inequalities between the sexes, and of oppression. Not a climate in which scientists can ask questions about mechanisms in nature. Today, the pendulum has settled sensibly in the middle of the nature–nurture debate, and scientists who care deeply about ending inequality and oppression can at the same time also talk freely about biological differences between the male and female brain and mind.

My own view is that the field of sex differences in mind needs to proceed in a fashion that is sensitive to this history of conflict by cautiously looking at the evidence and being careful not to overstate what can be concluded. Once again, the evidence says nothing about individuals. As we will see, the data actually require us to look at each individual on his or her own merits, as individuals may or may not be typical for their sex. In this chapter I will first look at the evidence from scientific studies of sex differences in the mind. At the end of the chapter, in keeping with the theme of this edited collection, I then consider the relevance of such work for our concepts of 'gender'.

Systemizing and empathizing

'Empathizing' is the drive to identify another person's emotions and thoughts and to respond to these with an appropriate emotion. Empathizing allows you to *predict* a person's behaviour and to care about how others feel. In this chapter, I review the evidence that, in general, females spontaneously empathize to a greater degree than do males. 'Systemizing' is the drive to analyse the variables in a system in order to derive the underlying rules that govern its behaviour. Systemizing also refers to the drive to construct systems. Systemizing allows one to *predict* the behaviour of a system and to control it. I review the evidence that, on average, males spontaneously systemize to a greater degree than do females (Baron-Cohen et al. 2002).

Empathizing is close enough to the standard English definition to need little introduction, and I will come back to it shortly. But systemizing is a new concept and needs a little more definition. By a 'system' I mean something that takes inputs and deliver outputs. To systemize, one uses 'if–then' (correlation) rules. The brain zooms in on a detail or parameter of the system and observes how this varies. That is, it treats a feature of a particular object or event as a variable. Alternately, a person actively, or systematically, manipulates a given variable. One notes the effect(s) of operating on one single input in terms of its effects elsewhere in the system (the output). The key data structure used in systemizing is [input–operation–output]. If I do x, a changes to b. If z occurs, p changes to q. Systemizing therefore requires an exact eye for detail.

There are at least six kinds of systems that the human brain can analyse or construct, as shown in Table 4.1. Systemizing is an inductive process. One watches what happens each time, gathering data about an event from repeated sampling, often quantifying differences in some variables within the event and observing their correlation with variation in outcome. After confirming a reliable pattern of association – that is, generating predictable results – one forms a rule about how a particular aspect of the system works. When an exception occurs, the rule is refined or revised. Otherwise, the rule is retained. Systemizing works for phenomena that are ultimately lawful, finite and deterministic. The explanation is exact, and its truth-value is testable. ('The light went on because the switch was in the down position.') Systemizing is of almost no use for predicting

Table 4.1 Main types of analysable systems

- **Technical** systems (e.g. a computer, a musical instrument, a hammer)
- **Natural** systems (e.g. a tide, a weather front, a plant)
- **Abstract** systems (e.g. mathematics, a computer program, syntax)
- **Social** systems (e.g. a political election, a legal system, a business)
- **Organizable** systems (e.g. a taxonomy, a collection, a library)
- **Motoric** systems (e.g. a sports technique, a performance, a musical technique)

moment-to-moment changes in a person's behaviour. To predict human behaviour, empathizing is required. Systemizing and empathizing are wholly different kinds of processes.

Empathizing involves the attribution of mental states to others and involves an appropriate affective response to the other's affective state. It not only includes what is sometimes called 'theory of mind', or mentalizing, (Morton, Leslie and Frith 1995) but also encompasses the common English words 'empathy' and 'sympathy'. Although systemizing and empathizing are in one way similar because they are processes that allow us to make sense of events and make reliable predictions, they are in another way almost the opposite of each other. Empathizing involves an imaginative leap in the dark in the absence of complete data. ('Maybe she didn't phone me because she was feeling hurt by my comment.') The causal explanation is at best a 'maybe', and its truth may never be provable. Systemizing is our most powerful way of understanding and predicting the law-governed inanimate universe. Empathizing is our most powerful way to understand and predict the social world. Ultimately, empathizing and systemizing depend on separate, independent regions in the human brain.

The main brain types

In this chapter I will argue that systemizing and empathizing are two key dimensions that define the male and female brain. We all have both systemizing and empathizing skills. One can envisage five broad types of brain, as Table 4.2 shows. This chapter concerns itself primarily with those on the extreme male brain end of the spectrum. Individuals who have this psychological profile may be talented

Table 4.2 The main brain types

Profile	Shorthand equation	Type of brain
Individuals in whom empathizing is more developed than systemizing	E>S	'female' (or Type E)
Individuals in whom systemizing is more developed than empathizing	S>E	'male' (or Type S)
Individuals in whom systemizing and empathizing are both equally developed	S=E	'balanced' (or Type B)
Individuals in whom systemizing is hyperdeveloped while empathizing is hypodeveloped (the autistic end of the spectrum). They may be talented systemizers, but at the same time, they may be 'mind-blind'	S>>E	extreme male brain
Individuals who have hyperdeveloped empathizing skills, while their systemizing is hypodeveloped. They may be 'system-blind'	E>>S	extreme female brain (postulated)

systemizers, but they are often, at the same time, 'mind-blind'. (Baron-Cohen 1995). The evidence reviewed here suggests that not all men have the male brain and not all women have the female brain. Expressed differently, some women have the male brain, and some men have the female brain. My central claim here is only that *more* males than females have a brain of type S, and *more* females than males have a brain of type E. I will review the evidence supporting these profiles. In the final section of this chapter, I will highlight the role of culture and biology in these sex differences.

The female brain: empathizing

What is the evidence for female superiority in empathizing? In the studies summarized here, sex differences of a small but statistically significant magnitude have been found.

- *Sharing and turn taking.* On average, girls show more concern for fairness, while boys share less. In one study, boys showed fifty times greater competition, as compared to girls, while girls showed twenty times greater turn taking, as compared to boys (Charlesworth and Dzur 1987).

- *Rough and tumble play or 'rough housing'* (wrestling, mock fighting, etc.). Boys show more of this than do girls. Although such activity is often playful, it can hurt or be intrusive. Lower empathizing levels are necessary to engage in rough and tumble play (Maccoby 1998).
- *Responding empathically to the distress of other people.* Girls from the age of 1 year show greater concern for others through sad looks, sympathetic vocalizations and comforting as compared to boys. Also, more women than men report frequently sharing the emotional distress of their friends. Women also show more comforting, even to strangers, than men do (Hoffman 1977).
- *Using a 'theory of mind'.* As early as 3 years of age, little girls are ahead of boys in their ability to infer what people might be thinking or intending (Happe 1995).
- *Sensitivity to facial expressions.* Women are better at decoding nonverbal communication, picking up subtle nuances from tone of voice or facial expression, or judging a person's character (Hall 1978).
- *Empathy.* Women score higher than men on questionnaires designed to measure empathic response (Davis 1994).
- *Values in relationships.* More women than men value the development of altruistic, reciprocal relationships, which by definition require empathizing. In contrast, more men value power, politics and competition (Ahlgren and Johnson 1979). Girls are more likely to endorse cooperative items on a questionnaire and to rate the establishment of intimacy as more important than the establishment of dominance. In contrast, boys are more likely than girls to endorse competitive items and to rate social status as more important than intimacy (Knight and Chao 1989).
- *Disorders of empathy.* Disorders such as psychopathic personality disorder or conduct disorder are far more common among males (Dodge 1980; Blair 1995).
- *Aggression.* Even in normal quantities, this can only occur with reduced empathizing. Here again, there is a clear sex difference. Males tend to show far more 'direct' aggression (pushing, hitting, punching, etc.), while females tend to show more 'indirect'

(relational, covert) aggression (gossip, exclusion, cutting remarks, etc.). Direct aggression may require an even lower level of empathy than indirect aggression. Indirect aggression needs better mind-reading skills than does direct aggression because its impact is strategic (Crick and Grotpeter 1995).

- *Murder*. This is the ultimate example of a lack of empathy. Daly and Wilson analysed homicide records dating back over 700 years, from a range of different societies. They found that 'male-on-male' homicide was thirty to forty times more frequent than 'female-on-female' homicide (Daly and Wilson 1988).
- *Establishing a 'dominance hierarchy'*. Males are quicker to establish such hierarchies. This in part reflects their lower empathizing skills because often a hierarchy is established by one person pushing others around to become the leader (Strayer 1980).
- *Language style*. Girls' speech is more co-operative, reciprocal and collaborative. In concrete terms, this is also reflected in girls being able to continue a conversational exchange with a partner for a longer period. When girls disagree, they are more likely to express their different opinion sensitively, in the form of a question rather than an assertion. Boys' talk is more 'single-voiced discourse'; that is, the speaker presents only his own perspective. The female speech style is more 'double-voiced discourse'; girls spend more time negotiating with their partner, trying to take the other person's wishes into account (Smith 1985).
- *Talk about emotions*. Women's conversations involve much more talk about feelings, while men's conversations tend to be more object- or activity-focused (Tannen 1990).
- *Parenting style*. Fathers are less likely than mothers to hold their infants in a face-to-face position. Mothers are more likely to follow through the child's choice of topic in play, while fathers are more likely to impose their own topic. Also, mothers fine-tune their speech more often to match their children's understanding (Power 1985).
- *Face preference and eye contact*. From birth, females look longer at faces, particularly at people's eyes, whereas males are more likely to look at inanimate objects (Connellan et al. 2000).

Females have also been shown to have better language ability than males. It seems likely that good empathizing would promote language development (Baron-Cohen, Baldwin and Crowson 1997) and vice versa, so these factors may not be independent.

The male brain: systemizing

The relevant domains to explore for evidence of systemizing include any fields that are in principle rule-governed. Thus, chess and football are good examples of systems, but faces and conversations are not. As noted previously, systemizing involves monitoring three elements: input, operation and output. The operation is what was done or what happened to the input in order to produce the output. What is the evidence for a stronger drive to systemize in males?

- *Toy preferences.* Boys are more interested than girls in toy vehicles, weapons, building blocks and mechanical toys, all of which are open to being 'systemized' (Jennings 1977).
- *Adult occupational choices.* Some occupations are almost entirely male. These include metalworking, weapon making, manufacture of musical instruments, and the construction industries, such as boat building. The focus of these occupations is on creating systems (Geary 1998).
- *Maths, physics and engineering.* These disciplines all require high systemizing and are largely male-dominated. The Scholastic Aptitude Math Test (SAT-M) is the mathematics part of the test administered nationally to college applicants in the United States. Males on average score 50 points higher than females on this test (Benbow 1988). Considering only individuals who score above 700, the sex ratio is 13:1 (men to women) (Geary 1996).
- *Constructional abilities.* On average men score higher than women in an assembly task in which people are asked to put together a three-dimensional (3-D) mechanical apparatus. Boys are also better at constructing block buildings from two-dimensional blueprints. Lego bricks can be combined and recombined into an infinite number of systems. Boys show more interest than girls in playing with Lego. Boys as young as 3 years of age are also faster at copying 3-D models of outsized Lego pieces. Older boys, from the age of 9 years, are better than girls at imagining what a 3-D object will look like if it is laid out flat. Boys are also better at constructing a 3-D structure from just an aerial and frontal view in a picture (Kimura 1999).

- *The Water Level Task.* Originally devised by the Swiss child psychologist Jean Piaget, the water level task involves a bottle that is tipped at an angle. Individuals are asked to predict the water level. Women more often draw the water level aligned with the tilt of the bottle and not horizontal, as is correct (Wittig and Allen 1984).

- *The Rod and Frame Test.* If a person's judgement of vertical is influenced by the tilt of the frame, he or she is said to be 'field dependent'; that is, their judgement is easily swayed by extraneous input in the surrounding context. If they are not influenced by the tilt of the frame, they are said to be 'field independent'. Most studies indicate that females are more field dependent; that is, women are relatively more distracted by contextual cues, and they tend not to consider each variable within a system separately. They are more likely than men to state erroneously that a rod is upright if it is aligned with its frame (Witkin et al. 1954).

- *Good attention to relevant detail.* This is a general feature of systemizing and is clearly a necessary part of it. Attention to relevant detail is superior in males. One measure of this is the Embedded Figures Test. On average, males are quicker and more accurate in locating a target object from a larger, complex pattern (Elliot 1961). Males, on average, are also better at detecting a particular feature (static or moving) than are women (Voyer, Voyer and Bryden 1995).

- *The Mental Rotation Test.* This test provides another example in which males are quicker and more accurate. This test involves systemizing because it is necessary to treat each feature in a display as a variable that can be transformed (e.g., rotated) and then predict the output, or how it will appear after transformation (Collins and Kimura 1997).

- *Reading maps.* This is another everyday test of systemizing, because features from 3-D input must be transformed to a two-dimensional representation. In general, boys perform at a higher level than girls in map reading. Men can also learn a route by looking at a map in fewer trials than women, and they are more successful at correctly recalling greater detail about direction and distance. This observation suggests that men treat features in the map as variables that can be transformed into three dimensions. When children are asked to make a map of an area that they have only visited once, boys' maps have a more accurate layout of the features in the environment. More of the girls' maps make serious errors in the location of important landmarks. Boys tend to emphasize routes or roads, whereas girls tend to emphasize specific landmarks (the corner shop, the park, etc.). These strategies of using directional cues versus using landmark cues have been widely studied. The directional strategy represents an approach to understanding space as a geometric system. Similarly, the focus on roads or routes is an example of considering space in terms of another system, in this case a transportation system (Galea and Kimura 1993).

- *Motoric systems*. When people are asked to throw or catch moving objects (target directed tasks), such as playing darts or intercepting balls flung from a launcher, males tend to perform better than females. In addition, on average men are more accurate than women in their ability to judge which of two moving objects is travelling faster (Schiff and Oldak 1990).

- *Organizable systems*. People in the Aguaruna tribe of northern Peru were asked to classify a hundred or more examples of local specimens into related species. Men's classification systems included more sub-categories (i.e., they introduced greater differentiation) and were more consistent among individuals. Interestingly, the criteria that the Aguaruna men used to decide which animals belonged together more closely resembled the taxonomic criteria used by western (mostly male) biologists (Atran 1994). Classification and organization involves systemizing because categories are predictive. With more fine-grained categories, a system will provide more accurate predictions.

- *The Systemizing Quotient*. This is a questionnaire that has been tested among adults in the general population. It includes forty items that ask about a subject's level of interest in a range of different systems that exist in the environment, including technical, abstract and natural systems. Males score higher than females on this measure (Baron-Cohen et al. 2003).

- *Mechanics*. The Physical Prediction Questionnaire (PPQ) is based on an established method for selecting applicants to study engineering. The task involves predicting which direction levers will move when an internal mechanism of cog wheels and pulleys is engaged. Men score significantly higher on this test, compared with women.

Culture and biology

At age 1 year, boys strongly prefer to watch a video of cars going past, an example of predictable mechanical systems, than to watch a film showing a human face. Little girls show the opposite preference. Young girls also demonstrate more eye contact than do boys at age 1 year (Lutchmaya and Baron-Cohen 2002). Some investigators argue that, even by this age, socialization may have caused these sex differences. Although evidence exists for differential socialization contributing to sex differences, this is unlikely to be a sufficient explanation. Connellan and colleagues showed that among *1-day-old* babies, boys look longer at a mechanical mobile, which is a system with predictable laws of motion, than at a person's face, an object that is next to impossible to systemize. One-day-old girls show the opposite profile (Connellan et al. 2000). These sex differences are therefore present very early in life. This raises the possibility that, while culture and socialization may partly determine the development of a male brain with a stronger interest in systems or a female brain with a stronger interest in empathy, biology may also partly determine this. There is ample evidence to support both cultural determinism and biological determinism (Eagly 1987; Gouchie and Kimura 1991). For example, the amount of time a 1-year-old child maintains eye contact is inversely related to the prenatal level of testosterone (Lutchmaya, Baron-Cohen and Raggatt 2002b). The evidence for the biological basis of sex differences in the mind is reviewed elsewhere (Baron-Cohen 2003).

Autism: an extreme form of the male brain

Autism is diagnosed when a person shows abnormalities in social development and communication and displays unusually strong obsessional interests from an early age (Task Force on DSM-IV 1994). Asperger Syndrome (AS) has been proposed as a variant of autism. It is seen in children who have normal or high IQ scores and who develop speech at the normal developmental age. Today, approximately 1 in 200 children have one of the 'autistic spectrum conditions', which include AS (Frith 1991). Autism spectrum conditions are far more common in males than females. Among individuals with high-functioning autism (HFA) or AS, at least ten males are affected for

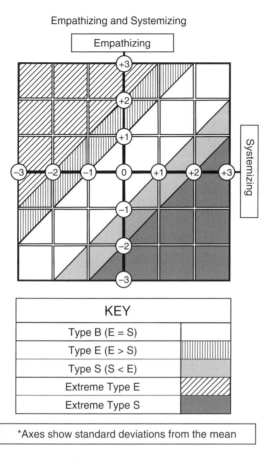

Figure 4.1. A model of the different brain types

every one female. These conditions are also strongly heritable (Bailey, Bolton and Rutter 1998) and neurodevelopmental in origin. Consider-able evidence supports structural and functional differences in certain regions of the brain. For example, the amygdala is abnormal in size in many individuals with austistic spectrum disorders, and it may not respond in the usual fashion to cues of emotional expression (Baron-Cohen et al. 2000).

The extreme male brain (EMB) theory of autism was first informally suggested by Hans Asperger in 1944. According to the 1991 transla-tion by Uta Frith, he wrote: 'The autistic personality is an extreme variant of male intelligence. Even within the normal variation, we find typical sex differences in intelligence ... In the autistic individual, the male pattern is exaggerated to the extreme' (Frith 1991). In 1997 this controversial hypothesis was re-examined (Baron-Cohen and Hammer 1997). We can now test the EMB theory empirically, as the female brain (E > S), the male brain (S > E), and the balanced brain (E = S) have been defined. According to the EMB theory, people with autism or AS should always fall in the dark grey zone as illustrated in Figure 4.1.

Evidence for the extreme male brain theory

Initial tests are beginning to provide positive proof of this theory (Baron-Cohen et al. 1999b; Baron-Cohen 2000). A number of studies utilizing different approaches and standard instruments indicate that people with autism show markedly impaired empathizing. Some of the convergent lines of evidence are summarized here.

- *Mind reading.* Girls score better than boys on standard 'theory of mind' tests, and children with autism or AS tend to perform even worse than do normal boys (Happe 1995). Children with autism have specific delays and difficulties in the development of 'mind reading', and they are unable to make sense of or predict another's feelings, thoughts and behaviour. Autism has been referred to as a condition of 'mind-blindness' (Baron-Cohen 1995).
- *The Empathy Quotient.* On this questionnaire, females score higher than males, and people with AS or HFA score even lower than males (Baron-Cohen et al. 2003).
- *The 'Reading the Mind in the Eyes' Test.* Females score higher on this test than males, but people with AS do not even score as well as males (Baron-Cohen et al. 1997a).
- *The Complex Facial Expressions Test.* Similar to the other tests mentioned, females score higher than males, and people with AS score even lower than do males (Baron-Cohen, Wheelwright and Jolliffe 1997).
- *Eye contact.* Females make eye contact more often and maintain it for longer periods of time than do males. People with autism or AS make less eye contact than males (Lutchmaya et al. 2002b; Swettenham, Baron-Cohen and Charman et al. 1998).

- *Language development.* Girls develop vocabulary faster than boys, and children with autism are even slower than males to develop vocabulary (Lutchmaya, Baron-Cohen and Raggatt 2002a).
- *Pragmatics.* Females tend to be superior to males at chatting with others and at understanding the pragmatics of conversation. It is precisely this aspect of language which people with AS find most difficult (Baron-Cohen 1988).
- *The Faux Pas Test.* Females are better than males at judging what would be socially insensitive or potentially hurtful or offensive. People with autism or AS have even lower scores on tests of this than do males (Baron-Cohen et al. 1999a).
- *The Friendship Questionnaire (FQ).* This instrument assesses empathic styles of relationships. Females score higher than males on this questionnaire, and adults with AS score even lower than do normal males on the FQ (Baron-Cohen and Wheelwright 2003).

There also exists a growing body of evidence that supports the superior systemizing abilities of individuals with autism spectrum disorders.

- *Islets of ability.* Some people with autism spectrum disorders have 'islets of ability' in mathematical calculation, calendrical calculation, syntax acquisition, music, or memory for railway timetable information to a precise degree (Baron-Cohen and Bolton 1993). For high-functioning individuals, this can lead to considerable achievement in mathematics, chess, mechanical knowledge, and other factual, scientific, technical or rule-based subjects. All of these areas are highly systemizable domains, and most are also domains that are more interesting to males than to females in the general population.
- *Attention to detail.* People with autism also tend to pay extra-fine attention to detail. For example, on the Embedded Figures Test (EFT) males score higher than females, and people with AS or HFA score even higher than males. This is not a systemizing test per se, but it is a measure of detailed local perception, which is a prerequisite for successful systemizing (Jolliffe and Baron-Cohen 1997). On visual search tasks, males demonstrate better attention to detail than do females, and people with autism or AS have even faster, more accurate visual search skills (O'Riordan et al. 2001).

- *Preference for rule-based, structured, factual information.* People with autism are strongly drawn to structured, factual and rule-based information. A male bias for this kind of information is also found in the general population.
- *Intuitive physics.* Males score higher than females on tests of intuitive physics. People with AS tend to score higher than males on such tests (Baron-Cohen et al. 2001a).
- *Toy preference.* In general, boys prefer construction-type and vehicle toys more than girls do. Clinical reports suggest that children with autism or AS demonstrate a very strong preference towards these types of toys as well (J. Lawson, S. Baron-Cohen and S. Wheelwright, unpublished data, 2002).
- *Collecting.* Boys engage in more collecting or organizing of items than girls, and people with autism show this characteristic to an even greater extent (Baron-Cohen 2003).
- *Obsessions with closed systems.* Most individuals with autism are naturally drawn to predictable things, such as computers. Unlike people, computers follow strict laws. Computers are closed systems; that is, all the variables are well defined within the system, and they are knowable, predictable and, in principle, controllable. Other individuals with autism may not make computers their target of understanding but may latch on to a different, equally closed system, such as bird migration or trainspotting (Baron-Cohen and Wheelwright 1999).
- *The Systemizing Quotient.* As noted previously in this chapter, males score higher on this test, and people with autism and AS score even higher than normal males on this instrument (Baron-Cohen et al. 2003).

Finally, some evidence rooted in biology and genetics supports the EMB theory of autism.

- *The Autism Spectrum Quotient (the AQ).* Males in the general population score higher than females, and people with AS or HFA score highest of all on this instrument (Baron-Cohen et al. 2001b).
- *Sexually dimorphic somatic markers.* Finger length ratio is a sexually dimorphic somatic marker. In general, males tend to have a longer ring finger compared to their second finger, which is

different than the ratio in females. People with autism or AS show an even greater difference in the ratio of ring finger to second finger length (Manning et al. 2001).

- *Puberty.* Males with autism are reported to show precocious puberty, which correlates with increased levels of circulating testosterone (Tordjman et al. 1997).
- *Familiality of talent.* Males are over-represented in occupations such as engineering, which require good systemizing but where a mild impairment in empathizing is not necessarily an impediment to success (Baron-Cohen et al. 1997b). There is a higher rate of autism in the families of those talented in fields such as mathematics, physics and engineering, as compared to those who are most talented in the humanities (Baron-Cohen et al. 1998). These findings suggest that the extreme male cognitive style is, in part, inherited.

Conclusions

The above evidence suggests that the male brain is characterized by type S (where S > E), the female brain by type E (where E > S), and the autistic brain is an extreme of the male brain (S >> E). Referring to Figure 4.1, development of an autism spectrum condition indicates that an individual's brain type is shifted towards the lower right quadrant. For males, it is a small degree of shift, from type S to extreme type S. For females, the movement is greater, from type E to extreme type S. The causes of this shift remain unclear, but candidate factors include both genetic differences and prenatal testosterone levels (Bailey et al. 1998).

The model in Figure 4.1 predicts that the extreme female brain (EFB) exists. How would such individuals behave? By definition, their brain type is in the upper left quadrant of Figure 4.1. Their ability to empathize is significantly better than that of other people in the general population, but their systemizing abilities are impaired. This category would include people who have difficulty understanding mathematics, physics, mechanical objects, chemistry, and the like as systems (Baron-Cohen et al. 2002) but who are extremely accurate at tuning in to others' feelings and thoughts. Would such a profile carry with it any disability? A person with EFB would be 'system-blind'. In our society, there remains considerable tolerance for such individuals. It is hoped that people who are 'mind-blind' will also enjoy the same tolerance by society.

We know something about the neural circuitry of empathizing (Baron-Cohen et al. 1999), but at present we know very little about the neural circuitry of systemizing. Research will hopefully begin to reveal the key brain regions involved in systems processing.

Finally, what are the implications of such research for our concepts of 'gender'? I think there are several. First, it appears that our behaviour and our psychology are a product not just of our experience (important as this is) but also of our biology. John Money, the now infamous paediatrician of the 1960s, ignored biology at his peril, in claiming that a child's gender could be determined purely by experience. The little boy whose parents were encouraged to bring him up as a girl, with a new name, new clothes and even surgical sex reassignment, grew up to feel she never fitted in as a woman, and felt deep down to be male, despite Money's strong insistence that she was female. Tragically, this dishonest sex reassignment recently led to suicide in this particular case. Second, the research suggests we should not expect that the sex ratio in occupations such as maths or physics will ever be 50–50 if we leave the workplace to reflect simply the numbers of applicants of each sex who are drawn to such fields. If we want a particular field to have an equal representation of men and women, which I think may be desirable for reasons other than scientific, we need to put in place social policies that will bring out that outcome. In other fields, it will not be necessary to intervene with policy. Medicine is a good example of a science where female applicants now outnumber male ones, probably because it is a science that favours the Type B brain (good systemizing and good empathy), and Type B is actually more common among females. But maths and physics may have little or no role for empathy, and so favour the Type S brain that is more common in males. Third, and most importantly, the research teaches us that there is no scientific justification for stereotyping, since none of the studies allow one to predict an individual's aptitudes or interests on the basis of sex. This is because – at risk of repetition – they only capture differences between groups on average. Individuals are just that – they may be typical or atypical for their group (their sex). Which means that to prejudge an individual on the basis of sex is, as the word 'prejudge' suggests, mere prejudice.

References

Ahlgren, A. and Johnson, D. W. (1979) 'Sex Differences in Cooperative and Competitive Attitudes from the 2nd through the 12th Grades', *Developmental Psychology* 15: 45–9.

Atran, S. (1994) 'Core Domains versus Scientific Theories: Evidence from Systematics and Itzaj-Maya Folkbiology', in L. A. Hirschfeld and S. A. Gelman (eds.), *Mapping the Mind: Domain Specificity in Cognition and Culture* (Cambridge: Cambridge University Press), 316–40.

Bailey, A., Bolton, P. and Rutter, M. (1998) 'A Full Genome Screen for Autism with Evidence for Linkage to a Region on Chromosome 7q', *Human Molecular Genetics* 7: 571–8.

Baron-Cohen, S. (1988) 'Social and Pragmatic Deficits in Autism: Cognitive or Affective?', *Journal of Autism and Developmental Disorders* 18: 379–402.

(1995) *Mindblindness: An Essay on Autism and Theory of Mind* (Boston, MA: MIT Press).

(2000) 'The Cognitive Neuroscience of Autism: Evolutionary Approaches', in M. S. Gazzaniga (ed.-in-chief), L. Cosmides and J. Tooby (eds.), *The New Cognitive Neurosciences*, 2nd edition (Cambridge, MA: MIT Press), 1249–57.

(2003) *The Essential Difference: Men, Women, and the Extreme Male Brain* (Boston: Basic Books).

Baron-Cohen, S., Baldwin, D. A. and Crowson, M. (1997) 'Do Children with Autism Use the Speaker's Direction of Gaze Strategy to Crack the Code of Language?', *Child Development* 68: 48–57.

Baron-Cohen, S. and Bolton, P. (1993) *Autism: The Facts* (Oxford: Oxford University Press).

Baron-Cohen, S., Bolton, P., Wheelwright, S., et al. (1998) 'Does Autism Occur More Often in Families of Physicists, Engineers, and Mathematicians?', *Autism* 2: 296–301.

Baron-Cohen, S. and Hammer, J. (1997) 'Is Autism an Extreme Form of the "Male Brain"?', in C. Rovee-Collier and L. P. Lipsitt (eds.), *Advances in Infancy Research* vol. 11 (Greenwich, CT: Ablex Publishing), 193–217.

Baron-Cohen, S., Jolliffe, T., Mortimore, C. and Robertson, M. (1997a) 'Another Advanced Test of Theory of Mind: Evidence from Very High Functioning Adults with Autism or Asperger Syndrome', *Journal of Child Psychology and Psychiatry and Allied Disciplines* 38: 813–22.

Baron-Cohen, S., O'Riordan, M., Stone, V., Jones, R. and Plaistead, K. (1999a) 'Recognition of Faux Pas by Normally Developing Children and Children with Asperger Syndrome or High-Functioning Autism', *Journal of Autism and Developmental Disorders* 29: 407–18.

Baron-Cohen, S., Richler, J., Bisarya, D., Gurunathan, N. and Wheelwright, S. (2003) 'The Systemising Quotient (SQ): An Investigation of Adults with Asperger Syndrome or High Functioning Autism and Normal Sex Differences', *Philosophical Transactions of the Royal Society, Series B* 358: 361–74.

Baron-Cohen, S., Ring, H. A., Bullmore, E. T., Wheelwright, S., Ashwin, C. and Williams, S. C. (2000) 'The Amygdala Theory of Autism', *Neuroscience and Biobehavioral Reviews* 24: 355–64.

Baron-Cohen, S., Ring, H. A., Wheelwright, S., et al. (1999) 'Social Intelligence in the Normal and Autistic Brain: An fMRI study', *European Journal of Neuroscience* 11: 1891–8.

Baron-Cohen, S. and Wheelwright, S. (1999) ' "Obsessions" in Children with Autism or Asperger Syndrome: A Content Analysis in Terms of Core Domains of Cognition', *British Journal of Psychiatry* 175: 484–90.

   (2003) 'The Friendship and Relationship Questionnaire', *Journal of Autism and Developmental Disorders* 33: 509–17.

Baron-Cohen, S., Wheelwright, S. and Jolliffe, T. (1997) 'Is There a "Language of the Eyes"? Evidence from Normal Adults and Adults with Autism or Asperger Syndrome', *Visual Cognition* 4: 311–31.

Baron-Cohen, S., Wheelwright, S., Lawson, J., Griffin, R. and Hill, J. (2002) 'The Exact Mind: Empathising and Systemising in Autism Spectrum Conditions', in U. Goswami (ed.), *Handbook of Cognitive Development* (Oxford: Blackwell Publishers), 491–508.

Baron-Cohen, S., Wheelwright, S., Scahill, V., Spong, A. and Lawson, J. (2001a) 'Are Intuitive Physics and Intuitive Psychology Independent? A Test with Children with Asperger Syndrome', *Journal of Developmental and Learning Disorder* 5: 47–78.

Baron-Cohen, S., Wheelwright, S., Skinner, R., Martin, J. and Clubley, E. (2001b) 'The Autism-Spectrum Quotient (AQ): Evidence from Asperger Syndrome/High-Functioning Autism, Males and Females, Scientists and Mathematicians', [published correction appears in *Journal of Autism and Developmental Disorders* 31: 603] *Journal of Autism and Developmental Disorders* 31: 5–17.

Baron-Cohen, S., Wheelwright, S., Stone, V. and Rutherford, M. (1999b) 'A Mathematician, a Physicist, and a Computer Scientist with Asperger Syndrome: Performance on Folk Psychology and Folk Physics Test', *Neurocase* 5: 475–83.

Baron-Cohen, S., Wheelwright, S., Stott, C., Bolton, P. and Goodyer, I. (1997b) 'Is There a Link between Engineering and Autism?', *Autism* 1: 101–8.

Benbow, C. P. (1988) 'Sex Differences in Mathematical Reasoning Ability in Intellectually Talented Preadolescents: Their Nature, Effects, and Possible Causes', *Behavioral and Brain Sciences* 11: 169–232.

Blair, R. J. (1995) 'A Cognitive Developmental Approach to Morality: Investigating the Psychopath', *Cognition* 57: 1–29.

Charlesworth, W. R. and Dzur, C. (1987) 'Gender Comparisons of Preschoolers' Behavior and Resource Utilization in Group Problem Solving', *Child Development* 58: 191–200.

Collins, D. W. and Kimura, D. (1997) 'A Large Sex Difference on a Two-Dimensional Mental Rotation Task', *Behavioral Neuroscience* 111: 845–9.

Connellan, J., Baron-Cohen, S., Wheelwright, S., Batki, A. and Ahluwalia, J. (2000) 'Sex Differences in Human Neonatal Social Perception', *Infant Behavior and Development* 23: 113–18.

Crick, N. R. and Grotpeter, J. K. (1995) 'Relational Aggression, Gender, and Social-Psychological Adjustment', *Child Development* 66: 710–22.

Daly, M. and Wilson, M. (1988) *Homicide* (New York: Aldine de Gruyter).

Davis, M. H. (1994) *Empathy: A Social Psychological Approach*, ed. J. Harvey. Brown and Benchmark Social Psychology Series (Boulder, CO: Westview Press).

Dodge, K. A. (1980) 'Social Cognition and Children's Aggressive Behavior', *Child Development* 51: 162–70.

Eagly, A. H. (1987) *Sex Differences in Social Behavior: A Social-Role Interpretation* (Hillsdale, NJ: Lawrence Erlbaum Associates).

Elliot, R. (1961) 'Interrelationship among Measures of Field Dependence, Ability, and Personality Traits', *Journal of Abnormal and Social Psychology* 63: 27–36.

Frith, U. (ed.) (1991) *Autism and Asperger Syndrome* (Cambridge: Cambridge University Press).

Galea, L. A. M. and Kimura, D. (1993) 'Sex Differences in Route-Learning', *Personality and Individual Differences* 14: 53–65.

Geary, D. C. (1996) 'Sexual Selection and Sex Differences in Mathematical Abilities', *Behavioral and Brain Sciences* 19: 229–84.

(1998) *Male, Female: The Evolution of Human Sex Differences* (Washington, DC: American Psychological Association).

Gouchie, C. and Kimura, D. (1991) 'The Relationship between Testosterone Levels and Cognitive Ability Patterns', *Psychoneuroendocrinology* 16: 323–34.

Hall, J. A. (1978) 'Gender Effects in Decoding Nonverbal Cues', *Psychological Bulletin* 85: 845–58.

Happe, F. G. (1995) 'The Role of Age and Verbal Ability in the Theory of Mind Task Performance of Subjects with Autism', *Child Development* 66: 843–55.

Hoffman, M. L. (1977) 'Sex Differences in Empathy and Related Behaviors', *Psychological Bulletin* 84: 712–22.

Jennings, K. D. (1977) 'People versus Object Orientation in Preschool Children: Do Sex Differences Really Occur?', *Journal of Genetic Psychology* 131: 65–73.

Jolliffe, T. and Baron-Cohen, S. (1997) 'Are People with Autism or Asperger Syndrome Faster than Normal on the Embedded Figures Test?', *Journal of Child Psychology and Psychiatry and Allied Disciplines* 38: 527–34.

Kimura, D. (1999) *Sex and Cognition* (Cambridge, MA: MIT Press).

Knight, G. P. and Chao, C.- C. (1989) 'Gender Differences in the Cooperative, Competitive, and Individualistic Social Values of Children', *Motivation and Emotion* 13: 125–41.

Lutchmaya, S. and Baron-Cohen, S. (2002) 'Human Sex Differences in Social and Nonsocial Looking Preferences at 12 Months of Age', *Infant Behavior and Development* 25: 319–25.

Lutchmaya, S., Baron-Cohen, S. and Raggatt, P. (2002a) 'Foetal Testosterone and Vocabulary Size in 18- and 24-Month-Old Infants', *Infant Behavior and Development* 24: 418–24.

(2002b) 'Foetal Testosterone and Eye Contact in 12 Month-Old Infants', *Infant Behavior and Development* 25: 327–35.

Maccoby, E. E. (1998) *The Two Sexes: Growing Up Apart, Coming Together* (Cambridge, MA: Belknap Press/Harvard University Press).

Manning, J. T., Baron-Cohen, S., Wheelwright, S. and Sanders, G. (2001) 'The 2nd to 4th Digit Ratio and Autism', *Developmental Medicine and Child Neurology* 43: 160–4.

Morton, J., Leslie, A. and Frith, U. (1995) 'The Cognitive Basis of a Biological Disorder: Autism', *New Scientist* 14: 434–8.

O'Riordan, M., Plaisted, K. C., Driver, J. and Baron-Cohen, S. (2001) 'Superior Visual Search in Autism', *Journal of Experimental Psychology: Human Perception and Performance* 27: 719–30.

Power, T. G. (1985) 'Mother– and Father–Infant Play: a Developmental Analysis', *Child Development* 56: 1514–24.

Schiff, W. and Oldak, R. (1990) 'Accuracy of Judging Time to Arrival: Effects of Modality, Trajectory, and Gender', *Journal of Experimental Psychology: Human Perception and Performance* 16: 303–16.

Smith, P. M. (1985) *Language, the Sexes, and Society* (Oxford: Blackwell Publishers).

Strayer, F. F. (1980) 'Child Ethology and the Study of Preschool Social Relations', in H. C. Foot, A. J. Chapman and J. R. Smith (eds.), *Friendship and Social Relations in Children* (Chichester: John Wiley & Sons), 235–65.

Swettenham, J., Baron-Cohen, S., Charman, T., et al. (1998) 'The Frequency and Distribution of Spontaneous Attention Shifts between Social and

Nonsocial Stimuli in Autistic, Typically Developing, and Nonautistic Developmentally Delayed Infants', *Journal of Child Psychology and Psychiatry and Allied Disciplines* 39: 747–53.

Tannen, D. (1990) *You Just Don't Understand: Women and Men in Conversation* (New York: William Morrow & Company).

Task Force on DSM-IV (1994) *Diagnostic and Statistical Manual of Mental Disorders*, 4th edn (Washington, DC: American Psychiatric Association).

Tordjman, S., Ferrari, P., Sulmont, V., Duyme, M. and Roubertoux, P. (1997) 'Androgenic Activity in Autism', *American Journal of Psychiatry* 154: 1626–7.

Voyer, D., Voyer, S. and Bryden, M. (1995) 'Magnitude of Sex Differences in Spatial Abilities: A Meta-analysis and Consideration of Critical Variables', *Psychological Bulletin* 117: 250–70.

Witkin, H. A., Lewis, H. B., Hertzman, M., Machover, K., Bretnall Meissner, P. and Wapner, S. (1954) *Personality Through Perception* (New York: Harper & Brothers).

Wittig, M. A., Allen, M. J. (1984) 'Measurement of Adult Performance on Piaget's Water Horizontality Task', *Intelligence* 8: 305–13.

5 | Sex and the social construction of gender

Can feminism and evolutionary psychology be reconciled?

SUSAN HURLEY

Standard opposition between sex and gender

These days it seems at best odd, at worst politically incorrect, to think sex has much to do with justice.[1] On this now standard view, sex is a system of biological reproduction, a matter of natural fact. Gender, by contrast, is a culturally constructed role; gender roles, such as hunter or gatherer, breadwinner or homemaker, are socially imposed. Sex is a matter of nature, gender of nurture. Feminists argue that gender, not sex per se, raises concerns of justice between men and women. They deny that the inequalities and restrictions that go along with a traditional division of labour between the sexes result from the different natures of men and women. What is natural is relatively unalterable. Recognizing that traditional gender roles are culturally constructed radicalizes us: it allows us to see their injustice and empowers us to challenge it. So feminists tend to criticize evolutionary psychological explanations of gender roles for naively attributing too much to nature, too little to social conditioning.

The standard feminist view gets a lot right. Social conditioning does contribute to traditional gender roles. And the resulting unfairness is deeply embedded in the structure of human society. We do need to be radicalized, to recognize and challenge the gender role injustices we are still too often blind to.

It is inadequate to reply that many women do not object to their restricted gender role. Amartya Sen (1985) and Nussbaum (2000) have shown, in work on 'adaptive preferences', that deprived women often

---

[1] For comments on earlier drafts (formerly entitled 'Feminism and Evolutionary Psychology: Can They Be Reconciled?'), I am grateful to Jude Browne, Paula Casal, Andrew Reeve and Chris Woodard.

do not feel dissatisfied, even when they are malnourished or ill because they are expected to eat less than 'more valuable' male members of the household. Limited experience may limit imagination and the desire for anything better. And people tend to adapt what they want to their deprived circumstances, to avoid the frustration of wanting what they cannot expect to get. If this is true even for food, why not also for education and job opportunities? If someone is content with her restricted gender role, we should not simply take this at face value, but should cast a critical eye on how this comes to be the case.

But there is also something wrong with the standard feminist view's choice of enemies. By looking harder at our sexual nature we can shed light on the cultural construction of gender. Perhaps surprisingly, arguments made by evolutionary psychologists can support feminism by removing obstacles to feminist arguments. Evolutionary psychology reveals the great variety of reproductive patterns in nature. The human pattern, social monogamy, is extremely rare and unstable in nature. Evolutionary psychologists explain why, and how the human pattern of reproduction required cultural support or 'construction' to survive.

Moreover, recent technologies, such as contraception and assisted reproduction, contradict not just the assumptions of evolution, but those of most of human history and culture as well. They have started a process of change in our sexual nature. We have not yet caught up with ourselves: if our old nature was adapted to the circumstances of our hunter-gatherer past, then it may be ill-adapted to our changed circumstances. To understand how best to respond to our present situation, we need to understand how it differs from the situation in which we evolved. Evolutionary psychology can help to open our eyes to the ruts we are stuck in and to the workable alternatives. Understanding the evolutionary forces that contribute to human and other forms of sexuality, far from condemning us to unalterable sexual roles fixed by nature, can help us to avoid a blinkered anthropocentric conception of sex. Understanding sex as a natural phenomenon can be a radicalizing force in relation to gender roles.

I shall argue for this suggestion by giving an exposition of two standard views, one held by some feminists and the other by some evolutionary psychologists, and relating them to each other. I shall use prominent proponents in each category as reference points, in particular Pateman and Okin for the feminist view and Ridley and Wright for the evolutionary psychology view. Both views are explained in part through the use of just-so stories, and it turns out that these converge in an interesting way. My point here is not to defend these two views or their details. It is rather to draw attention to their mutual compatibility and indeed to the ways in which the story from evolutionary psychology not only is not in tension with the feminist story but furthermore can remove obstacles to it.

Feminists on the social contract and the sexual contract

Essential background to a feminist reading of evolutionary psychology are classic feminist arguments such as those made by Carole Pateman in *The Sexual Contract* (1988) and Susan Moller Okin in *Justice, Gender, and the Family* (1989). These criticize social contract theories of justice for focusing exclusively on the public realm and ignoring injustices in the private realm, within the family.

Social contract theories explain the legitimacy of political power and the demands of justice in terms of an agreement to form a political state out of pre-political society. Liberal social contracts are especially concerned to limit the resulting power of the state to intrude into private life. The family is regarded as a private space that should properly be governed by natural instinct and sympathy, not by rules of justice such as govern public life. The social contractors are thought of as rational, autonomous, mature individuals; how they get to be that way is not a concern of justice (Pateman 1988: 43, 49). Feminists argue that the social contractors are implicitly assumed to be male heads of households, with families at home in the shadows. The social contract they reach is a deal struck between males (Pateman 1988: ch. 4). It might regulate the distribution of income to households, but not what happens to income within the household. It might require equality of opportunity among male breadwinners, but not across gender roles. It might protect the privacy of men, keeping men out of other men's households and bedrooms, but not the privacy of women against male control within the household. How labour and benefits and opportunities are divided within the family is discreetly veiled, beyond the purview of justice.

Okin argues that the line drawn by social contract theories between the public and private realms makes injustice within the household invisible. Most men manage to offload most domestic and childcare labour onto women, even if the women also have careers. As a result most women are handicapped in career structures that assume the worker has someone else at home to care for children. They thus face a choice between family and high-flying career that most men do not face. Such unequal gender relations are mired in the kind of restrictions, based on birth and status, that liberals reject in feudalism. But social contract theory looks the other way. Since these relations hold in the private realm, they are not concerns of justice, but personal matters properly governed by the different sexual natures of males and females.

Okin rejects the public/private distinction and the convenient rationalization it provides for ignoring injustice between men and women. In her view, procreation is not outside the scope of justice. Culture, not nature, dictates that marriage has such different consequences for men and women, and it can be challenged. Having a family should not preclude having a career, and the unavoidable costs of having a family should be shared fairly between men and women. Questions of fairness and justice do arise within the family. The fight against injustice must extend to private as well as public injustice. The failure to confront injustice within the family is a betrayal of liberal principles of equal opportunity and individuality.

The veil drawn by social contract theories over family injustice can be seen as a symptom of a sexual contract among men tacitly presupposed by the social contract (Pateman 1988: 93–4). Pateman illustrates this using the mythical story that Freud tells in *Moses and Monotheism*. In this story the patriarchal father is a kind of alpha male, who hoards women and deprives junior males of access to females. His dominion over women leads his sons to rebel and murder him. The brothers then enter a contract of sexual equality, renouncing incest and the aspiration to hoard women, and establishing an orderly system of equal access by each man to an unrelated woman: socially regulated monogamy, or marriage. Conjugal rights over women are distributed equally among men. Marriage reflects an agreement among men to share women rather than a fair agreement between the marriage partners. The 'initial momentous step from nature to culture' is marked by the sexual contract among men (see Pateman 1988: 110). These cultural arrangements are then taken for granted as the 'natural' foundation for the subsequent social contract, and are carried over implicitly into the new social order. The presupposed sexual contract defines the players in the social contract and removes from the stage injustice in the private realm (Pateman 1988: 103–15).

Surprisingly, there are echoes of this feminist just-so story in recent evolutionary psychological arguments about social monogamy.

Evolutionary psychology on the variety of mating patterns in nature: parental investment and sexual selection

To understand why I say this, it is first necessary to see marriage in the context of the variety of reproductive patterns in nature. These are explained by Matt Ridley in *The Red Queen* (1993) and Robert Wright in *The Moral Animal* (1994), whose accounts I paraphrase below. Note that these are popular science accounts that represent and distil certain standard views about the evolutionary psychology of sex, to which feminists may react negatively; I choose them deliberately, in order to make an argument about the compatibility of these standard views with standard feminist views and their potential to support feminism. I do not suggest that these accounts represent the latest and best, state-of-the-art thinking in these areas. However, if my compatibility argument works here, it may be worth pursuing the reconciliation strategy further, drawing on recent scientific work on the evolutionary psychology of sex. The general point illustrated is that feminists should not be too quick to assume that 'nature' is not on their side.

Pioneered by Robert Trivers (1972), the concepts of parental investment and sexual selection are basic to the evolutionary psychology of sex. He argued that the difference between male and female genetic interests can be understood in terms of the sacrifice or investment required to reproduce. Parental investment in one offspring increases the chance of that offspring surviving to reproduce, at the cost of the parent's ability to invest in other offspring. The sex that invests more in rearing the young makes the least marginal profit, in evolutionary terms, from an extra mating. Among mammals, the female carries the offspring internally and provides essential food to the newborn. Extra matings do not contribute much to her fecundity; she can only deal with a few offspring at a time (Ridley 1993, 128ff, 173). The quality of the genes donated to her offspring matters more. Offspring who get better genes from their father are more likely to survive, taking her genes with them. Any help she can get from a partner in feeding and protecting offspring is also valuable: it increases their, and her own, chances of surviving for further reproduction. The female mammal is thus biased to seek quality of mate rather than quantity of mates. The male mammal invests less in each offspring, so is more likely to be interested in quantity of mates. He can increase his fecundity by taking more mates.

These are generalizations. There is tremendous variety in mating patterns even among mammals, let alone the rest of the animal kingdom. Females do not always carry young; for example, male seahorses do. Sometimes both sexes invest equally. The point here is not that females must invest more in offspring than males, but to distinguish the heavier investors from the less heavy investors and to explain sexual behaviour accordingly. Usually, though not always, the heavier investors are female. But when they are male, they behave as heavy parental investors should: small male jacanas, for example, form a male harem, sit on eggs, rear the chicks, and are controlled by a large, fierce female (Ridley 1993: 170).

The degree of male parental investment, or MPI, varies between species a great deal. Human MPI is high compared to MPI in most other primates. While human females invest more than human males, the imbalance is not as great as it is in many other mammals (Wright 1994: 42, 57ff). This is partly because human babies have such large brains that they must be born early. They are so helpless at birth that significant contributions from both parents are often needed to keep them alive at all. Thus relatively high MPI makes sense from the point of view of the male's genes: they do not benefit if the young are eaten while the mother hunts (Wright 1994: 58).

If the heavier investors are females, then females tend to seek quality, and males to seek quantity in sex. So males compete for females. As a result, males have a greater chance than females of leaving a large number of offspring. But they also have a greater chance than females of leaving no offspring at all. Ridley explains that males act as a 'genetic sieve' or filter: only the 'better' males get to breed, and nature throws the rest away (Ridley 1993: 129). The reproductive expendability of less fit males purges weak genes from the population. This filtering process is an aspect of sexual selection. Notice it can operate without polygamy: monogamous males might compete to win the first females ready to breed. If earlier breeders breed more, getting there first has a genetic advantage (Ridley 1993: 135).

Sexual selection can take different forms: males can fight for females, or females can choose males (Ridley 1993: 132ff, 136ff). Nature uses both techniques: males are equipped with weapons to fight other males, like horns and antlers, and ornaments to display their fitness to females who might choose them, like the peacock's tail and elaborate songs. In many species, males congregate at breeding time, each marks out his own space, and they parade their wares to the females, who wander through the market inspecting and choosing. Males can also be choosy, especially in species with high MPI. High MPI males will seek females who are fertile but coy: it is not in their genetic interest to invest in another male's offspring.

Exaggerated ornaments can threaten the survival of males – an absurdly long tail might prevent a male bird from flying efficiently, for example. But such ornaments will still evolve, if females like them so much that they increase the male's likelihood of breeding enough to outweigh their threat to his survival (Ridley 1993: 135). So we can see why males will evolve the traits that females choose. But why should females choose traits that burden males, like long tails?

One theory says that the female preference may be arbitrary to start with. But once most females prefer long tails, females who choose a short-tailed male will probably have short-tailed sons who will not attract mates. Females who do choose long-tailed males will probably have 'sexy sons', so will be at a genetic advantage. The process can spiral onward: males evolving ever longer tails, females choosing ever longer-tailed males (Ridley 1993: 138ff).

Another theory is that females might prefer males whose long tails say: 'I have such incredibly good genes that I can get by even with this ridiculous handicap' (see Ridley 1993: 138, 142ff). Ornaments and displays may be more than just promises of sexy sons. They may also reveal the underlying quality of the genes, such as disease resistance and vigour. Indeed, males have a genetic incentive to advertise better genes than they actually have. Ornaments that are actually handicaps may be a female way of forcing honesty on males: only really good genes can afford really big handicaps.

The point here is that selection pressures do not result in just one 'natural' pattern of sexual behaviour, but many. It is more common for the female to invest more in offspring and the male to aspire to a harem, as in gorillas or elephant seals, but it can go the other way, as in jacanas. Alternatively, both sexes may be promiscuous, as in chimpanzees. Or, a group of related females who hunt together may share a small group of related males whose only parental contribution is to protect their own offspring from other males who would kill them, as in lions. Or, animals may mate with one individual for life and share parenting equally, as in the albatross.

Human sexuality, and the rarity and instability of social monogamy in nature

Where amongst all this natural variety does human nature lie? Are we naturally polygamous? Our hunter-gatherer ancestors seem to have been largely monogamous, with occasional turns to polygamy (Ridley 1993: 186). In past civilizations, rich and powerful men often monopolized thousands of women in harems, cutting many males out of the genetic stakes entirely. Though most human beings today aspire to monogamous marriage, many tribal cultures are polygamous (Ridley 1993: 171; Wright 1994: 90). Moreover, Wright argues that the serial monogamy so common today is equivalent in many ways to polygamy: one male monopolizes the reproductive years of more than one female, but in a series rather than simultaneously.

However, human beings do not have the physiology of full-fledged harem polygamists. In the animal kingdom there is a strict correlation between harem polygamy and a large size difference between males and females, as in gorillas. The size difference between human males and females does not qualify them as true polygamists (Ridley 1993: 170). And our ancestors lived in social groups containing multiple sexually active males and females, unlike harem polygamists – probably as a result of food pressures.

Food pressures also give chimps cause to live in social groups (Ridley 1993: 206). Chimps practise promiscuity, initiated by females as well as males. Female chimp promiscuity can be a way of extracting resources from various males: she trades sex for extra food, which benefits her young. Moreover, male chimps, like lions, often kill the young of other males, which makes their mothers sexually available sooner. Female promiscuity sows the seeds of confusion among males and thus helps to avoid infanticide: the more males there are who sense they might be the father of her young because they have often had sex with her, the fewer males who are inclined to kill her young (Ridley 1993: 207; Wright 1994: 68–9).

But human beings do not have the physiology characteristic of promiscuity either. Promiscuity like that of chimpanzees or right whales requires sperm competition: large quantities of sperm are needed to flush out rivals' contributions. So testicle size correlates with promiscuity: the more promiscuous, the larger. Human testicle size does not qualify us as truly promiscuous (Ridley 1993: 211–12; Wright 1994: 71).

On the other hand, human beings are not as utterly monogamous as the asocial gibbons, where bonded pairs retreat into their own territories and defend them against all others. Human beings are highly social. Nevertheless, we most commonly aspire to monogamy, and our MPI is relatively high.

This combination, social monogamy, has built-in difficulties. It is rare and unstable in nature, and where it is found it is ridden with adultery, as in the human case. Group-living in other mammals almost always goes with promiscuity or polygamy; MPI and monogamy are almost always found in isolated, asocial pairs. Social monogamy is delicately balanced in between. Some of the closest comparisons to human mating patterns are not with other primates or even mammals, but with colonial birds, where monogamy and high MPI survive despite frequent adultery by both sexes (Ridley 1993: 180, 213, 215ff).

Unlike promiscuous chimp sex, which is overt, adultery in human beings and many monogamous birds is covert (Ridley 1993: 227). But genetic research on the offspring of social monogamous birds has shown that a surprisingly large percentage result from adultery. The monogamous male has genetic incentives to play a mixed strategy: to play daddy with one high-quality (fertile and coy) female to guarantee some offspring, while maximizing his genetic fitness by covert adultery whenever possible. The monogamous female also has genetic incentives to adultery. Extra mates may not increase the quantity of her offspring, as they do for the male, but may increase their quality. Females need not just parental investment from males, but also good genes: adultery can be a way of getting both. A female may be genetically better off with a monogamous but mediocre daddy than in a big rich male's harem. But she may be better off still if the big fancy male fathers her offspring in secret and the unsuspecting monogamous male helps to raise them. To protect their parental investment, males in turn will evolve anti-cuckoldry strategies (Wright 1994: 66). However, the female's parental investment is not equally threatened by her mate's infidelity, as long as he maintains his parental investment dutifully. Thus a 'double standard' may emerge (Ridley 1993: 229; Wright 1994: 66).

Cultural support of social monogamy

Given the rarity and inherent instability of social monogamy in nature, and the variety of more common alternatives, what explains social monogamy in human beings? Evolutionary psychology suggests an answer that shows how human reproductive patterns do indeed depend on social and cultural support.

Our ancestors' sexual division of labour into hunters and gatherers was a distinctively human form of social life, uncharacteristic of other primates (Ridley 1993: 93–185). Initially, it was probably a response to drier habitats with more seasonal food supplies. Meat became an important food, to fill the gaps in seasonal supplies. Hunting was done most efficiently by teams of cooperating males, while females, pregnant or with children, gathered fruit and greens. Males had to help females rear their helpless young if these were to survive at all, so MPI was relatively high. Moreover, team hunting had relatively egalitarian results for males; it did not generate the food hoarding or inequalities that would be needed for harem polygamy (Ridley 1993: 187).

We have seen that genetic pressure to monitor mates against adultery, and to avoid monitoring by one's mate, is inherent to social monogamy. This generates ever more refined strategies for monitoring, cheating, deceiving, and detecting cheating and deception. But the hunter/gatherer system makes social monogamy even more problematic and generates further communicative pressures. The sexual division of labour meant that hunting males were not around to guard their gathering females (Wright 1994: 56). This provided built-in opportunities for adultery, which appears to have been far more common among hunter-gatherers than overt polygamy. In response, males may have assigned guard duty to other family members. Symbolic and cultural support for monogamy – in effect, marriage – may have been needed to hold the whole system together.

A recent argument to this effect is made by Terence Deacon in his book *The Symbolic Species* (1997: ch. 12). He asks why symbolic language evolved, and suggests that it may have helped to solve the uniquely human evolutionary dilemma our ancestors faced. Males had both to hunt cooperatively and to provide meat to females and their young. They needed assurance that the offspring who benefited were their own, even though they could not guard their mates themselves while hunting. So they came to rely on social mechanisms to verify and enforce fidelity (see also Ridley 1993: 221; Wright 1994: 56). Pairbonding became a public promise and the object of joint social attention and ritual. Social support was needed to make monogamy work: recognition of established pairs, enforcement of the pairing, detection and punishment of the cheaters who inevitably arose and who found ever more subtle ways of avoiding the enforcement mechanisms. We are the only species in which the whole group gets involved in maintaining pairbonding and punishing cheaters. Marriage is the uniquely human way of regulating social monogamy, an essentially symbolic relationship involving rituals that refer publicly to abstract social relations and future expectations, to reciprocal obligations, prohibitions and expected social consequences. Deacon suggests that the heavy informational demands made by social monogamy in the hunter-gatherer context may thus explain the origins of symbolic language and culture. In effect, they countered the evolutionary instability of social monogamy by making it possible to establish a sexual contract.

Evolutionary psychology on the sexual contract and the social contract

Feminists should take note. Evolutionary psychology points out not only the striking variety of reproductive styles in nature, but also that the human style is distinctly unusual – and indeed so unstable in nature that it appears to require cultural support: to be a matter of nurture as much as nature. If this is correct, the 'initial momentous step from nature to culture' is indeed marked by a sexual contract. Can evolutionary psychology throw any further light on the sexual contract and its relationship to the social contract?

There are evolutionary pressures both towards monogamy and towards deviating from monogamy, for both sexes. Consider a polygamous population of birds, in which females invest more in the young and males attempt polygamy. Remember that to attempt is not to succeed: where a few males have big harems, many males do not mate at all. There are never enough females for most males to be polygamous (Ridley 1993: 174). The more polygamous a species is, the more males are excluded from reproduction altogether. Females, by contrast, will nearly always find mates and have offspring under polygamy.

Suppose you are a junior male without a harem. As Ridley explains it (at pp. 177ff), you have two strategies. The high-risk 'macho' strategy is to emulate the harem masters, to hope one day to follow in their footsteps. The safer 'daddy' strategy is to offer high MPI: find an unattached female and help to rear your joint offspring, thus increasing their chances of survival. You won't have as many offspring as a polygamist, but at least you'll have some. Females now have a choice: they can choose a rich polygamist, with flashy genes or a big territory. Or they can select a monogamist, who'll help with the kids.

The sexual selection trade-off between good genes and high MPI can go either way. A species can be taken over by monogamy, as more females choose 'daddy' males to get extra care for their offspring. But if a polygamist is big or rich enough, females will choose him over a monogamous male, even though they share him and can't expect much help with their offspring; their offspring will still be better off if the polygamist's genes or his territory are good enough.

Is this kind of reasoning relevant to human beings? Women in some societies appear to prefer to be one of several wives of a rich man rather than the only wife of a poor man (Ridley 1993: 178). This raises the question: in whose interests is polygamy anyway? We tend to assume it is in men's interest, and that outlawing it is in women's interest. But Wright and Ridley argue that we should think again.

Wright reasons as follows (at pp. 93–7; see also Ridley 1993: 179). Suppose marriage and polygamy were strictly voluntary, and imagine 100 men and 100 women, ranked in order of whatever determines reproductive status: wealth, power, intelligence, etc. Each woman is betrothed to her opposite number, the man who shares her status. Each would like to marry higher, but the higher-status types are already taken. Suppose a few low-status women decide that they and their offspring would do better if they become the second wives of men with higher status than their own opposite numbers. Such upward mobility by a few women allows all the women below them to move up in the pecking order of mates, should they wish. Every woman who makes this choice, however, leaves behind a man at the bottom of the pecking order with no mate at all. Equality among women increases along with inequality among men; the more women who opt for polygamy, the more low-status men are left mateless. In this sense most men may be better off under enforced monogamy and most women worse off. In the human case it is natural to consider this claim not just in terms of the reproductive interests of women, but also in terms of their interests as persons in commanding resources per se.

Wright's reasoning suggests that if no one is coerced to marry and polygamy is not outlawed, then female interests determine whether polygamy or monogamy results; it could go either way. But polygamy necessarily gives men unequal access to women and cuts out low-status males. Official monogamy may do less to protect the interests of women than to enforce sexual equality among men. Monogamy ensures that most men have a chance of at least one mate and protects males against the ravages of sexual selection and their 'natural' sexual expendability (Wright 1994: 96; Ridley 1993: 179).

What is the relationship between such sexual inequality and other dimensions of inequality? Enforced monogamy can have inegalitarian effects on the distribution of resources among women; we have seen how polygamy can, under certain conditions at least, more evenly distribute resources among women (Wright 1994: 98; Ridley 1993: 179–80, 185). However, overt polygamy appears to depend on inequalities of wealth or power among men. Anthropologists classify more than half of known monogamous societies as non-stratified (Wright 1994: 94). Our hunter-gatherer ancestors were usually monogamous in part because co-operative hunting made men relatively equal. Agriculture opened the door to hoarding, inequality, and thus increasing polygamy (Ridley 1993: 88). The more economically and socially stratified a society, the more extreme the polygamy. Ancient despots hoarded women as they did wealth, in the tens of thousands, and maximized their offspring by practices such as monitoring ovulation, providing wet nurses, and fiercely guarding their concubines. The number of wives an official was allowed increased with his power and status (Ridley 1993: 191–2; Wright 1994: 99). Higher-status folk preferred male children, who could reproduce more extravagantly than their sisters, while lower-status folk preferred female children. Females could always reproduce, but low-status males were in danger of being excluded altogether from reproduction.

Wright suggests that increasing political equality and democracy among males seals the fate of official polygamy. Monogamy is a response to egalitarianism among men: a sexual contract among brothers. High-status men still get the highest-status women, but at least they only get one each. This is to explain the sexual contract in terms of the changing social contract (Wright 1994: 94, 98–9).

However, inequalities of wealth and power may be necessary but not sufficient for polygamy. Wright is puzzled by economically stratified yet monogamous cultures, such as western culture appears to be (Wright 1994: 94). In fact, they present a problem for his view: if egalitarianism among men explains monogamy, why are these societies still so inegalitarian in other respects?

Though Wright does not ask this question, both he and Ridley make a point that suggests a possible answer. The mateless low-status males produced by polygamy are, in the absence of despotic power, likely to be violent and socially destructive. They may threaten the privileges and lifestyle of higher-status males. Monogamy distributes sex and weighs low-status males down with the burdens of family, so reducing this threat (Wright 1994: 98, 100; Ridley 1993: 195, cf. 199). Sexual equality is a kind of sop, a shower of gold coins among the masses of the sexually dispossessed. By giving up their sexual privileges under polygamy, higher-status males may protect their other privileges, of wealth and power. Monogamous sex is the opium of the people, and keeps the lower strata in their places – at least for a while, until pressure may arise for a more thoroughgoing social contract. This suggestion invokes interests of men that are not purely reproductive, interests in wealth and power per se. However, ultimately maintaining their wealth and power may be the best way for high-status males to secure reproductive success, even at the cost of 'official' monogamy.

If so, then the relationship of the sexual contract to the social contract is more complex, in a way that resonates with Pateman's feminist account. A contract of sexual equality among males would mediate between despotic inequality and the terms of the modern social contract. In this way the social contract may indeed presuppose the sexual contract, and the identities of the male sexual contractors may be carried over implicitly into the social contract, leaving no conceptual space for injustice within the family.

Wright offers a different response to the puzzle of stratified monogamous societies. Many western nations, he explains, are no longer truly monogamous. They are riddled with serial monogamy, a form of sexual inequality that is equivalent to polygamy, or worse (Wright 1994: 101). The high-status man who marries while young and has one family, then divorces and marries another much younger woman and has another family, is a functional polygamist: he monopolizes the reproductive years of more than one woman. As a result, I would point out, giving up polygamy officially may not be such a sacrifice after all for high-status males, since they can resort to serial monogamy instead. Wright argues that this tendency on a large scale must have the effect of leaving many other men without fertile partners, given roughly equal numbers of men and women – just as polygamy does. And men at the bottom of the social scale will face the greatest scarcity of mates. If official polygamy is indeed wrong, inegalitarian in its effects on men and socially destructive, then the de facto polygamy of serial monogamy is wrong for the same reasons. In some ways it is worse than legalized polygamy, in its effects on women and children. True, the second wives of rich men have their options increased. But divorced men are far more likely to remarry than divorced women, and divorce tends to leave ex-husbands better off and ex-wives worse off (Wright 1994: 88, 91). And stepfathers are more likely to mistreat children than their fathers are. Who benefits from insisting the man divorce the first wife before marrying the second?

Inequalities of wealth and power again lead to sexual inequality. Wright suggests that social and economic inequalities undermine monogamy; distributing income more equally would strengthen monogamy (Wright 1994: 105). But should that be our aim today, in circumstances very different from those in which human social monogamy first evolved?

Kymlicka (1991) calls for more imagination in designing sexual justice and integrating it with other aspects of justice. He asks whether we should give social support to monogamy, or whether some other family structure might be better suited to our present circumstances – which include contraception, work that can be done by both sexes, and babies who can be fed by both sexes. Some responses keep monogamy intact, and have various pros and cons. For example: (1) many women with demanding careers have delayed child-bearing until their careers are well established and they can afford high-quality childcare; but such delay often leads to fertility problems and health problems, with high personal and financial costs. (2) More equal parental leave for both sexes should make women more desirable employees relative to men and would remove the implication that childcare is woman's work, so mothers need parental leave while fathers do not. If such parental leave were paid for from taxes, a larger portion of this funding would initially come from higher male salaries, and over time there would probably be a redistribution of income from men to women. However, that should be predicted to produce protests from male earners and their employers, who may wish to protect the status quo in these respects. (3) Tax-funded state childcare continuous with school hours would reduce the difficulties of combining job and family, though it might be argued to be unfair to the childless if they were equally taxed on this account. Whether such an unfairness argument holds up may depend on whether children are regarded as a kind of expensive consumption item, a kind of public good – or a mixture of both. (4) Reduced working hours so that state school/childcare and standard working hours coincide would also reduce the difficulties of combining job and family, and help to erode the implicit assumption of many mainstream male job structures that 'someone else' is doing the childcare, since it is not compatible with the job. However, the childless could still work overtime, which might again tend to redefine the fairness issue from one between men and women to one between parents and non-parents. But this shift might itself be regarded as an advance, given the long history of unfairness between men and women, as it would engage men in securing fairness for parents. In practice, a compromise between (3) extended childcare and (4) reduced working hours may be best for both children and parents.

Other responses may be more radical in departing from the standard monogamous model and calling for socially supported alternatives. Perhaps non-standard family structures should receive institutional support. (5) For example, some women might take a cue from the lioness sisterhood and adopt a feminist version of polygamy, choosing to share a man who fathers their children, with all contributing to child-rearing. (6) Or, women might separate sexual relations with men from their domestic arrangements with other women, and divide child-related labour amongst themselves in fair and flexible ways that provide freedom of choice and career support, whilst also insulating childrearing from the instability of sexual relations.

Conclusions

Recall that my point has not been that we must agree with the evolutionary psychologists (or the feminists) whose views I have explained and considered. Rather, I take their views as representative, in order to explain how the perspective of evolutionary psychology can actually be friendly to many feminist concerns. It is not that we can infer feminist norms or values from evolutionary psychology, but rather that evolutionary psychology can remove (rather than present!) obstacles to feminist arguments. I have developed this point in three ways. First, evolutionary psychology brings to our attention many of nature's alternatives to monogamy, some of which may be better suited to our contemporary circumstances. Second, it points out the natural instability of the human reproductive pattern and the way it depends on social and cultural reinforcement and support. Thus, we can survey nature's alternatives in the recognition that our own pattern may be culturally malleable. It can of course be very difficult to change cultural features. Nevertheless, a mating pattern is at least less entrenched overall if it is not stable without cultural support than if it is stable purely biologically. Third, evolutionary psychology underscores the way equality among men can conflict with equality among women, and the critical social role of the sexual contract. In contrast to the standard feminist view, I have illustrated here how it might be possible for understanding the nature of sex to help us understand the social construction of gender. With a better sense of the range of possible patterns of sexual behaviour, their need for stabilizing social support, and their interaction with other socio-economic issues, we will be better equipped to reconsider the standard sex/gender opposition, our societal ideals and where we should head from here.

References

Deacon, Terence (1997) *The Symbolic Species* (London: Penguin).
Kymlicka, Will (1991) 'Rethinking the Family', *Philosophy and Public Affairs* 20: 77–97.
Moller Okin, Susan (1989) *Justice, Gender and the Family* (New York: Basic Books).
Nussbaum, M. (2000) *Women and Human Development* (Cambridge: Cambridge University Press).
Pateman, Carol (1988) *The Sexual Contract* (Cambridge: Polity Press).

Ridley, Matt (1993) *The Red Queen* (London: Penguin).

Sen, Amartya (1985) *Commodities and Capabilities* (Amsterdam: North Holland).

Trivers, Robert (1972) 'Parental Investment and Sexual Selection', in Bernard Campbell (ed.), *Sexual Selection and the Descent of Man, 1871–1971* (Chicago: Aldine de Gruyter), 136–79.

Wright, Robert (1994) *The Moral Animal* (London: Little, Brown and Co.).

6 | 'Trans' trouble
Trans-sexuality and the end of gender

TERRELL CARVER

C URRENT DEVELOPMENTS in trans-sexual technologies, and trans-gender identities, may seem marginal to the traditional concerns of ethics, and to mainstream moral issues. They are not. Ethics is concerned with the human person in relation to the good, as a matter of judgement and action (see, for example, Aristotle 2000, esp. Book I). Ethical discourses, as they are repetitively (yet variably) articulated in society, produce the human individual conceptually and socially as a physical and ethical subject. This is done through the construction of stereotypes (which are of course never fully realised by any one individual) and the elision of 'difficult' or 'intermediate' types (through marginalisation, erasure or 'forgetting'). Any ethical subject also has a 'constitutive outside', a set of overt and contrasting categories and stereotypes through which 'others' are understood as different from the ethical subject itself (but without which the ethical subject is not fully intelligible). These may be human others, distinguished by age, sex, race/ethnicity, religion, language, class or any other set of markers, to which an ethical authority or discourse may appeal (see, for example, Aristotle 1996, esp. Books I–III). Or indeed these others may be animals, divinities or spirits (which resemble animals or humans in various ways), or mythological or cult entities of ambiguous status.

Ethical communication is not always dialogical in the sense of communication amongst moral persons who construe themselves as equals. In fact most of it is not, given the role that religious texts and teachers, and various forms of authorised representation of entities or authorities over and beyond the human, play in the processes through which moral judgements take place and obtain institutional sanctions. The modern (and supposedly secular) form of ethical discourse through which equal human persons arrive at principled judgements of a disinterested and universal character is of course quite distinct in human experience.[1] While European in origin, and Eurocentric in character, it attracts both widespread global support and localised trenchant critique, both external and immanent. The most powerful immanent critique is the feminist one, which focuses on the concept of the human person (Prokhovnik 2002).

Feminists have comprehensively gendered social life (in theory, and in many practical ways) by making women visible as subjects and objects of knowledge, and by making gender problematic as a power structure of presumptions, disciplines and legislation. They have also successfully challenged the abstract or generic human person as in fact covertly male in body and masculinised in mind (Pateman 1988, 1999). Men's studies and masculinities perspectives have made men's gendered behaviours more visible and problematic, and exposed the easy slide between the masculine and the humanly 'normal' (Carver 1996, 2004). Post-structuralist feminisms, gender and sexuality studies, and queer theory have questioned the univeralising and binarising strategies employed in ethical theory and political practice, emphasising instead Nietzschean individuality, transgression, subversion, imagination and performativity (Butler 1999, 2004).

This chapter argues that 'trans' trouble represents a practical critique, at the most profound level, of the naturalising discourses through which commonplace conceptual and practical binaries and generalisations are constructed about the human person or ethical subject. This critique fulfils in practical terms the radical deconstructions that post-structuralist theorisations have articulated with respect to individual identity, which in themselves followed on from the feminist 'troubling' of gender. Feminist critique has made both binary sex (as male and female) and heteronormative construals of sexuality highly problematic.[2] To some extent this process has ironically undermined the category 'woman', through which feminism was (and still is) necessarily constructed in theory and practice (Grant 1993; Kinsella 2005). Certainly many if not most feminists would not choose to go as far down the deconstructive path as others, and indeed there are distinguished woman-centred contributions to

---

[1] I say apparently secular because from non-western, non-Christian perspectives, Kantian and post-Kantian ethical systems are likely to look like translations of Christian values into a supposedly non-religious and worryingly universalising discourse and political practice.

[2] I attend to the gay liberation and queer critique of heteronormativity below.

dialogical ethics and social policy (Tronto 1993). Nonetheless the most radical questioning of naturalised concepts of sex and sexuality have been those from the feminist margins, where the politics of sexuality meets queer theory (Fausto-Sterling 1985; Phelan 2001). The concepts of sex and sexuality are the ones through which gender (as a power-sensitive theory of oppression) has been constructed, and it is that understanding of gender which has made the term itself ambiguous: sometimes it seems to be a synonym for sex, and sometimes it seems to signal 'woman'. 'Woman' as a category famously stands in for reproduction of the human species and for 'family life' in human societies, and many feminists are indeed struggling to square their concerns as, and on behalf of, women, with masculinised conceptions of equality in social and personal relations (Squires 1999).

This chapter argues further that the theory and practice of trans-sexuality, together with the technologies of assisted reproduction and the politics of same-sex marriage, mark an important stage in redefining the human person, and therefore the ethical subject. These campaigns and practices include recharacterised subjects that effectively deconstruct and resignify the human. Ethics must there-fore catch up with political practice and develop more complex and realistic concepts of the person. These will have to be less committed to commonplace binarisations characteristic of gender as it is currently and commonly understood, and more overtly cognisant of the complex gradations and hybridities through which social, political and legal change is taking place. In some areas this is very rapidly indeed.

Identity

The adult human, coincident with the contemporary ethical subject, is a culturally complex and regularly contested conceptual artefact presupposing physical singularity and psychological centredness. Both are of course constructed through a constitutive 'outside' of borderline or anomalous cases or syndromes. For present purposes I will leave to one side the *psychological* 'others', whether multiple personalities, insanity however defined, lesser degrees of rationality (e.g. through racialised or gendered presumptions), religious categor-isations (who is, or is answerable to, a deity), or mere unreliability of character or memory (beloved of lawyers who cross-examine). Instead I will focus on the *physical* singularity that functions increasingly as a point of overt contention in current social, political and legal struggles.

The first issue is simply whether the human person is always singular, as ethical discourses generally presume, or if not, what precisely this might mean. In making women visible and valued, feminists have necessarily engaged with pregnancy, though rather more on the assumption that two (or sometimes more) physical individuals are involved than on the specific issue of the physical non-singularity of the human person (see, for example, Young 1990: 160–8). The well-known issues surrounding abortion, whether conceptualised from an overtly religious or a self-avowedly secular point of view, generally focus on the point at which a second (or sometimes further) individual achieves recognition of some sort (whether in the eyes of a divinity or of a legal system). While these struggles concern the chronological point at which (otherwise unremarkable) human tissue is said to become a singular person, the debates proceed on the assumption that a binarising line exists in virtue of some theological test (e.g. a soul) or physiological test (e.g. a primitive nervous system), or that binarising moralities require such a line of principled distinction in order to demarcate rightful from wrongful practice (e.g. the role of the UK Human Fertilisation and Embryology Authority and similar agencies elsewhere) (Warren 2000).

The above discussion relates most clearly to the politics of abortion, technologically assisted pregnancy, embryo disposal, experimentation on embryos and foetal tissue, production of stem cells from fertilised and cloned embryos, and the like (Harris 2004). It also applies to the practice in the USA of criminally charging pregnant women with harming their foetuses through drug use, and the rather more speculative lawsuits brought there on behalf of embryos and foetuses for false imprisonment (Scharnberg 2003). What is almost never in question is the necessary singularity of the human individual.

Conjoined twins have raised the issue of singularity very strikingly. Some have survived conjoined for various lengths of time, including rare cases into adulthood. Typically the situation is read as two singular individuals sharing a body (or at least some vital body parts), although a more profoundly psychologised interpretation is less clear about a binary separation between personalities or wills in that set of circumstances (Dreger 2004). My point is that despite the common-place 'eating for two' comment on pregnancy, the discourses and practices of identity, some of them at the extremes of invasive disciplinarity, relentlessly impose the one body/one mind model as the only *intelligible* way to be a human person. Perhaps an extreme example of this was the case of conjoined twins in which UK courts intervened (against the parents' wishes) that there should be no surgical separation of the two, even though both babies would otherwise inevitably die (i.e. one first, and then the other necessarily). Given that the circumstances were such that separation would cause certain death to one twin, and that one twin was in fact going to kill the other one anyway (because one was larger and stronger), the judgement ruled that the 'killer' twin should be sacrificed, rather along the lines that this would prevent the murder of an innocent (see Locke 1988: 271–6). Not only were singular individuals constructed in this case, but motives and responsibilities were read into their 'separate' selves and culpable 'actions', and conclusions drawn on that basis (McCall Smith 2000).

This is not to quarrel with any decision or rule, but rather to note the pattern of finding or making one body/one individual on the one hand, and the persistence of hard cases or anomalies on the other. Perhaps more thought should be put into the pregnancy/conjoined twins scenarios, before taking swift recourse to the norm. It could well be that with developing technologies more conjoined twins will survive, or that this could be a possibility. It could also be that women's experience of pregnancy could be an even more intriguing object of feminist research than it is already, e.g. personal accounts which would no doubt be highly varied. My view is that the philosophical, legal and popular approach to this issue is so reductionist that little is known about the variety of experiences involved, and that far more scientific resources are turned towards in-womb foetal experiences than to anything like woman-centred research, given that a woman can be a pregnant person. Pregnancy is an experience that obviously defies or at least complicates the one person/one body presumption, and in this chapter I have used it to 'trouble' the notion of individual singularity before moving on to reproduction, sex, sexuality/ies and gender.

Reproduction

Human management of sexual relations (widely construed), pregnancy (or its avoidance), parturition, lactation and childcare is traceable throughout the history of human culture, and in that sense is denaturalised. Nonetheless, such management and regulation take place within disciplinary discourses of the natural, the sacred, the traditional and the like, and ethical systems characteristically have crucial commitments in these areas. This leads, through an anxiety-driven circularity, to questioning these 'realms', which are of course discursive, in order to obtain answers, judgements and principles, through which ethics is characteristically enacted. The natural, the sacred and the traditional are accessible not in themselves, but only through discursive activity in a continuing present, even though the discourse itself may be one of timeless truth extracted from age-old, other-worldly or universalistic resources (Stevens 1999; Howarth 2000).

Modern methods of contraception have in practice broken the link between heterosexual and reproductive activity in an obvious and widespread way, and counter-discourses (e.g. the teachings of the Roman Catholic Church) on this subject are testimony to the global power of biomedical science and technology. Unsurprisingly if heterosexual relations cannot be persuasively naturalised in a 'family' centred set of ethical principles and relationships (where 'family' relates to some cultural stereotype), other sexualities and practices will then look much less 'unnatural' and so no longer worthy of marginalisation, exclusion and disdain (Blasius 1994; Phelan 1994; Warner 1999). From this perspective, the ethical subject therefore need no longer be construed as naturally heterosexual because naturally human. This means not that ethical dialogues will take no interest, or less interest, in these areas, but rather that the persons and issues involved in 'the family' will be unbundled into interpersonal concerns. In that way the human person, sexuality, reproduction and childcare will reveal ethical subjects of considerable diversity, but no less human for that (Weston 1991; Minow and Shanley 1996; Weeks et al. 2001).

Technologically assisted reproduction represents an even larger leap into diversity, and a much more profound deconstruction of the traditional 'family-centred' account of ethical life through which, and against which, ethical subjects must be understood. In recent years techniques of in-vitro fertilisation and embryo implantation, surrogacy and adoption, have exploded the man/woman/family narrative that typically opens an ethical system, or underpins its principles. Constitutions, legislation and public authorities (charged with ethical management, practical regulation and public consultation) struggle to maintain the naturalised language through which, at present, ethical life is understood, in defiance of the otherwise prosaic language of the practices involved: one egg-donor, or sometimes two egg-donors, contributes to the construction of a mature ovum; another person donates sperm; fertilised eggs are implanted in another person's womb for gestation and parturition; one or two other persons may then adopt the child (or children). Given that fertilised ova may be frozen and implanted successfully, this may all go on over quite some time, and indeed questions of death, consent, preservation and destruction have all been legally tested (Harris and Holm 1998).

Ethical and legal authorities in present circumstances must then arrive at judgements concerning 'mother', 'father', 'suitable parent(s)' and similar categories which clearly no longer conform (as traditionally construed) to the new array of bodily activities and procedures just described. However, the participants in these new activities and procedures will have already given undertakings related to, or made contracts drawing on, the older terminology. Taking some of these activities and procedures across international borders then raises further conflictual issues about the rights and ethics of citizenship, legal residence, access to technologies, and legalisation of parental status and 'family life'. Perhaps there will be no other way of understanding human experience, and constructing the ethical subject than with reference to the naturalised model (which, as I have suggested, has been a 'culturalised' appeal to an unstable concept of nature from the start). However, the current strain between the new activities and the older terminology is obvious, and it would be reasonable to expect the strains to show even more in the media, government regulation and grassroots politics.

Recategorisation is already underway on an incremental model. Interestingly, 'real' and 'natural' are no longer so likely to figure as discursive attachments to 'mother' or 'father', but rather we have womb-mother, sperm-father (or the terms mother and father sometimes prefixed with 'biological' as a useful gesture towards the body), 'birth-mother', 'adoptive parents', etc. While there are various contractual and voluntary/non-pecuniary ways of construing the rights and obligations involved (and the consequences of changing one's mind at various points), the general trend of judgements has been woman-centred, child-centred and 'family-centred', understood in this updated way. In itself this is profoundly different even from 'western'[3] cultures of the mid-nineteenth century, where patriarchal rights over wives and children were nearly absolute (Vogel 1994, 1995; Shanley 1982, 1989). In terms of aligning traditional terms with current practices, though, there is an obvious tension between stereotypical exclusivity (i.e. it takes two, and only two parents, of 'opposite' sex, to have a baby) and the various persons, roles and claims that technologically assisted reproduction brings into existence.

While there have been claims of male or father's rights over the unborn, on the whole ethical and judicial judgements tend not to equate the bodily practices and experiences of sperm-donors equally with that of egg- and womb-donors (Gavanas 2002). Quite where this leaves adoptive mothers as ethical subjects, in relation to adoptive fathers, given that neither (in many circumstances) has contributed to the bodily processes through which ethical subjects have traditionally been understood in a naturalised way, is an interesting question. Given the deconstructive character of recent theoretical, practical and political work on sexual difference, it would seem that social or psychological claims about women and motherhood in this particular instance may be wearing rather thin. On the other hand, these claims are often well defended in such cases, though at the cost of reinforcing the woman/mother/family stereotype that feminists have frequently identified as demeaning.

And what about two female adoptive parents (where neither has contributed bodily to the reproductive process)? Or two males? The 'gay dads' in Essex were a case in point, in that they were separately sperm-donors to an egg-mother (whose embryos were implanted in a birth-mother) in the USA (whereas such arrangements are not legally sanctioned in the UK). Rather unusually, before implantation, one

---

[3] I use 'western' to signify wealthy countries in the 'global north' where mass cultures of liberal rights and market commodification are crucial drivers in politics.

fertilised egg divided into twins, one embryo of which was frozen. This child was then born to another birth-mother more than a year later. The 'half-fraternal-twins' of the first birth-mother have the same egg-mother, but different sperm-fathers. The third child is an identical twin genetically to one of the older children, but quite a different age. The children have US birth certificates naming both men as parents. The UK Home Office initially refused to make the initial two adoptive children British subjects or to give them permanent right of abode (a decision later reversed in respect of residence, on grounds that they – all four – were in fact a genuine family) (Tremlett 2004). My point here is that social, legal and ethical practice is now in realms so far removed from the heteronormative model of the ethical subject, and from the two different and variously unequal 'halves' of a 'naturally' reproductive couple, that the naturalised narrative of human reproduction must necessarily be receding from the terms and presuppositions of dialogical ethics.

Sex

If reproduction and 'family life' are dropping out of the picture through which an ethical subject can be consistently constructed as a matter of principle and in equitable practice, then what about bodily sex itself? Again, the appearance of, and management of, intersex bodies is not new, nor were pre-modern reactions necessarily those of exclusion and horror. Rather, as has been famously argued, modernising medical practice has been obsessively concerned with regularising 'deviant' bodies, such that the human person is made to conform physically and behaviourally to binary sexual difference. Crucially binary sexual difference underpins the hierarchies of signification and symbolism that constitute gender as an intelligible and practical system of 'normality' (Foucault 1990–2).

While the previous sections of this chapter have explored the history and current practicalities of the imbrication of gender with heteronormativity and with 'family-centred' reproduction, in this section I turn to the biology and increasingly variable morphology of what counts in medical, social and personal terms as male and female. The invariability traditionally associated with the 'naturalness' of the biological, physical world arises, in fact, in the *language* of invariability through which biologists and doctors have striven to describe, explain and understand humans as a particular form of animal life, and not in what they, strictly speaking, have observed (Fausto-Sterling 2000). Rather more importantly, in terms of my argument, it is becoming apparent that sex categories other than male and female (including the category 'other'!) are on the horizon, and that ethical subjects will no longer be required to conform to bodily and social stereotypes of biological maleness and femaleness, since biologically these are quite variable. This variability will become more and more visible, and less subject to medical and other 'correction' to a categorial norm.

This is happening in two ways: trans-sexuality and intersex. Changing sex through medical interventions on (and in) the body has a history dating from the first part of the twentieth century. This is to be distinguished from cross-dressing in some temporary way, for various practical or erotic purposes, and from trans-gender, which involves psychological and social transformation into the other sex in terms of identity and behaviour, but not bodily configuration, removing any sense of 'drag' or impersonation. Both of these practices – cross-dressing and trans-gender – have a long history (Whittle 1996; Kates 2001). As surgical techniques have improved, and as legal and ethical systems have relaxed, trans-sexual change has developed considerably to include female-to-male, as well as the initial male-to-female, transformations, which themselves typically involve both surgery and hormone therapies. These come in varying degrees of sophistication (and expense), and generally include trans-gender counselling, 'practice', adjustment therapies and, controversially, changes in legal documents specifying sex. Particularly with female-to-male trans-sexuals, there are various medical stages or stopping points in the process, such that different approximations to stereotypical maleness are produced. There are also reverse procedures for those who want to change back (Great Britain 2000).

Intersex simply illustrates human genetic and developmental variability, in that the stereotypical normality of male and female development to adulthood requires considerable genetic and chromosomal processual regularities (not just the mere presence of XX and XY chromosomes), hormonal interactions (crucially in the womb and at puberty) and gender-identification that 'matches' the body in some sufficient social sense. An array of anomalies and syndromes have been documented, from various forms of true hermaphroditism through numerous other physical deviations from the supposed norm, right down to slight misplacements of the urethral opening just shy of the tip of the penis.

Fausto-Sterling's (2000) definitive work documents the way that doctors and other scientists (almost wholly male) were demonstrably driven by a variety of pre-observational goals. She suggests these included a fixation that there must be two (and only two) sexes, that they must be sharply different, that maleness must diverge (heroically) from a female baseline of inferiority and 'lack', that sex must be caused by the minimum of purely physical agents (whether chromosomes or hormones), and that the two sexes must in some biological sense be conflicting or competitive. Her work recounts and confirms a thorough critique of invasive practice on individuals, and she produces counter-evidence to suggest that those who escaped these interventions were not necessarily scarred psychologically or disadvantaged socially as had commonly been predicted.

Fausto-Sterling's conclusion is that sex does not exist, but human physical and psychological variability does, and that the two interact in important and demonstrable ways. Moreover she rejects the obvious circularity of arguing from nature that reproduction is natural, so variability must be naturalised (in the name of nature). While estimates on the frequency of intersex births vary somewhat, it is clear that any sizeable city will have several hundreds or thousands of such persons living in it at any one time. There are registered charities and support groups offering advice and support to those with an intersex body and in some instances an intersex identity (http://www.ukia.co.uk/about.htm). My conclusion is that this work either casts doubt on the sex or sexing of the ethical subject, or reveals that a sexed subject can also be intersex. If the human subject can then be construed as intersex, this will 'trouble' considerably the experiential presumptions through which ethical dialogue normally proceeds. The fact that sexed pronouns will not in some sense properly apply will be no small matter. And, as Fausto-Sterling observed, the spectre haunting trans-sexuality is same-sex marriage, that is, surgeons and psychologists would be creating lesbian or gay male marriages, in those circumstances where one married partner changes sex and divorce does not occur. This is indeed a fact, as at least one notable male-to-female trans-sexual (Jan Morris) is still married to 'his' (as was) female partner.

Sexuality/ies

Sexuality research as a formal scientific study dates from the later nineteenth century, and is subject to many of the same kinds of criticism that Fausto-Sterling has levelled against sex research. The development of a binary conceptualisation of sexuality, namely heterosexuality and homosexuality (and with a clear hierarchy of ethical esteem between the two) took some time to develop (Katz 1995; Carver 1998). Some studies did not see human sexual behaviour in binary terms, notably Kinsey, and the suppositions that a sexuality is something that one 'has', and that it is in itself an identity, or an important factor in one's identity/ies, represent further developments in the concept (Reinisch 1991). Much of this development has been politically driven by campaigns for gay and lesbian rights and equalities, a process which clearly necessitated conceptual diversification within the presumed binary (which in itself does not necessarily represent or presage a stable 'homosexual' coalition between self-identified men and women).

Conventional characterisations of homosexuals require a conventional characterisation of the sexed body, just that two similarly sexed bodies become engaged in what all (now) agree is sexual activity, even if it cannot be reproductive in the 'normal' way. Of course considerable heterosexual activity is non-reproductive owing to any number of circumstances ranging from timing, to infertility (from known or unknown causes), to design (using contraception). And of course both individual heterosexuals and homosexuals, and the same in couples, may have various ways of acquiring children with or without genetic connections of various sorts. I leave aside the half-siblings and step-children that result from heterosexual marriage patterns and constitute the 'normal' family in receding stages, drifting away from a monogamous, married stereotype (Shanley 2004).

Questions concerning the validity of trans-sexual marriage have arisen in the past, that is, can surgical trans-sexuality trump birth-sex or chromosome sex or some other sex test? What, indeed, makes a man a man in the requisite sense? And a woman a woman? Presumed (or tested) reproductive capacity has never featured as a marital test in 'western' societies. As with birth-sex, where superficial examination suffices, so it is with marriage where, generally, the tests are even more superficial. Only if man/woman or male/female can truly be defined and stabilised can a marriage then conform to an 'opposite sex' stereotype, and trans-sexuality presents exactly this deconstructive challenge. Is sex in the chromosomes, the genitalia, the (unassisted) hormones, in dress and deportment (Currah 2001)?[4] Judicial and legislative (and indeed constitutional) decisions and debates have taken up various positions on this question, including the UK Gender Recognition Act, which merely requires that a person 'has lived in the acquired gender throughout the period of two years ending with the date on which the application is made' (UK Gender Recognition Act 2004: ch. 7, sect. 1). Clearly the only consistent position would be the one that said, 'marriage must be between two persons', though this begs numerous questions concerning the institution of marriage, the relation between the state and sexual relations (and childcare), and the worthiness of individuals who are unmarried (for any reason) in relation to their fellow citizens (Josephson 2005).

The sexuality binary has been subjected to queer critiques, emphasising individuality and protesting the disciplines of categorisation and regulation. More intuitively, trans-sex and trans-gender make it difficult to sustain the stereotypical model of gay male and lesbian sexuality, e.g. a male-to-female trans-sexual attracted to women ... while dressing as a man. The influence of sexualities not obviously rooted in genital (and secondary sex) identifications, such as sado-masochism, has also strained a politicised identity that presumes a defensible binary (homosexual/heterosexual) (Warner 1993). Paralleling the sex research tracked by Fausto-Sterling, a scientific and socio-biological search for 'gay' fixity in something 'natural' (the brain, the genes, psychosexual development, etc.) is currently operating as a defence against the categorial dissolution that political practice continually generates.

Gender

There has been a lot of gender trouble since *The Feminine Mystique* (1963), Stonewall (1969) and the first test-tube baby (1978). Whether gender is viewed as naturalised or as performative, it is a complex

---

[4] Racial classifications under apartheid were rather similarly subject to naturalising definitions and deconstructive fragmentation, and featured a rather similar pastiche of bodily and behavioural characteristics, including bizarre examinations and tests.

conceptual and experiential system. If it is viewed as naturalised, it represents masculine and feminine behaviours (culturally mediated) that are thought to fit (in some normal or normalising sense) with bodies that are sexed as male and female, and therefore presumed to fit in with heterosexual desire, reproductive sex and a normal (or at least overwhelmingly majoritarian) heterosexual order (Lorber 1994). If it is viewed as performative, then gender is an order of binary and hierarchical concepts and codes of masculinities and femininities, mapped onto bodies which are then viewed (or made to represent) maleness and femaleness in terms of genital and other physical signifiers of sex (itself a pastiche of indicators variously related to reproduction and eroticism). Gender is then enacted in practice through repetitive citation of this mélange in every kind of thought and action through which human subjects are understood and valued (Butler 1999).

The codes of sex, sexuality/ies, reproduction and gender (meaning masculine and feminine behaviour, dress, self-identification as a man or woman, etc.) through which human life has traditionally been understood (especially in 'western' ethical systems) were rooted in naturalising accounts of biology and sacralising or pseudo-sacralising 'ethical' accounts of 'the good'.[5] The effect of these naturalising and sacralising discourses was to fix or at least stabilise human bodies, sexual and reproductive practices and moral identities in a realm of facts and/or values such that judgements, disciplines and hierarchies could be justified with certainty. It should be noted that the line between the naturalising and the sacralising, between secular or scientific and religious or quasi-religious discourses, is extremely porous, and the two apparently 'opposite' categories are characteristically intermingled. Roman Catholic teaching on the body, reproduction, sexual activity and the like has depended historically on conceptions of science current at the time, and has taken moral stands on what good science must be.[6] Conversely science that claims to be objective has been shown to be driven by the value-laden but unexamined presumptions of scientists themselves in numerous fields, especially medicine and human biology (Kuhn 1996; Fausto-Sterling 2000).

---

[5] Religious moralities are obviously sacralising. Natural law and transcendental ethical systems privileging a realm of human values seem to me to be pseudo-sacralising.

[6] As it still does, most recently in respect of Darwinian biology.

By drawing together political developments related to bodily sex, reproduction and sexuality/ies, I have shown that the traditional naturalising and sacralising discourses, including pseudo-sacralising 'ethical' ones, through which gender is commonly understood and enacted, are fragmenting, and with that they are departing further and further from the originary stereotypes. This process has been taking place over a very long period of time as marriage (in the 'West') was both democratised and moved from the religious to the civil realm; the same occurred with divorce, and the stigma of illegitimacy has largely vanished in legal terms. Complex codes relating to adoption, child support for half- and step-children, and increasingly abstruse kinship relations[7] are becoming commonplace, all of which make the monogamous, lifetime, fecund family a near-minority practice.

Legal enforcement of sanctions against adultery, fornication or so-called deviant heterosexual practices has largely fallen away, and the politics of gay liberation is currently targeting same-sex marriage as a goal (though this is controversial within gay liberation circles, as well as outside them).[8] Technologically assisted reproduction has strained the mother/father/child model to breaking point by striking crucially at the (supposedly) basic biological facts of sexual reproduction, and the mapping of those facts onto two individuals of 'opposite' (meaning potentially fertile) sex. Human cloning, should this be successful through to parturition, will confuse the naturalised and sacralised version of human normality to the point where kinship systems, derived from exogamously 'mated' reproductive (and stereotypically parenting) partners will make no sense when applied to certain human individuals. As with intersex people, and their ambiguous relation to the language through which binary gender (and binary sex) are expressed and understood, these individuals born 'out of order', so to speak, will be 'impossible', but they will have rights, a voice and citizenship (Butler 2000).

---

[7] For example, Jackie Onassis and Gore Vidal were credited with 'sharing a step father', in that Jack Bouvier was married to both their mothers (at different times), and was the father of neither.

[8] The larger picture here includes controversy over 'civil association', over marriage generally, and over other goals, such as broader notions of sexual liberation and critiques of state regulation or privileging of some arrangements, rather than others, in the first place.

I do not mean to suggest that gender and gendered language
will disappear overnight, and I do not mean to minimise the
naturalising and sacralising political forces that will struggle to keep
the stereotypical 'family' arrangements of sex, gender and sexuality
(singular) centred in a system of coordinated facts and values. While
a concern for human rights, for equal treatment and for moral
consistency has driven many of the judicial, executive and legislative
decisions through which the developments, charted above, have
transpired (in a piecemeal way), the strain on conventional language,
and therefore on conventional characterisations of human identity, is
clearly starting to show. Witness non-gender-specific locutions such as
person, parent, carer, partner and spouse,[9] which commonly (though
not universally) occur in 'western' societies, in the media, in everyday
life and in judicial and political judgements.

The retreat from gendered language (man/woman, she/he, husband/
wife, etc.) acknowledges the gendered inequality built into these
terms, and is not just an acknowledgement of intersex or trans-sexual
people. Indeed they are still very largely invisible. Same-sex marriage
will be especially disturbing in this regard: which partner will be the
husband and which the wife? Using these terms within an increasingly
egalitarian framework has been a heterosexual struggle, given the
history of gendered hierarchy involved. Same-sex marriage will
consolidate this equality, and with same-sex parenting the gendered
expectations enshrined in mother and father will follow.[10] These
linguistic markers are telltale signs of social change, as practices and
language mutually adapt to create social intelligibility of a different
kind. One of the results, of course, is resistance and backlash; the
democratising politics of the human subject, on the rise since the
'western' middle ages, has no unshakeable foothold, even in 'western'
political systems.

Conclusions

My conclusion is that gender trouble is here to stay, but that current
practices with respect to bodily sex, reproductive technologies, caring

---

[9] These terms could, of course, refer to individuals of 'either sex', but I take
them to be referring, increasingly, to persons irrespective of sex, gender and
sexuality.
[10] I leave aside psychoanalytic debates on this subject.

responsibilities for children and the social visibility of sexuality/ies, taken together, represent a very considerable challenge to philosophical conceptualisations of the human subject. These are still centred in traditional naturalising and sacralising frameworks, albeit ones which admit exceptions. These exceptions are consistently proving the rule, and producing profound alterations in everyday practice. Many individuals and groups, bringing legal cases, mounting political campaigns and pursuing highly varied individual and collective goals, are driving this process by using the rights-governed frameworks of liberalism and the full range of modern democratic institutions, not least an independent judiciary (Evans 1993; Lister 2003). A conception of the human subject in dialogical ethics will have to embrace these varied conceptions of the 'other' in new and complex ways. This will mean finding new terms of inclusivity rooted in specifics, and then amending or expunging contrary concepts.

References

Aristotle (1996) *The Politics and The Constitution of Athens*, ed. and trans. S. Everson (Cambridge: Cambridge University Press).

(2000) *Nicomachean Ethics*, ed. and trans. R. Crisp (Cambridge: Cambridge University Press).

Bindel, J. (2004) 'If We Wanted To Be Straight, We Would Be'. www.guardian.co.uk/comment/story/0,,1372971,00.html

Blasius, M. (1994) *Gay and Lesbian Politics: Sexuality and the Emergence of a New Ethic* (Philadelphia: Temple University Press).

Butler, J. (1999) *Gender Trouble*, 2nd edn (London: Routledge).

(2000) *Antigone's Claim: Kinship between Life and Death* (New York: Columbia University Press).

(2004) *Undoing Gender* (London: Routledge).

Carver, T. (1996) ' "Public Man" and the Critique of Masculinities', *Political Theory* 24: 673–86.

(1998) 'A Political Theory of Gender: Perspectives on the "Universal subject" ', in R. Randall and G. Waylen (eds.), *Gender, Politics and the State* (London: Routledge), 18–28.

(2004) *Men in Political Theory* (Manchester: Manchester University Press).

Currah, P. (2001) 'Queer Theory, Lesbian and Gay Rights, and Transsexual Marriages'. in Mark Blasius (ed.), *Sexual Identities, Queer Politics* (Princeton: Princeton University Press), 178–99.

Dean, C. and Goodstein, L. (2005) 'Leading Cardinal Redefines Church's View on Evolution' www.nytimes.com/2005/07/09/science/09cardinal. html (12 July 05).

Dreger, A.D. (2004) *One of Us: Conjoined Twins and the Future of Normal* (Cambridge, MA: Harvard University Press).

Evans, D.T. (1993) *Sexual Citizenship: The Material Construction of Sexualities* (London: Routledge).

Fausto-Sterling, A. (1985) *Myths of Gender: Biological Theories about Women and Men* (New York: Basic Books).

(2000) *Sexing the Body: Gender Politics and the Construction of Sexuality* (New York: Basic Books).

Foucault, M. (1990–2) *The History of Sexuality*, 3 vols, trans. R. Hurley (Harmondsworth: Penguin).

Gavanas, A. (2002) 'The Fatherhood Responsibility Movement: The Centrality of Marriage, Work and Male Sexuality in Reconstructions of Masculinity and Fatherhood', in B. Hobson (ed.), *Making Men into Fathers: Men, Masculinities and the Social Politics of Fatherhood* (New York: Cambridge University Press), 213–42.

Grant, J. (1993) *Fundamental Feminism: Contesting the Core Concepts of Feminist Theory* (London: Routledge).

Great Britain (2000) *Report of the Interdepartmental Working Group on Transsexual People* (London: Home Office).

Harris, J. (2004) *On Cloning* (London: Routledge).

Harris, J. and Holm, S. (eds.) (2000) *The Future of Human Reproduction: Ethics, Choice and Regulation* (Oxford: Oxford University Press).

Howarth, D. (2000) *Discourse* (Buckingham: Open University Press).

Josephson, J. (2005) 'Citizenship, Same-Sex Marriage and Feminist Critiques of Marriage', *Perspectives on Politics* 3: 269–86.

Kates, G. (2001) *Monsieur d'Eon Is a Woman: A Tale of Political Intrigue and Sexual Masquerade*, new edn (Baltimore: Johns Hopkins University Press).

Katz, J.N. (1995) *The Invention of Heterosexuality* (New York: Dutton).

Kinsella, H. (2005) 'Securing the Civilian: Sex and Gender in the Laws of War', in M. Barnett and B. Duvall (eds.), *Power and Global Governance* (Cambridge: Cambridge University Press), 249–72.

Kuhn, T. (1996) *The Structure of Scientific Revolutions*, 3rd edn (Chicago: University of Chicago Press).

Lister, R. (2003) *Citizenship: Feminist Perspectives*, 2nd edn (Basingstoke: Palgrave Macmillan).

Locke, J. (1988) *Two Treatises of Government*, ed. P. Laslett (Cambridge: Cambridge University Press).

Lorber, J. (1994) *Paradoxes of Gender* (New Haven: Yale University Press).

McCall Smith, A. (2000) 'The Separating of Conjoined Twins'. bmj. bmjjournals.com/cgi/content/full/321/7264/782 (11 July 2005).

Minow, M. and Shanley, M. L. (1996) 'Relations, Rights and Responsibilities: Revisioning the Family in Liberal Political Theory and Law', *Hypatia* 11: 4–86.

Pateman, C. (1988) *The Sexual Contract* (Cambridge: Polity Press).
(1999) 'Beyond the Sexual Contract?', in G. Dench (ed.), *Rewriting the Sexual Contract* (New Brunswick, NJ: Transaction), 1–9.

Phelan, S. (1994) *Getting Specific: Postmodern Lesbian Politics* (Minneapolis: Minnesota University Press).
(2001) *Sexual Strangers: Gays, Lesbians, and Dilemmas of Citizenship* (Philadelphia: Temple University Press).

Prokhovnik, R. (2002) *Rational Woman: A Feminist Critique of Dichotomy*, 2nd edn (Manchester: Manchester University Press).

Reinisch, J. (1991) *The Kinsey Institute New Report on Sex: What You Must Know To Be Sexually Literate* (Harmondsworth: Penguin).

Scharnberg, K. (2003) www.come-over.to/FAS/ProsecutePregnant.htm (11 July 2005).

Shanley, M. L. (1982) 'Marriage Contract and Social Contract in Seventeenth Century English Political Thought', in J. B. Elshtain (ed.), *The Family in Political Thought* (Amherst: University of Massachusetts Press), 80–95.
(1989) *Feminism, Marriage, and the Law in Victoran England 1850–1895* (Princeton: Princeton University Press).

Shanley, M. L., Cohen, J. and Chasman, D. (2004) *Just Marriage* (New York: Oxford University Press).

Squires, J. (1999) *Gender in Political Theory* (Cambridge: Polity Press).

Stevens, J. (1999) *Reproducing the State* (Princeton: Princeton University Press).

Tremlett, G. (2004) http://observer.guardian.co.uk/uk_news/story/0,,1143435,00.html (11 July 2005).

Tronto, J. (1993) *Moral Boundaries: A Political Argument for an Ethic of Care* (London: Routledge).

UK Parliament (2004) Gender Recognition Act. www.opsi.gov.uk/acts/acts2004/40007-a.htm#2 (11 July 2005).

Vogel, U. (1994) 'Marriage and the Boundaries of Citizenship', in B. van Steenbergen (ed.), *The Condition of Citzenship* (Thousand Oaks, CA: Sage), 76–89.
(1995) ' "But in a Republic, men are needed": Guarding the Boundaries of Liberty', in R. Wokler (ed.), *Rousseau and Liberty* (Manchester: Manchester University Press), 213–30.

Warner, M. (ed.) (1993) *Fear of a Queer Planet.* (Minneapolis: Minnesota University Press).

Warner, M. (1999) *The Trouble with Normal: Sex, Politics, and the Ethics of Queer Life* (New York: Free Press).

Warren, M. A. (2000) *Moral Status: Obligations to Persons and Other Living Things* (Oxford: Oxford University Press).

Weeks, J., Heaphy, B. and Donovan, C. (2001) *Same-Sex Intimacies: Families of Choice and Other Life Experiments* (New York: Routledge).

Weston, K. (1991) *Families We Choose: Lesbians, Gays, Kinship* (New York: Columbia University Press).

Whittle, S. (1996) 'Gender Fucking or Fucking Gender?' in R. Ekins and D. King (eds.), *Blending Genders: Social Aspects of Cross-Dressing and Sex Changing* (Routledge: London), 196–214.

Young, I. M. (1990) *Throwing Like a Girl and other Essays in Feminist Philosophy and Social Theory* (Bloomington: Indiana University Press).

7 | *Gender and social change*

TONY LAWSON

OW IN THE CONTEXT of the currently developing global order (and consequent ever-changing local political frameworks) might feminists most sensibly seek to transform the gendered features of society in such a manner as to facilitate a less discriminating scenario than is currently in evidence? This is a question that motivates much of the thinking behind this book. But posing it carries certain presuppositions. In particular it takes for granted the notion that *gender* is a meaningful as well as useful category of analysis. And it presumes, too, that, whatever the socio-political context, it is always feasible to identify some forms of emancipatory practice, at least with respect to gender discrimination. Or at least there is an assumption that such emancipatory practice is not ruled out in principle. Both sets of presuppositions have been found to be problematic. Specifically, various feminist theorists hold that there are conceptual and political difficulties to making use of the category of gender in social theorising (see e.g. Bordo 1993; Spelman 1990). And the reasoning behind such assessments tends in its turn to be destabilising of the goal of emancipatory practice.

In this chapter I focus on these latter concerns rather than the more specific question posed at the outset. For unless the noted difficulties can somehow be resolved any further questioning of appropriate local and global strategies appears to beg too many issues.

I shall suggest that the difficulties in question can indeed be resolved, but that this necessitates a turn to explicit and systematic ontological elaboration, a practice that feminists have tended to avoid (see Lawson 2003), but which, I want to suggest, needs now to be (re)introduced to the study and politics of gender inequality.

By ontology I mean the study of the nature and structure of (a domain of) reality, including the identification of its most fundamental components; and here my concern is primarily with *social* ontology, the study of social being. I must acknowledge at the outset

136

that philosophy in the guise of ontology can never be a substitute for substantive theory. However, it can serve a ground-clearing role, facilitating substantive theoretical and political advance and/or clarification. Here, I shall be using ontology to under-labour for substantive socio-political analyses concerned with addressing the question posed at the outset.

Specifically, after suggesting that ontological theorising, as here conceived, can render the category of gender meaningful – and given the relative neglect of ontology in feminist theorising I shall set out in some depth the ontological conception I believe to be the most sustainable – I draw out various optimistic implications of the analysis regarding the possibility of emancipatory change, including change concerned with undermining gender-based hierarchies and forms of discrimination.

Some problems of gender

I start, though, by rehearsing some of the problems often associated with the study of gender. A first difficulty, one frequently raised, is that it is not at all clear what *sort* of thing the category signifies. Within modern feminist thought the standard definition of gender is something like 'the social meaning given to biological differences between the sexes' (Ferber and Nelson 1993: 9–10; Kuiper and Sap 1995: 2–3).[1] Though this is widely accepted, a problem with this sort of formulation is that it allows of various interpretations (for example, gender as a subjective experience, a psychological orientation, a set of attributes possessed, a normative image or ideal, and so forth), whilst a satisfactory elaboration has proven elusive.

Further, whatever the precise interpretation of the category, and despite the significant use made of the sex/gender distinction by early (second-wave) feminists, numerous theorists now appear sceptical about its analytical usefulness. Let me briefly recap.

In the late 1970s and early 1980s feminists began increasingly to emphasise the partiality of all knowledge, and to criticise the tendency

---

[1] The distinction between sex and gender on which this conception builds derives from the work of the psychologist Robert Stoller (1968) who first formulated it to differentiate the socio-cultural meanings ('masculinity' and 'femininity') from those of biological sex differences ('male' and 'female') on which they were erected (see Oakley 1972).

of (typically white and male) scientists to presume their views to be uninfluenced by local biases, and personal histories and values. The dominant message of these feminists was that a fuller vision of reality could be uncovered by drawing attention to gendered locations, that a theorising of gender was a useful way of uncovering previously hidden aspects of the social process (see, for example, Chodorow 1978 and Keller 1985). These gender theorists argued that concepts commonly used to evaluate behaviour (such as calculative rationality in economics) do not express universal values or ideals but male ones.

Although insightful, by the late 1980s this early feminist contribution was being challenged by other feminists for making the same sorts of ('essentialist') mistakes that it itself criticised. Specifically, the earlier (typically white, middle-class) feminists were charged with treating their own particular experience of gender differences as universal; they were criticised for taking 'the experience of white middle-class women to be representative of, indeed normative for, the experience of all women' (Spelman 1990: 1x). In so doing, these early feminists were accused of marginalising differences of race, ethnocentricity, culture, age and so forth; women of colour, lesbians and others found their history and culture ignored in the ongoing discussions relating to gender.

As a result of this criticism there emerged an epistemological position often referred to as gender scepticism, characterised precisely by its 'scepticism about the use of gender as an analytic category' (Bordo 1993: 135). Gender sceptics argue that an individual's gender experience is so affected by that individual's experience of class, race or culture, etc., that it is meaningless to consider gender at all as a useful category. For once we are attentive to differences of class, ethnic origin, sexual orientation, and so on, the notion of gender disintegrates into fragments unusable for systematic theory. According to this assessment it is impossible to separate facts about gender from those about race, class, ethnic origin, and so on. Spelman writes:

If it were possible to isolate a woman's 'womanness' from her racial identity, then we should have no trouble imagining that had I been Black I could have had just the same understanding of myself as a woman as I in fact do ... It is thus evident that thinking about a person's identity as made up of neatly distinguishable 'parts' may be very misleading. (Spelman 1990: 135–6).

In short, early feminist (and other) gender theorists were criticised for assuming cross-cultural stability of facts about gender, and a separability of the parts of a person's achieved identity.

If the intent of this criticism was to be corrective, it was soon to be pushed to destructive extremes. Specifically, some 'post-modernists' came to argue that, because of differences of ethnic origin, sexual orientation, culture and so forth, not only is each individual's experience unique but no category can legitimately be treated as stable or separable. The fact of differential historical experiences means that each 'woman' differs from every other and it is impossible or meaningless to talk of the 'authentic woman' and so to unify different individuals under the signifier 'woman'. There is no woman's (or of course man's) experience, situation or point of view. As a result, it is difficult to make sense of feminist projects of collective emancipation. For who is to be emancipated, and from whom? The sort of perspective in question leads to a view of a world only of differences, an individualist perspective in which it is impossible to make much sense of any system or collectivity, whether oppressive or otherwise.

This post-modernist critique of (interpretations of) early gender theorising contains much insight and can indeed be read in part as a corrective of the excesses or errors of naïve essentialist positions. However, the critique itself is ultimately not satisfactory, in that it loses the central insight of the earlier feminist contribution entirely. For according to the logic of this critique there is no basis for systematic forces of societal discrimination.[2] Yet it cannot really be denied that there are systematic forms of domination in society as we experience it, and in particular that biological females are very often dominated or oppressed by males, and in ways that have little if anything to do with sexual as opposed to social differences[3] (see Bryson, this volume).

---

[2] As Kate Soper complains: 'the logic which challenged certain kinds of identity thinking and deconstructed certain notions of truth, progress, humanism and the like, has pushed on to question the possibility of *any* holistic and objective analysis of societies of a kind which allows to define them as "capitalist" or "patriarchal" or indeed totalitarian, together with the transformative projects such analyses advocate. It gives us not new identities, not a better understanding of the plural and complex nature of society, but tends rather to collapse into an out and out individualism' (Soper 1991: 45).

[3] This is indeed manifest in the orientations, language, values and priorities of academic disciplines, as economics, my discipline, illustrates as well as anything else (see e.g. the contributions in Ferber and Nelson 1993).

Put differently, the post-modernist critique, in highlighting the problems of essentialism, loses the insight for which gender analysis was originally formulated, namely the discrimination of individuals classified as 'women' in ways that have little directly to do with the quality of being female.[4] If it is widely recognised that there are many types of differences between members of society, specifically between those classified as men and women, we need to attend to ways of disentangling rather than neglecting the types that there are.[5]

Such considerations suggest that what is needed is a conception of gender that can sustain both (1) the insights underpinning the noted criticisms of early gender theorising, specifically the fragmented experiences of us all and the difficulties of partialling out the gendered aspects of our experiences, as well as (2) the (widely recognised) feature of our world that gender is an objective category that (currently) marks the site of the domination of one (gendered) group by another.

We need a conception that can sustain the insight that we all are different, that our experiences and identities are historically, culturally and socially, etc., variable and indeed unique, as well as the deep intuition that there is a need for, and legitimacy to, collective organisation and struggle.

We need, in short, a conception that transcends the opposition of difference and unity with a clear basis for achieving both, a conception precisely of unity in difference. I now want to indicate that ontological elaboration can facilitate a conception of the sort required.

---

[4] As Susan Bordo summarises the situation: 'Assessing where we are now, it seems to me that feminism stands less in danger of the totalizing tendencies of feminists than of an increasingly paralysing anxiety over falling (from what grace?) into ethnocentrism or "essentialism" ... Do we want to delegitimate a priori the exploration of experimental continuity and structural common ground among women? ... If we wish to empower diverse voices, we would do better, I believe, to shift strategy from the methodological dictum that we foreswear talk of "male" and "female" realities ... to the messier, more slippery, practical struggle to create institutions and communities that will not permit *some* groups of people to make determinations about reality for *all*' (Bordo 1993: 465).

[5] As Anne Phillips has observed: 'Notwithstanding the conceptual difficulties feminists have raised around the distinction between sex and gender, we will continue to need some way of disentangling the differences that are inevitable from those that are chosen, and from those that are imposed' (Phillips 1992: 23).

Ontology

By social ontology, let me recall, I mean the study (or a theory) of the basic nature and structure of social being.[6] And by the social, I just mean the domain of those phenomena whose existence, at least in part, depends on us. Thus the domain includes artefacts, technology, wars, pollutions, social relations, institutions, and so forth.

Now a first fundamental feature of the social realm, one of significance to the issues being addressed here, is that it is *structured* in the sense of comprising more than one ontological level. Specifically, it consists in far more than actualities such as (actual) human behaviour including its observable patterns. It also comprises features

---

[6] It is no secret (though somewhat puzzling) that feminist theorists have tended to fight shy of ontology/metaphysics. Sally Haslanger's recounting of her own experience captures this situation: 'Metaphysics has never been without critics. Plato's efforts have repeatedly been a target of attack; Hume ranted against the metaphysicians of his day; and one of the founding missions of logical positivism was to show that metaphysical claims are meaningless. More recently, feminist theorists have joined the chorus. To reveal among academic feminists that one's specialization in philosophy is metaphysics is to invite responses of shock, confusion and sometimes dismissal. Once after I gave a presentation at an American Philosophical Association meeting on social construction, a noted senior feminist philosopher approached me and said, "you are clearly very smart, and very feminist, so why are you wasting your time on this stuff?" Academic feminists, for the most part, view metaphysics as a dubious intellectual project, certainly irrelevant and probably worse; and often the further charge is levelled that it has pernicious political implications as well' (Haslanger 2000: 107). Why should ontology be so treated? Some seem to suppose ontology must be foundationalist. But ontology is just an epistemological project, and like any other must be recognised as situated, practically conditioned, partial, and in parts at least probably transient. Sandra Harding (1999: 132) suggests that existing ontological/realist presuppositions of science can be entrenched, and that epistemic standards are an easier target for criticism. But surely the insights of recent feminist theorising have stemmed from the fact that almost all claims suppositions, no matter how entrenched, have been regarded as legitimate targets of deconstruction or other forms of criticism. Harding (1999: 132) also gives a Kuhnian argument as to why implicit and naïve ontological presuppositions may be worth persevering with anyway. Whether or not this can be shown to be provisionally the case with regard to some branches of natural science, it is certainly not so with regard to studies of the social realm, as I have shown at length elsewhere (Lawson 2003). A final explanation is that ontology may reveal objective grounds for identifying groups, and so group-memberships, whereas such a finding does not help the overriding cause of being non-exclusive (see Fricker 2000 or Haslanger 2000). As Donna Haraway (1985: 372) puts it, 'Consciousness of exclusion through naming is acute.' This is a line of reasoning I briefly address in the main text below.

such as social rules, relations, positions, processes, systems, values, meaning, and the like, that do not reduce to human behaviour. Nor do features such as these exist just in their instantiation or manifestation in behaviour. Rather they are mostly ontologically distinct from behaviour. Such features that do not reduce to behaviour can be termed *social structures*, constituting, in their entirety, *social structure*.

How do I defend the claim that social reality includes structure that is ontologically irreducible to human agency or behaviour? I go into this at length elsewhere (e.g. Lawson 1997, 2003). Basically the argument is that a conception of social reality as structured is required if we are to explain numerous widespread features of everyday life.

Most clearly the distinction is required if we are to make sense of the widespread observation of a gap between cultural norms or stipulations and patterns of individual behaviour. More precisely, the distinction is necessitated if we are to explain the fact of practices in which rules affect action, but are systematically contravened in it. For example, workers in conflict with their employers or management could not threaten to 'work-to rule', as they do in the UK, if any rule (or set of rules) in question just reduces to the norm or average form of the work activities that are already being undertaken. Nor could the workforce sensibly make such 'threats' if they did not have the power or agency to do so, a power that is not reducible to what in the event happens (whatever the outcome).

Also in the UK, not all, but some, motorway drivers regularly exceed the legal speed limit. In some cities of the world (for example Naples) most drivers pass some (but rarely all) red lights, and so on.

In short, rules and the practices upon which they bear are sometimes aligned but at other times are systematically out of phase. This is a feature of reality we can render intelligible only by recognising that social structures and the practices they condition, though presupposing of each other, are irreducible each to the other. For it is only because they are ontologically distinct and irreducible that they can be aligned on occasion, or that any 'threat' (promise or request) to align them makes sense.

Human beings too are structured. Individual agents have capacities and dispositions, for example, which are irreducible to the behaviour patterns we produce. Each of us has capacities that may never be exercised. And, individually, we are continually reflexive, even having ('inner') conversations with ourselves as well as other first-person experiences that are not open to inspection by others. These clearly have their conditions of possibility, presumably including processes in the brain. But the subjective aspects appear irreducible to any neurobiological activity. Most clearly, what we can do does not reduce to the patterns of behaviour that others can observe; and nor even does all of what we actually do.

Notice that this irreducibility of social structure and human subjectivity can be rendered intelligible only if we further recognise the reality of processes of *emergence*, underpinning *emergent* social and psychological realms in particular (see e.g. Lawson 1997, especially chapters 6 and 13, 2003). Let me briefly elaborate.

A stratum of reality can be said to be emergent, or as possessing emergent powers, if there is a sense in which it (1) has arisen out of a lower stratum, being formed by principles operative at the lower level; (2) remains dependent on the lower stratum for its existence; but (3) contains causal powers of its own which are both irreducible to those operating at the lower level and (perhaps) capable of acting back on the lower level. Thus organic material emerged from inorganic material. And, according to the conception I am defending, the social realm is emergent from human (inter-)action, though with properties irreducible to, yet capable of causally affecting, the latter. For example language systems have emerged from human interactions, and bear powers that act back upon, but remain irreducible to, the speech acts which they facilitate.

So interpreted, the theory of emergence commits us to a form of materialism which ultimately entails the unilateral ontological dependence of social upon biological upon physical forms coupled with the taxonomic and causal irreducibility of each to any other. Thus, although, for example, the geohistorical emergence of organic from inorganic matter and of human beings from hominids can be acknowledged, when we come to explain those physical and biological states that are due, in part, to intentional human agency it is necessary to reference properties, including powers, not designated by physical or biological science (again see Lawson 1997).

So the social realm consists, in part, of (emergent) social structures and human subjects that are reducible neither to each other nor to human practices. It may already be clear how I am going to argue that the category gender can be retained as a meaningful object of reality with a degree of stability. For I will argue that gender is in large part a feature of (emergent) social structure, i.e. something that is irreducible to human practices or experiences. First though let me say something more about the forms of social structure as well as its (processual) mode of being.

Social positions and relations

In emphasising the structured nature of social life I have so far focused upon social rules. But this is not all there is to social being. For society is also constituted in a fundamental way by both *social relations* and *positions*. These features are essential to understanding the precise manner in which human agency and structure come together.

The significance and fact of social relations and positions are easily recognised once we take note (and inquire into the conditions) of that general feature of experience that there is a systematic disparity across individuals regarding the practices that are, and apparently can be, followed. Although most rules can be utilised by a wide group of people it by no means follows that all rules are available, or apply equally, to everyone, even within a given culture. To the contrary, any (segment of) society is highly differentiated in terms of the obligations and prerogatives that are on offer. Teachers, for example, are allowed and expected to follow different practices from students, government ministers to follow different ones from lay-people, employers from employees, landladies/lords from tenants, and so on. Rules as resources are not equally available, or do not apply equally, to each member of the population at large.

What then explains the differentiated ascription of obligations, prerogatives, privileges and responsibilities? This question directs attention to the wider one of how human beings and elements of social structure such as rules come together in the first place. If these elements such as rules are a different sort of thing from human beings, human agency and even action, what is the point of contact between human agency and structure? How do they interconnect? In particular how do they come together in such a manner that different individuals achieve responsibilities and obligations available to some but not all others, and thereby call on, or come to be conditioned in their actions by, different social rules and so structures of power?

If it is clearly the case that teachers have different responsibilities, obligations and prerogatives from students, and government ministers face different ones from the rest of us, then it is equally apparent that these obligations and prerogatives exist independently of the particular individuals who happen, currently, to be teachers, students or ministers. If I, as a university teacher, were to move on tomorrow, someone else would take over my teaching responsibilities and enjoy the same obligations and prerogatives as I currently do. Indeed, those who occupy the positions of students are different every year. In short, society is constituted in large part by a set of *positions*, each associated with numerous obligations, rights and duties, and into which agents, as it were, slot.

Internal relations

Something more about this system of societal positions can be expressed if we take note of the additional observation that practices routinely followed by an occupant of any position tend to be orientated towards some other group(s). The rights, tasks and obligations of teachers, for example, are orientated towards their interactions with students (and vice versa), towards research funding bodies or governing institutions, and so forth. Similarly the rights and obligations of landladies/lords are orientated towards their interactions with tenants, and so on.

Such considerations indicate a causal role for certain forms of *relation*. Two types of relation can be distinguished: *external* and *internal*. Two objects or aspects are externally related if neither is constituted by the relationship in which it stands to the other. Bread and butter, coffee and milk, barking dog and mail carrier provide examples. In contrast, two objects are internally related if they are what they are, or can do the sort of thing they do, by virtue of the relationship in which they stand to one other. Landlady/lord and tenant, employer and employee, teacher and student, magnet and its field are examples that spring easily to mind. In each case it is not possible to have the one without the other; each, in part, is what it is, and does the sort of thing it does, by virtue of the relation in which it stands to the other.

Now the intelligibility of the rule-governed and rule-differentiated social situation noted above requires that we recognise first the internal relationality of social life, and second that the internal relationality in question is primarily not of individuals per se but of social positions; it is the positions (say of teachers and students) that are relationally defined.

The picture that emerges, then, is of a set, or network, of positions characterised by the rules and so practices associated with them, where the latter are determined in relation to other positions and their associated rules and practices. On this conception the basic building blocks of society are *positions*, involving, depending upon or constituted according to social rules and associated tasks, obligations and prerogatives, along with the practices they govern, where such positions are both defined in relation to other positions and are immediately occupied by individuals.

Systems and collectivities

Notice further that notions of social *systems* or *collectivities* can be straightforwardly developed using the conceptions of social structure as rules, practices, relationships and positions now elaborated. Most generally, social systems and collectivities can be viewed as ensembles of networked, internally related positions with their associated rules and practices. All the familiar social systems, collectivities and organisations – the economy, the state, international and national companies, trade unions, households, schools and hospitals – can be recognised as depending upon, presupposing or consisting in internally related position-rule systems of this form.

Sub-distinctions can be drawn. If a social *system* is best conceived as a structured process of interaction, a social group or *collectivity* can be understood as consisting in, or depending upon, or as a set of people distinguishable by, their current occupancy of a specific set of social positions. Notice that at any one time a particular individual will occupy any number of positions. That is, the same person may be a parent and a child, a worker and a boss, a teacher and a student, immigrant and native, old and young, a member of religious or political or community organisations and so on. The resulting conception then is one that (1) renders intelligible the often noted, but reputedly difficult to sustain, sense of a group or collective interest and thus the basis for a theory of collective action, and yet (2) allows the possibility of a conflict of interest at the level of individuals.

Put differently, on this relational conception any specific collectivity can be understood in terms both of its relations to other groups, especially those against which it is defined and/or is opposed, and of the complex of internal relationships within the collectivity itself. Amongst the many advantages of this conception is the feature that it allows a meaningful focus not only upon production and exchange activities but also upon a range of distributional issues as well, such as resources to groups as well as people to positions (or positions to people).

To anticipate the discussion of gender that follows shortly, my contention will be that gender is usefully viewed as intimately bound up with nexuses of internally related positions to which perceived-to-be biological females and males are (differentially) assigned in any context (or which are assigned (differentially) to individuals identified as biological females or males), along with the associated rules, rights and obligations and so forth. This enables us to locate the site of domination (and recognise that feminist distributional studies ought indeed to be concerned with the allocation of positions) whilst allowing that every individual's path is unique, just as her or his occupancy of positions is variable and complex and again unique. This conception thus allows uniqueness at the level of the actual, including experience, the focus of post-modernists, whilst maintaining the ability to locate the forces of discrimination so many also regularly experience.

Social being as process

If the above account is to prove sustainable, it clearly follows that the societal positions that individuals occupy and the rules associated with them be (or can be) relatively *enduring*. Yet the whole question of the fixity or otherwise of social structure, as well as of the human individual, is a topic that has yet to be broached. These are issues that must be addressed, especially if we are ultimately concerned with questions of emancipatory change.

It is instructive at this point to consider the mode of being of social structure. To focus the discussion, let me again consider the example of a system of language. Clearly we are all born into language systems; none of us creates them. At the same time, being social phenomena, language systems depend on us, and specifically on transformative human agency. So they do not determine what we do, they do not create our speech acts; they merely facilitate them. So in theorising the relationship of agency and structure, the categories of creation and determinism are out of place here. Rather we must view matters in terms of the categories of *transformation* and *reproduction*. For any given language system, its structure of rules, etc., is given to the individual when he or she comes to speak, and it is reproduced and/or transformed through the sum total of individuals engaging in speech acts. The social structure in question, then, is the (typically unacknowledged) condition of a set of practices; just as its reproduction and/or transformation is the (typically unintended) result of these practices.

Now what is true of the mode of being of a language system holds for all social structure; social structures exist as processes of reproduction and transformation. A market or a university or a language system does not exist in a primarily static form, subject at most to moments of change (owing to new technology or whatever). Rather change is essential to the mode of being of such structures; they exist as continuous processes of transformation and/or reproduction. Even where aspects of certain social structures appear a posteriori to remain intact, this is only and always because they have been actively (if mostly unintentionally) reproduced. On this conception, which has elsewhere in economics been systematised as the *transformational model of social activity*, no aspects are fixed and out of time. All are subject to processes of transformation. So there is no ontological prioritisation of continuity over change (or vice versa); continuity and change are ontologically equivalent. And each, when it occurs, is open to, and for understanding necessitates, (a causal) explanation (see e.g. Lawson 1997, 2003).

Social structure, then, is reproduced and transformed through human practice. But so is each individual human agent. For, as we have seen, the human individual too is structured. To speak a language such as English presupposes the capacity to do so. To possess the capacity to speak English presupposes the more basic capacity for language acquisition, and so on. Human individuals are far more than their behaviours. And the ways in which capacities and dispositions are developed and maintained or transformed, depends on individual practices. The same applies, of course, to tastes, or preferences, long-term and short-term plans, other features, psychological make-up, and so forth. So the individual agent, just like social structure, is continually reproduced and transformed through practice.

The social world, including both structure and human agency, then, turns on human practice. Social structure and human agency each condition the other, although neither can be reduced to the other, nor to the practices through which both are reproduced and/or transformed.[7]

The foregoing is a brief overview of aspects of a transformational model of social activity. It is a model that is seen to be appropriate once social reality is conceptualised as being structured. And a conception of social reality as structured is found to be a requirement of explaining familiar aspects of everyday experience. The overall transformational conception is a thoroughly non-reductionist account of linked or co-development. Neither structure nor agency has analytical priority, for each depends irreducibly on the other. And although each develops at its own ontological level, it does so only in

---

[7] One further component of this transformational conception is that there are both synchronic and diachronic aspects to agency–structure interaction. It is, of course, human beings that make things happen. And it is only through the mediation of human agency that structures have a causal impact. Now if a person who speaks only English makes a short (possibly unplanned) visit to a region where English is not spoken, the inability to speak the local language (or the existence only of languages other than English) will be experienced by the traveller as a constraint. It forces her or him to seek a translator or whatever. If, however, English is spoken as a second language, this will be experienced by the traveller as an enabling (as well as constraining) feature of the local social structure. Here, with the momentarily enabling and/or constraining aspects of social structure we have the *synchronic* aspect of agency–structure interaction.

However, if the individual who speaks only English decides to settle in a non-English speaking region, then, if he or she is to become competent it will be necessary to acquire the local language (and indeed become competent in numerous aspects of the local culture). The process through which this happens is the *diachronic* aspect of agency–structure interaction. If at a point in time structure serves to constrain and enable, over time it serves more to shape and mould. As new practices are repeatedly carried out they become habitual as dispositions are moulded in response. This, of course, cannot happen without the collusion of the individual in question (and the mediation of his or her practices). If the individual remains for a long time in the new language or culture zone, he or she may even lose the capacity to speak English, or at least to do so competently. Just as human capabilities, etc., can be transformed via the relocation, so the maintenance of those previously held may require active reproduction. Experience suggests that individuals can lose a significant degree of competence in languages with which they once were fluent (also, of course, what is true of capabilities and dispositions applies equally to tastes, preferences, and the like).

conditions set by the other. Thus each is significantly dependent on, though not created or determined by, the other. Social life, then, is intrinsically dynamic, and interdependent.

Theorising gender

So how does all this help with theorising the category of gender? Let me stress once more that ontology cannot do the work of substantive social theorising. Although I now want to suggest an interpretation of gender consistent with the ontological framework elaborated, it will not be the only possibility. Even so, in that the interpretation provided evades the charges levelled by gender sceptics whilst retaining the ability to explain domination and discrimination, it is one that does seem worth considering seriously.

The key to combining the insights both of gender theorists and of gender sceptics lies in recognising ontological distinctions between social structure, human agency and practice. These distinctions allow that individuals can indeed have unique, including fragmented, experiences and social identities, and yet be conditioned (and facilitated) by relatively enduring, if always space-time specific, social structures, including internally related positions, and associated rights and practices that allow the systematic subjugation or oppression of some by others.

For if the continually reproduced and transformed social structures, comprising networks of internally related positions and associated rights and obligations, provide the sites, the objective bases, for forms of discrimination, it warrants emphasis that there is no one-to-one mapping from social structure to individual pathways, experience or personal identities.

Furthermore, each individual occupies many positions simultaneously, and life is a unique path of entering and exiting. So the perspective sustained is quite consistent with the insight of multiple or fragmented experiences.

Of course, the fact of systematic discrimination presupposes there is nevertheless a way or sense in which some individuals, whatever their experiences, are nevertheless marked as similar (and different from some others). The markers can be age, skin colour, language, accent and a host of other (actual or perceived) human qualities.

Gender, I suggest, is bound up with one such system of identification and differentiation, one that (as it happens in seemingly all societies so far) serves to privilege some over others.

Essential to such a system are the following two components:

(1) a distinction repeatedly drawn between individuals who are regularly/mostly observed or imagined to have certain bodily features presumed to be evidence of a female's biological role in reproduction and others who are regularly/mostly observed or imagined to have certain bodily features presumed to be evidence of a male's biological role in reproduction;

(2) a set of mechanisms or processes which work in any given society or locality to legitimise/motivate the notion that individuals regarded as female and those regarded as male ought to be allocated to, or to have allocated to them, systematically differentiated kinds of social positions, where the nature of the allocations encouraged need not, and typically does not, reflect any commonalities or differences located at the biological level.[8]

Currently, as I say, in seemingly all societies, the positions characterised as being for women are in fact mostly subordinate along some prominent set of axes, whilst those for men are typically privileged.

What precisely is gender on this conception? I would define it neither as a substance, nor *simply* a category of analysis, but rather as a social totality, a social system. It is a system of processes and products (of processes in product and products in process). The processes in question (which are always context specific) are precisely

---

[8] I hope it is clear that in advancing this conception I neither assume fixity, nor deny variability (if within limits), at the biological level, and nor do I suppose that any biological sex form, or for that matter form of sexuality, is more natural than any other (nor, of course, do I endorse any such differences as there are, or perceptions of them, being used to legitimate social inequalities). I do hold that if biological differences/commonalities, as they are perceived, affect emergent social structure, then equally the (emergent) social structure can act back on the biological. However, the two domains, the biological and the socio-structural, remain ontologically distinct, though causally interacting; neither is reducible to, or explicable completely in terms of, the other. It will be clear, then, that however I suggest we conceptualise gender as an aspect of social structure (see below), I am accepting the reality (and the explanatory significance), of maintaining the sex/gender distinction.

those that work to legitimise/motivate the notion that individuals regarded as female and those regarded as male ought to be allocated to, or to have allocated to them, systematically differentiated kinds of (relationally defined) social positions. The products are the (equally transitory and spatially/culturally limited) outcomes of these processes. If the processes serve *to gender,* i.e. are gendering processes (or processes of genderation), the products (aspects of social relations, positions (with associated rights and norms) practices, identities) must be regarded as *gendered.*

Where precisely is the gender system? So conceived, I do not think the gender system can be isolated from the rest of social reality; rather it is the whole of social reality considered under a particular (albeit only one[9]) aspect. That is, the gender system comprises all social processes/products viewed under the aspects of gendering/being rendered gendered. In all our practices we draw upon the structures of society as we (momentarily) find them, including their gendered aspects. And through our acting, these structures – whether bearing on issues of material distribution, status, power or whatever[10] – are, wittingly or not, continually reproduced and/or transformed. This transformational activity is the mode of being of all social processes. And all structures and their processes of reproduction seemingly have gendered aspects.

Often processes of gendering are intended/fully conscious. Such processes will include not only overtly sexist practices of some adults but also perhaps the differentiating practices of rival siblings responding to the 'trauma' of discovering differences.[11]

---

[9] In viewing gender as everything considered under only *one* aspect (but without wishing to detract from the emphasis on *everything*) I concur with Fraser (this volume) in viewing 'gender struggles as one strand among others in a broader political project aimed at institutionalizing democratic justice across multiple axes of social differentiation'.

[10] See Fraser (this volume) on the need to hold distributional and status issues together in considering matters of gender inequality.

[11] This view is advanced by Juliet Mitchell who argues that 'sibling trauma instigates the construction of gender difference. Gender is engendered in the sibling (or sibling equivalent) relationship' (2003: 216). When 'the child is overwhelmed by the trauma of one who, in the mind, was supposed to be the same as itself inevitably turning out to be different, it finds ways to mark this difference – age is one, gender another' (216). This trauma ensures that violence is latent and always possible between either the actual siblings or their replacements in the wider world. 'The cradle of gender difference is both

But mostly, I suspect, gendering processes are implicit and unnoticed; with specific gendered structures or features being the typically unacknowledged conditions as well as the usually unintended outcomes of our practices[12] (where gendering processes of this sort will include, significantly, those in which already prevalent gendered categories – e.g. leadership (male), dexterous (female) – are reinforced through being used in turn to signify relationships of power – e.g. through being used to signify typical characteristics of, respectively, employers and employees).[13]

If gender is a (intrinsically dynamic and open) system comprising processes of gendering and the (again always open and dynamic) products of such processes, it is the forces for continuity and change, along with the changing nature of gender, that are analytically interesting.

Personal identities

Parenthetically, I might note that nothing in this analysis undermines the possibility of our establishing personal identities, albeit identities which are always unique, changing and relational.

Such identities, if and where established, will be conditioned by our experiences, fallible knowledge of situations, perceived possibilities, normative ideals, plans and constraints. As such they are open to evaluation. Indeed, in that we continually reproduce and transform our identities, they are something of an (ongoing) achievement.

An individual's experiences will of course vary according to social positions entered and retained and others previously exited. But there is no strict correspondence between the structures experienced and

narcissistic love and violence at the traumatic moment of displacement in the world. Gender difference comes into being when physical strength and malevolence are used to mark the sister as lesser' (219–20).

[12] And more subtly gendering will probably be implicated even within discussions of gender discrimination, such as this chapter, so that the successful eradication of gender inequalities will require that, amongst other things, we continually challenge the frameworks within which equality is debated (see Bryson, this volume).

[13] As such the conception advanced here encompasses the distinction between sexual difference and gender advanced elsewhere in this volume by Juliet Mitchell. However, in emphasising how siblings reveal how crucial a force is sexuality in a psychosocial dynamics, Mitchell is wary of any conception of gender that does not place sex or sexuality at the centre.

identities formed. Like everything else, experiencing is fallible. Moreover we mostly recognise this. Just as we each regularly find we experience a given situation differently from others, we can also come to reinterpret our experiences over time.

But, if the reduction of identities to conditions experienced is a theoretical error, it remains the case that the conditions we experience do nevertheless make a difference. If we ultimately make our own identities, we do so only with the resources available, and in conditions not all of our own choosing. In particular the nature of gender positions we occupy or have occupied, along with all other features of our specific social situations, many of which have been allocated to us, causally impinges on our experiences and so constitutes conditioning factors of our identities.[14] Our identities are themselves a form of emergent, relationally conditioned, social structure in process.

Overview

My overall contention, then, is that the conception defended here retains the insights both of the early gender theorists and of their post-modernist critics. It retains the latter's emphasis on multiple or fragmented experiences, whilst also sustaining the wider feminist insight that our societies provide an objective basis for the discriminating tendencies already noted.

The central idea underpinning my arguments is that there is an ontological distinction between (emergent) social structure and human agency, whereby neither can be reduced to the other, though each is continually transformed through practice in a process of linked or co-development.

In the light of the perspective defended we find that gender sceptics portray early (supposedly essentialist) feminists as, in effect, reducing agency to specific (gender) structures, or at least to specific aspects regarded as fixed, whilst gender sceptics themselves have responded by more or less cutting the individual free of structural forces of determination entirely. However, we can now recognise the initial

[14] Although the conception here is derived by way of first elaborating the ontological conception discussed above and defended more fully elsewhere, others have reached a similar position on certain aspects via alternative routes. See for example, Mohanty 2000, and Moya 2000.

(essentialist) form of gender theorising as well as the out and out deconstructive response to be polar degenerate cases of the range of real possibilities, with the deconstructive response in particular achieving its credibility only by situating essentialism as the only alternative. There are additional possibilities. And once the conception elaborated above is accepted we have a basis for sustaining the insights of both essentialist and post-modernist perspectives, whilst avoiding the limit weaknesses of each.

The broad implications for theorising are clear: the study of gender requires attention not just to individuals and their experiences but equally to explaining specific networks of internally related position-practice systems, including their conditions and how they are reproduced and/or transformed over time and space. The focus is precisely on specific examples of social reproduction and social transformation (methodological aspects of this are discussed elsewhere – see Lawson 2003, especially chapter 4).

The possibility of emancipatory practice

Of central interest here is that implications also follow at the level of emancipatory practice. Specifically, the ontological conception sustained allows us to acknowledge the relativity of knowledge as well as the uniqueness of experiences and yet still entertain the possibility of progressive, including emancipatory, projects. For it is now clear that there is no contradiction in *both* recognising each of us as a unique identity or individuality, resulting (in part) from our own unique paths through life, and *also* accepting that we can nevertheless stand in the same or similar positions and relations of domination to those of others around us, including gender relations. From this perspective there is no contradiction in recognising our different individualities and experiences *as well as* the possibility of common interests in transforming certain forms of social relationships and other aspects of social structure. Fundamental here once more is the fact that human subjectivities, human experiences and social structure cannot be reduced one to another; they are each ontologically distinct, albeit highly interdependent, modes of being.

I re-emphasise that I make no presumption that any aspects of social structure, including its gendered features, are other than intrinsically dynamic, or are everywhere the same. It is evident that gender relations in most places (still) serve to facilitate (localised) practices in which men can dominate/oppress women, or appear in some way advantaged. But the extent of commonality/difference across time and space is something to be determined a posteriori.

This conception also allows that although the individualities/ personalities of people from quite diverse backgrounds may be quite different, when they arrive in the same location they are likely to be subject to, or forced to stand within, similar, i.e. *local*, gender (and other) relations, whether or not they are aware of this, and whether or not they learn to become locally skilful. For example, it seems that currently in parts of the UK any (person identified as a) woman going alone to a pub in the evening is likely to meet with harassment by some 'men' whatever the former's previous experiences, realised capacities, acknowledged needs, expectations, self-perceptions or understandings of the local gender relations, and so on.

Gender relations with a degree of space-time extension along with practices they facilitate can be *transfactually* operative irrespective of the knowledges or understandings and wishes of those affected. The existences of multiple differences in manifest identities and individual experiences is not inconsistent with this insight – any more than the unique path of each autumn leaf undermines the hypothesis that all leaves are similarly subject to the transfactual 'pull' of gravity.

In short, once a structured ontology is recognised, multiplicity in the course of actuality is found to remain coherent with a degree of uniformity at the level of underlying causes or structure. The conception defended thus secures the basis for an emancipatory politics rooted in real needs and interests. In so doing it provides grounds, in particular, for feminist projects of transforming gender relations, in an awareness that the existence of multiculturalism or of differences in general need not in any way undermine or contradict such emancipatory practice. It also preserves, without strain, the possibility of strategies of solidarity or meaningful affiliated action between groups. In short, it transcends the sorts of tensions that currently seem to pervade much of feminist epistemology and political theory.

Social transformation and the good society

A more specific implication of the framework is that emancipatory social change is found to be a matter not only just of ameliorating events but also, and especially, of social transformation. Now given that social structures depend on our practices, then, whatever the appropriate feminist orientation to the state, we can recognise that social change may be brought about not just through central state action, but equally through each of us changing the conceptions which guide our practices. Radicals of all sorts have always understood this, that we can transform social reality by increasing our awareness and understanding of it, and in turn change the practices via which existing structures are reproduced.

What more can be said? I think the framework defended here bears implications, albeit still at a very abstract level, about the (conception of the) sort of society that might reasonably inform our emancipatory structural transformations. I think it is an inescapable conclusion that the ultimate goal of emancipatory practice *is* a form of society. Moreover, given the interconnectedness of social life, entailing that all actions are affecting of others, the basic unit of emancipatory analysis is presumably (at least) the whole of humanity. However, emancipatory practice must equally recognise our differences. My suggestion here is just that (given both our (structured) interrelatedness as well as differences at the level of each individual) the concern of emancipatory action must be with the possibility of a society so constituted as to allow that the flourishing of each is a condition of the flourishing of all and vice versa; or, as Marx put it: 'an association in which the free development of each is a condition of the free development of all' (Marx and Engels 1952 [1848]: 76).

I emphasise that in proposing this formulation of the 'good society' I do not presuppose any fixity; the formulation allows for the openness of everything to the future, including human 'nature', society, knowledge, technology, science, and all else. But anything short of this formulation, as a goal, it seems to me, is likely to beg the questions of the sort as to whose interests are to be met.

Is the above conception of the good society consistent with one constituted in large part by social positions? Now in the light of the analysis sustained it appears feasible that society will for a long time, if not always, be in large part constituted by networks of internally related social positions, marking divisions of labour, or of age or of political, religious or other attachments. But there is no obvious reason to suppose that a structuring of society cannot be achieved that, though in some part constituted by objective (though always transient) positions, nevertheless avoids being hierarchically organised. That is, (always transient) positions can conceivably be facilitating without providing the basis for the unreasonable privileging of some over subjugated others. Also, social positions can be rotated amongst the population. Perhaps participating first as a speaker, then as a member of the audience, and later perhaps as a chair, at a feminist meeting is a relevant illustrative model; objective positions all, but surely non-discriminatory in any necessarily excluding fashion and acceptable.[15]

A sustainable conclusion, then, is that the theorising of strategy for a developing global order, including the adoption of an appropriate orientation to the state, is reasonably informed by such an (open) conception of the good society. Specifically, in proposing measures to transform social reality it seems that a criterion of relevance is whether such measures appear capable of moving us in the direction of a society in which the flourishing of each is consistent with, and a condition of, the flourishing of all others, and vice versa.

From this perspective the strategy adopted by some post-modernists of emphasising an ontology of mere difference – on the reasoning that if no objective basis is admitted for including only some individuals, there is equally no basis admitted for excluding any[16] – can be seen

---

[15] This seems consistent too with Nancy Fraser's 'status model' which encourages a politics aimed at overcoming subordination by recognising all individuals as full members of society whatever their socio-cultural positions, or perceived identities, etc. (see Fraser 2000). This conception of justice is advanced in the current volume with Fraser's formulation of 'the principle of *parity of participation*' according to which 'justice requires social arrangements that permit all (adult) members of society to interact with one another *as peers*'. See Fraser (this volume) for a discussion of the preconditions for such 'participatory parity'.

[16] Miranda Fricker (2000: 148) captures the motivation of the latter well: 'Postmodernists typically advocate a social ontology of fragmentation not on grounds of social accuracy, but on the political ground that any other ontology would be exclusionary ... In feminist postmodernism ... to recognise difference is to meet an obligation to political inclusiveness rather than empirical adequacy'.

Sally Haslanger (2000: 122) summarises how this works in the arguments of Judith Butler in particular: 'Remember how the move to nominalism functions in the structure of Butler's strategy: if there is no objective basis for distinguishing one group from another, then no political regime – especially the dominant one – can claim authority by grounding itself in "the way the world is"; instead ... the choice will have to be made on normative argument. The

not only as based on an unrealistic assessment of the nature of social reality, but also as marking a scenario that is but a degenerate special case of the above conception of the good society, one in which all positions, all divisions of labour and of other practices, have all but disappeared.

Even where the latter scenario is believed to constitute a real possibility, there is, to put it differently, little reason to suppose it is the only feasible structure of an emancipated society, and even less reason to suppose that we have reached it already, or can achieve it just by denying the objective structures including positions of gender system in which we currently live. Though we can change the world by becoming more aware of the way it is constituted, and thereby adjust our practices, it does not follow that we can achieve a particular social structure merely by wishing that the (thought-to-be) desirable features are already in place (or undesirable ones absent). More to the point, by focusing on only one version of the good society, we unnecessarily constrain our options for bringing an emancipated society about.

Conclusions

I have defended a conception that preserves and endorses, indeed itself incorporates, the impulse behind the 'deconstructive' turn in recent feminist theory, but which simultaneously, through its emphasis on ontology, avoids complete self-subversion, maintaining, amongst other things, the basis for an intelligible account of gender as well as the possibility of emancipatory action.

The particular theory of reality defended is of a structured and open world. It is a conception which recognises that in our everyday practices we, all of us, as complexly structured, socially and culturally situated, purposeful and needy individuals, knowledgeably and capably negotiate complex, shifting, only partially grasped and contested structures of power, rules, relations and other possibly relatively enduring but nevertheless transient and action-dependent social resources at our disposal. Ontological analysis provides an insight into this reality.

worry seems to be that if we allow objective types, then we are politically constrained to design our social institutions to honour and sustain them.'

My primary focus here has been gender and the possibility of transforming gender aspects of society that are found to be discriminatory. In the light of the framework sustained, gender can be understood as turning on a positioned feature of human life, specifically a network of internally related positions with associated rule-governed rights and practices. In fact, according to the conception defended, gender is very likely a feature of everything social. It is nothing less than the social system as a whole viewed under a particular aspect, that whereby social discriminations are made between individuals solely on their being identified or perceived as being of different biological sexes, discriminations that mostly have nothing to do with any differences that may be found at the biological level. Transforming the undesirable gender features of society, then, amounts to a generalised project of social transformation.

In discussing the specific implications of the analysis for projects of social emancipation, I have argued that whatever the orientation of feminists and others to the state, the goal of a society in which the flourishing of each is a condition of the flourishing of all is appropriately brought to bear in formulating substantive measures or political strategies. It is the task of formulating the latter measures or strategies that now requires our attention.

I re-emphasise, finally, that the orientation of the chapter has been ontological. It is noticeable that the study of gender, and indeed feminist theorising quite widely, has tended to neglect ontology in favour of epistemology. My own view is that this is an error, and that the two activities, along with all other forms of theorising – ontology, epistemology and substantive analysis – need to be co-developed. Indeed, it seems quite possible that if feminists allow explicit ontological analysis more fully out of the margin the opportunities for advance thereby opened up will prove to be quite significant.

References

Bordo, S. (1993) 'Feminism, Post Modernism and Gender Scepticism', in *Unbearable Weight: Feminism, Western Culture, and the Body*, The Regents of the University of California; reprinted in Anne C. Herrmann and Abigail Stewart (eds.), *Theorizing Feminism: Parallel Trends in the Humanities and Social Sciences* (Boulder, San Francisco and Oxford: Westview Press, 1994) (page references to the latter).

Chodorow, N. (1978) *The Reproduction of Mothering: Psychoanalysis and the Sociology of Gender* (Berkeley: University of California Press).

Collins, P. (1991) *Black Feminist Thought: Knowledge, Consciousness and the Politics of Empowerment* (London and New York: Routledge).

Ferber, M. and Nelson, J. (eds.) (1993) *Beyond Economic Man: Feminist Theory and Economics* (Chicago: University of Chicago Press).

Fraser, N. (2000) 'Rethinking Recognition', *New Left Review* 3, May–June: 1–10.

Fricker, M. (2000) 'Feminism in Epistemology: Pluralism without Post Modernism', in M. Fricker and J. Hornsby (eds.), *The Cambridge Companion to Feminism in Philosophy* (Cambridge: Cambridge University Press), 146–65.

Haraway, D. (1985) 'A Manifesto for Cyborgs: Science, Technology, and Socialist Feminism in the 1980s', *Socialist Review* 80: 65–108.

— (1988) 'Situated Knowledges: The Science Question in Feminism and the Privilege of Partial Perspective', *Feminist Studies* 14, 3: 575–99.

Harding, S. (1993) 'Rethinking Standpoint Epistemology: What Is "Strong Objectivity"?', in L. Alcoff and E. Potter (eds.), *Feminist Epistemologies* (New York: Routledge) 49–82; reprinted in E. Fox Keller and H. Longino (eds.), *Feminism and Science* (Oxford and New York: Oxford University Press), 235–48 (page references to the latter).

— (1995) 'Can Feminist Thought Make Economics More Objective?', *Feminist Economics* 1, 1: 7–32.

Hartsock, N. (1983) 'The Feminist Standpoint', in S. Harding and M. Hintikka (eds.), *Discovering Reality: Feminist Perspectives on Epistemology, Metaphysics, Methodology, and Philosophy of Science* (Dordrecht: Reidel), 283–310; reprinted in (for example) L. Nicholson (ed.), *The Second Wave: A Reader in Feminist Theory* (London and New York: Routledge), 216–40 (page references to the latter version).

Haslanger, S. (2000) 'Feminism in Metaphysics, Negotiating the Natural', in M. Fricker and J. Hornsby (eds.), *The Cambridge Companion to Feminism in Philosophy* (Cambridge: Cambridge University Press), 107–26.

Keller, E. (1985) *Reflections on Gender and Science* (New Haven: Yale University Press).

Kuiper, Edith and Sap, Jolande (eds.) (1995) *Out of the Margin: Feminist Perspectives on Economics* (London and New York: Routledge).

Lawson, T. (1997) *Economics and Reality* (London and New York: Routledge).

— (2003) *Reorienting Economics* (London and New York: Routledge).

Longino, H. (1990) *Science as Social Knowledge: Values and Objectivity in Scientific Enquiry* (Princeton: Princeton University Press).

Marx, K. and Engels, F. (1952 [1848]) *Manifesto of the Communist Party* (Moscow: Progress Publishers).

Mitchell, J. (2003) *Siblings: Sex and Violence* (Cambridge: Polity Press).

Mohanty, Chandra Talpade (2000) 'Under Western Eyes: Feminist Scholarship and Colonial Discourses', in *Feminism without Borders: Decolonizing Theory, Practicing Solidarity* (Durham, NC: Duke University Press), 333–58.

Moya, P. (2000) 'Postmodernism, "Realism", and the Politics of Identity: Cherríe Moraga and Chicana Feminism', in P. Moya and M. Hames-Garcia (eds.), *Reclaiming Identity: Realist Theory and the Predicament of Postmodernism* (Berkeley: University of California Press), 67–101.

Oakley, A. (1972) *Sex, Gender and Society* (London: Temple-Smith).

Phillips, A. (1992) 'Universal Pretensions in Political Thought', in M. Barrett and A. Phillips (eds.), *Destabilizing Theory: Contemporary Feminist Debates* (Cambridge: Polity Press), 10–30.

Seiz, J. (1995) 'Epistemology and the Tasks of Feminist Economics', *Feminist Economics*, 1, 3: 110–18.

Smith, Dorothy (1987) *The Everyday World as Problematic* (Boston: Northeastern University Press).

(1990) *The Conceptual Practices of Power* (Boston: Northeastern University Press).

Soper, Kate (1990) *Troubled Pleasures: Writings on Politics, Gender and Hedonism* (London and New York: Verso).

(1991) 'Postmodernism, Critical Theory and Critical Realism', in Roy Bhaskar (ed.), *A Meeting of Minds* (London: The Socialist Society), 42–9.

Spelman, Elizabeth V. (1990) *Inessential Woman: Problems of Exclusion in Feminist Thought* (London: The Women's Press).

Stoller, Robert (1968) *Sex and Gender* (London: Hogarth Press).

8 Procreative mothers (sexual difference) and child-free sisters (gender)

JULIET MITCHELL

Feminism and femininity[1]

Gender, sexual difference and demographic change

In order that the future does not miss out ('pass') on feminism, it is necessary for us to consider what feminism we are able to hand on ('pass on') to the next generation. Why does it seem to be the case that some benefits but little politics are transmitted? Has feminism created or reflected, or both, a change in the position of women?

The aim of this chapter, then, is to consider the relationship of feminism to social change. In particular my concern is second-wave feminism as it started in the West in the late 1960s. Although my focus is historical, this is not in any way a historical account; instead I have selected specific instances or events which stand as icons for my thesis. The major social change which concerns me is the demographic transition to non-replacement populations. How far did feminism spearhead this, thus putting politics in command, and how far was its advent a reflection of a wider historical process which had thrown up feminism as one of its effects? The connection between feminism and fertility changes has been well noted (Banks and Banks 1964). Here, however, I want to suggest that we have omitted half the equation: the fertility decline not only has women (and men) not reproducing so prolifically as hitherto, but has as its other side the rise to prominence of non-reproductive gender relations which are, to a degree, socially and psychologically autonomous.

---

[1] The first section was originally a talk for a conference in Amsterdam organised by the *European Women's Journal* under the title 'Passing on Feminism'; earlier versions of this paper were also given as talks at the 'Women and Society' conference, University of Seoul, Korea, 2003 and Panteion University, Athens, 2004. The second section arose out of a contribution to the conference 'Looking again at Sisterhood', Zagreb, 2005.

The two major concepts which I will be interrogating in this enquiry are therefore, on the one hand, the notion of 'sexual difference' which feminism initially deployed to analyse female/male divergence (femininity and masculinity as a necessary minimal difference from each other) and, on the other, 'gender' as a more inclusive concept which embraces the sexuality of both different- and same-sex relations, but which is also deployed in a range of places which are not necessarily primarily or determinatively sexual. As Princeton historian Joan Scott once wrote: 'The rise of gender emphasizes an entire system of relationships that may include sex, but is not directly determined by sex, nor directly determining of sexuality' (Scott 1996: 156).[2]

My suggestion is that the two concepts of 'sexual difference' and 'gender' can be understood as two equally significant dimensions of feminism's relationship to demographic change. The first relates to the psychosocial construction of heterosexual procreative sexuality and gender to its other side – non-procreative sexuality. Another social trend should be held in tension with the triptych of gender, non-procreative sexuality and population decline: this is the prevalence and increase of sibling support and childcare in the so-called developing world to which UNICEF has recently drawn anxious attention.

Feminism and fertility decline: a brief recent history

The long and uneven demographic transition will always interlink with changes in sexual and gender relations. What interests me here is the specific moments when a particularly acute transition from high to low fertility interacts both with sexual and gender relations and with active political feminism. I shall start by mentioning first-wave feminism in the late nineteenth century in order to give a point of historical reference for second-wave feminism in the latter part of the twentieth century. It is important to note that there is no simple equation between fertility decline and feminism – the one can occur without the other. This does not, however, mean that their

---

[2] Scott has recently argued against the use of 'gender', in her revised preface (2003) to Butler and Scott, *Feminists Theorize the Political*.

connection, when it occurs, is incidental or insignificant. The late nineteenth century in the western world saw the birth-rate plummet (Seccombe 1995). There were many different causes, but most, if not all, were related. Here I am concerned only with the interrelationship between declining fertility and the intensification of demands for equal rights of women made under the political banner of feminism.

The extreme paternalism of Victorian England shifted from a pride in the quantity of children to a demand for the quality of children. There was a sharp decline in fertility and the rise of feminism which, as well as its dominant struggle for the vote, stressed the urgency of effective birth-control. Christabel Pankhurst notoriously proclaimed: 'Votes for Women and Chastity for Men.' During the second industrial revolution from 1871 to 1911 there was an absolute fall of 36 per cent in marital fertility. Fertility continued to decline until 1931, with the number of fecund women marrying also declining (Szreter 1996). A century to a century and a quarter ago, the main demands were for equal rights in education, the professions and civic responsibilities and in relation to property and children, and most notoriously, the gaining of the vote – in England first in 1918 and then fully in 1928. The discussion around freeing women into safe and hence restricted sexuality and maternity was central to all issues.

Lateral relations and child-free femininity

When the fertility decline of the last decades of the nineteenth century is analysed, all the explanations for changing birth-rates are offered in terms of family practices. My contention is that there is another side to the coin of family demise that needs to be read in to the picture. In the hegemonic middle classes, not only are women having fewer children but the opening of education and the professions means that a significant number of women in the same hegemonic social class not only are having *no* children but are not imagining or intending to do so. We need to think about child-free women not as mothers manquée but as deploying another part of a feminine psyche – a femininity that comes from a different social practice which therefore in turn makes use of different aspects of the psychic structure which might otherwise only be latent.

Florence Nightingale deplored the absence of a social class of British nurses and admired the French situation in which, thanks to Roman Catholicism, there was already in place a religious population of celibate nursing sisters. We can see what Nightingale achieved as the creation of a lay sisterhood: the nursing sisters cared for the brotherhood of soldiers. Slightly less obviously there was the growing band of women teachers trained to train a new professional elite of girls and young women. On the surface, generations of schoolgirls chanted of their great teachers, the famous pioneers of girls education, 'Miss Buss and Miss Beale Cupid's darts do not feel they are not like us, Miss Beale and Miss Buss', thus equating their own sexuality with heterosexuality and marking their teachers as negative – missing out on love as they missed out on procreation. Yet, despite this chant, in fact the girls and their teachers formed two social groups relating to each other, not to men. Similarly it has been argued that there were no models for women's education unless it imitated male education, which the pioneers did not entirely want to do (Strathern 2000). The ideological framework was either the brotherhoods of male teachers and male students or women in relation to men. However, once again despite this framework, women professionals of all kinds formed a sisterhood, women relating to women. So too did the feminists who can be seen as the political dimension of this band of women bonding to each other and demanding to be let into (or respected by and as parallel to) the brotherhood – of soldiers, doctors, lawyers, university professors, male students.

Job segregation along gender lines is astoundingly prevalent. We must remember how not only this segregation in jobs but also celibacy ruled all the women's professions for more than half the twentieth century: women teachers and civil servants in England were not allowed to be married until the 1950s. There are women's friendships, single sisters or friends as 'Auntie' co-parenting with the overworked mother – wherever, whenever and however, women (like men) have always formed same-sex groups. This in some languages, which don't have the Anglo-Saxon 'gender', is called 'social sex'. Finding a sisterhood already present in religious orders, both nursing and educational, can help us shift the framework and consider that women entering paid work with industrialisation should not be seen as either a regiment of failed mothers or of surrogate men. Their job segregation, although the basis for exploitation, is not only a result of the work, but also a precondition of it.

If there were two dimensions both to the population decline during the second industrial revolution of the late nineteenth century and to its feminism, this was no less true, although somewhat differently, of the second dramatic phase of both in the latter decades of the twentieth century. What is the significance of the uneven development of the demographic transition to non-replacement birth-rates among the dominant social classes such as we are witnessing everywhere today, but particularly in the 'developed' world, and the similarly uneven development of feminism and the demand for gender equality? Today's demographic transition, the social position of women and feminist political movements are intimately connected – and their connection is important.

Non-procreative gender

Central to my argument about this connection within second-wave feminism is my contention that the rise of the concept of 'gender' (initially in Anglo-Saxon languages) is an unconscious reflection of a move towards non-reproductive sexual relations, particularly for the highest economic groups. 'Gender' has come to replace 'women', as in 'Gender Studies' versus 'Women's Studies', at exactly that point where the intimate association between women and procreation is tending to become obliterated. It is not, as is commonly argued, that 'gender' allows men in that is significant, it is that 'gender' throws babies out. It is not that 'fatherhood must be reclaimed' but that the welding of true womanhood and maternity and hence of manhood and paternity has become unstuck.

To think of 'women' is to think of 'women and children'; to think of 'gender' is to think of 'men and women' but it is also to think of 'women and women' or 'men and men'. I do not agree with the central contention of Judith Butler's study *Gender Trouble* (1992) or her debates with Nancy Fraser during the nineties that same-sex relations subvert the centrality and dominance of heterosexuality – they are always (and always have been) its alternative, latent or dominant in different contexts. Butler fails to link the growing, if ambivalent, acceptance (here more relevant than practice) of female and male homosexuality, and trans-genderism to the prevalence of non-procreative sexuality which is crucial to the demographic transition to non-replacement populations particularly in the western world and in the upper social echelons of the developing world.

Against Butler I would point out that all societies tolerate or institute some version of non-procreative gender relations alongside reproductive heterosexuality; we can think of nuns and monks, clients and prostitutes, eunuchs and castrati, brotherhoods and sisterhoods. However; what takes place unevenly with industrialisation is a growing centrality of non-procreative gender and the relative marginalisation of reproduction, either within a society or to other societies, or both. The issue is complicated and no aspect is unique, however, as a generalisation we may witness this shift of non-procreative gender from the edge to the centre in changing marriage patterns, declining fertility and reproductive *technology* (as opposed to reproductive *relationships*). A related issue is the feminisation of poverty exemplified by the lone mother: the lone mother is the woman whose motherhood is disallowed. Population decline would seem to be an effect not of political-economic systems (capitalism or socialism) which merely articulate them, nor indeed of feminism, but of processes of industrialisation.

The concept of 'gender'

'Gender' was introduced in the early 1970s to distinguish the acquisition of social attributes from biological ones for which the term 'sex' was reserved. 'Gender' addressed the social prescription of which gender can or cannot drive trains. Sex and reproduction were effectively fixed in biology; gender could be changed. This meant that the social practices following reproduction, such as being primary carers, fell under the flexibility of gender roles (see Chodorow 1978) – the processes of reproduction did not. 'Gender' gradually came to cover all relationships which had a sexual element even if marked by its repression as amongst nuns or soldiers: the other sex is present in its absence; or, more dominantly, same-sex relations. 'Gender' is now an inclusive term that ultimately has come to include even biology.

As a new concept, gender did not have a history or a psychology. The history of women was tied to the concept of sexual difference, it was the history of one side of the sexual difference equation and it was utterly bound up in the family; so much so that many texts of second-wave feminism, of which Shulamith Firestone's 1971 *Dialectics of Sex* was perhaps only the most far-reaching, proclaimed that women would only be free from oppression when freed from childbirth. Firestone's argument for test-tube babies illustrates the absence of procreative relationships within the rise of reproductive technologies. Thus the argument was made entirely within the terms of the ideology: women were mothers; women were oppressed; not to be oppressed meant to be not mothers or, at most, only part-time mothers. It was this thinking about the interrelationship between women's position and the family (even if the opposition to the equation led to feminism with its demand for women to be child-free or birth-free as in Firestone's account) which was then held to be responsible for a crisis of fatherhood and the decline of the family. An accusation which surely mis-reads the relationship.

There was indeed an explicit challenge to family values from both the sixties youth movement and women's liberation groups, but more important was the fact that the presence of the social movements rather than their political challenges signified an alternative non-intergenerational familial position. I would argue that it was the peer group of the one (the youth/students) and the sisterhood (a lateral same-generation relationship) of the other (women's liberation) that can be seen to indicate an alternative gender position. The women's liberation movement arose in part because women in the radical youth movements and the left-wing generally felt excluded from the brotherhoods of which they thought they had formed a part. They formed a sisterhood instead. Sisterhood, like brotherhood, is an organisation of non-reproductive relationship – gendered womanhood without children (whether or not there are actual children). In our introduction to *What is Feminism?* sociologist Ann Oakley and I wrote of the difficulties of sisterhood. Relationships have their pains and pleasures – the point is that these are not the same as reproductive relationships although the actors can be predominantly one or the other or both.

We can select two iconic moments to illustrate the dual aspects – declining reproduction and non-procreation – both of the fertility decline and of feminism. My Anglo-Saxon examples can easily be transposed onto others from elsewhere. For the first, at least on the surface level, there is the 1964 publication of *The Feminine Mystique* in the United States and soon worldwide; for the second, in Britain, the Ford women machinists' strike for equal pay in 1968.

Sexual difference and The Feminine Mystique

In 1964, Betty Friedan published *The Feminine Mystique*. *The Feminine Mystique* tackled not 'gender' but 'sexual difference' – it challenged the heterosexual relationship which had man as the breadwinner and woman as 'helpmeet', or in Parsonian terminology (which still has relevance) 'instrumental' men out in the world of work and 'expressive' women at home. Far from the two complementing each other as they were supposed to do, Friedan's research revealed women's distress and discontent with their so-called better part of the deal. Friedan's portrait of frustrated 1950s mothers and housewives in New England suburbia became instantly famous – it addressed the hegemonic familism of patriarchy exemplified by the Boston middle-class women Friedan interviewed. It challenged the world of sexual difference institutionalised in rigid segregation of roles – male breadwinner/female housewife with appropriate psychosocial distinctions. Friedan's book was emblematic of the revolt against the oppression of women in their sexual difference. At least on the surface, *The Feminine Mystique* attacked the side of the equation in fertility decline that relegated women to motherhood, and by implication proposed their liberation from its exclusive hold. In fact we might wonder how far it spearheaded the underlying socio-economic shift towards 'Women's Two Roles', where women have two jobs, being both instrumental in the labour force and expressive at home, or have one role but then employ other women to be women in their homes. Recent decades have seen an unprecedented growth in the servant class.

Sexual difference applies to a psychosocial difference which uses the biological fact that two sexes are (still) needed to reproduce. (Reproductive technology avoids the psychosocial but not the biological difference – at least until we have cloning.) In her *Dialectics of Sex* (1971), because she argued that the oppression of women would only end with the obliteration of sexed reproduction, American radical feminist Shulamith Firestone foresaw current reproductive technologies – test-tube babies independent of male progenitors and female procreators. Her account too, although it 'negatived' the psychosocial dimension of reproduction, was within the framework of 'sexual difference'. Indeed sexual difference in the service of reproduction was the only framework within which women were seen until the advent of 'gender'. The point was, women were not men. Why not? Because they were mothers. To look for the category 'women' in the 1960s was not to find them; as Sheila Rowbotham wrote (1977), women were 'hidden from history'. The varied and numerous writings that had 'found' the hidden women during first-wave feminism were out of print and unavailable, even unknown. What was there was not women but the families that defined them. In a vituperative attack on my own attempt to deconstruct the family in a 1966 article, "Women: The Longest Revolution", Quintin Hoare wrote: 'the whole *historical* development of women has been within the family ... women have lived and worked within *its* space and time ... any discussion of the position of women which does *not* start from the family as a mode of her relation with society becomes abstract." (1967: 79)[3] Studies of the family abounded. If women were not mothers or potential mothers, they were nothing. The family, housework and motherhood, all of which were areas outside the domain of politics, hid women. Women's other roles were invisible and remained untheorised. To be a woman could only be to be a mother and a daughter; whatever else a woman did, she did within the range of this framework.

There is, however, another text in *The Feminine Mystique* – one that was first picked up by Simone de Beauvoir. Simone de Beauvoir, the well-established author of *The Second Sex* (1947[1952]) and a political radical, but not at the time of Friedan's book a feminist, read *The Feminine Mystique* shortly after its appearance. De Beauvoir published in *Les Temps Modernes* Friedan's chapter on magazine images of women during World War II: teams of women were working, driving the ambulances, producing munitions and so forth – no motherhood, not even the lone motherhood of wartime, was in sight in the iconography that recorded and encouraged them.

We know that in England, following World War II, many women were happy to leave employment and enter the feminine mystique of the 1950s. This does not, however, mean that our analysis should

---

[3] For a brilliant analysis of this vituperation, see Jardine and Swindells (1989).

follow suit – understanding women only as wives and mothers. The other side of women, the side of sisterhood, of non-procreative sexuality, had been evident in the war. As with the critique of the mystique of motherhood, it too contributed its psychology to the fertility decline. World War II offers a crucible for understanding this second dimension.

Women, war and work: World War II and the 1968 Ford women machinists' strike

In fact, contrary to expectation and also contrary to the general assumptions of hindsight, fertility did not decline in the war (Kiernan et al. 1979). It had declined in the preceding years of the Depression. One suggested explanation for wartime fertility compared with the pre-war period is that the late age of pre-war marriage made people realise that it was now or never if they were to have children. Pro-natalist policies were also encouraged from the 1930s. But also, during the war, there was good social provision for children. The war provided both high employment for all and the welfare facilities of childcare so women could work. These latter may have been the main reasons for relatively high fertility during the war, as where these have persisted or been reintroduced, for example in France today, the birth-rate has been maintained (in France it is 2:2 as distinct from Italy's 1:2 (Kiernan et al. 1998)). What is important is that although, for whatever reason, wartime women were reproducing, to be a woman was other than a maternal definition. In neither World War was 'Rosie the riveter' a surrogate man, a lesbian or a mother manquée: she was a woman at work – with other women. Women have always worked; women have always formed sisterhoods or had the potential for such relationships, be it in the harem or in feminist struggles. Although different (they do not have rules and regulations), they parallel brotherhoods, and are to some degree independent of the patriarchate or an autonomous feature within it.[4]

It is commonplace to argue that the worldwide phenomenon of unequal pay despite egalitarian legislation in 'advanced' countries can

---

[4] On this point, I disagree with Carole Pateman's interesting analysis (Pateman 1990). See Mitchell (2003).

be explained at least in part by gender job segregation: women are doing different and hence lower-status, lower-paid jobs. What the analysis fails to point out is that the factor of women as a group pre-exists this distribution: girls and boys are differentiated as children in relation to each other and they organise themselves along gender lines irrespective of their future role as differentiated parents. Women may like working with women, men with men – their same-sex friendships were set down in childhood. Rather than the job categorising the worker, the worker is predisposed to same-gendered work not through the supposed quality of sex (caring, delicate fingers, low ambition, etc.) but through same-gendered relationships. Women's work is not suited to women qua some psychological sex difference emanating from actual or potential motherhood, but because of the pre-existent social relation of women along gender-different lines, through the lateral relations of girls to girls and boys to boys. It is then downgraded simply because the workers are women (for which read 'mothers', not to be counted in the workforce).

The Ford women's strike for equal pay, which was one of the initiators of second-wave feminism in England, is emblematic. Women machinists were doing essentially the same job as men machinists – but the argument was made that the job was somewhat different in accordance with gender skills. As I write, women who maintain the Cambridge college to which I belong are paid less than men who do so, on the grounds that women work indoors and men work outdoors because of their gender propensities. Although outdoors/indoors, front-seats/back-seats of cars are attached as gender attributes, these I believe only play on the social gender distinction already in place: women would not machine front-seats or work outdoors because they are socially constructed to form a group with other women – often still called 'other girls', indicating not just class denigration but the gender provenance in a childhood of girls and boys. That much is recognised; what is not taken into account is that this social group is not constructed along the line of women as mothers.

Sisterhood is always present

My argument is that these lateral gender groups, as distinct from the sexual difference derogated from maternity and paternity, are, like the latter, set up in earliest childhood, through differentiation of siblings, peers, school-children. They are already present to assist job segregation, or the segregation of mental illness, of criminality or the formation of feminist movements. This can be seen if we look at the actors who initiated second-wave feminism. Feminism highlights a propensity to emphasise lateral gender difference over vertical sexual difference. Being girls together rather than mothers of the nation might also be traceable to the Second World War. The 1960s saw the introduction of an effective means of birth-control. The population decline which followed (not necessarily causally linked) is only one side of the equation – the other is the exceptional suitability of the young people concerned to form non-reproductive groups along gender differentiated lines. It was not only that Friedan's 1950s mothers had been war-workers, it was also that their children were socially cared for in peer groups. 'British Restaurants' where even young children could eat on their own without their parents, day care and crèches, the evacuations of cohorts of school-children, all provide an extraordinary resource for contemplating peer group interaction, children who identified with each other as well as with their absent parents. The evacuation programmes referred to the evacuees as children not of their parents, but of the nation – 'our children' fed with free national orange-juice, milk, radium malt and cod-liver oil.[5]

The Second World War demonstrates very vividly the tension between a need to produce parents and the creation of strong lateral gender cohorts. Women have a social and psychological history other than the potential motherhood that it is claimed defines them. With the demographic transition, this other history is coming to the forefront; it needs feminism to take control of it. There is an urgent need not only to hand on but to develop further a critical (and self-critical) politics of feminisms. Virginia Woolf rightly contended that we need to look back through our mothers – we do. We need also to look forward through our daughters. But both backwards and forwards and in the present, we need also to look sideways through sisters, peers and friends.

---

[5] For a description of the importance of this for the subsequent generation of feminists see Steedman (1987).

Looking again at sisterhood

Psychoanalysis and feminism

Post-modernism initially attacked the preoccupation with origins in the grand narratives of modernism. From the viewpoint of feminism and psychoanalysis, it was exactly such a modernist question of origins – how sexual difference originates – that had led to their conjuncture: could psychoanalysis help with feminist questions about the installation of sexual difference as a *sine qua non* of the human psyche? I would argue that it was the subsequent querying of the validity of this question that made an early contribution to the rise of the post-modern. The modernist question of the origins of difference put heterosexual division at the centre of both life and enquiry. Yet feminism had arisen in its second wave in the 1960s to challenge that centrality. The sixties 'sexual revolution' displaced reproduction (or took place precisely because reproduction was sidelined) and in doing so opened the way to a radical challenge to heterosexism. The subsequent history with gay politics and queer theory as its most visible manifestation is familiar terrain. The argument against origins still bears these marks – it inhabits the either/ or space which post-modernism came into being to challenge.

Post-modernism also challenged modernism's universalistic claims by pointing to the difference which was occluded within concepts of sameness. Second-wave feminism straddled modernism and post-modernism, opening with questions to the one that led to an initiation of the other. My argument here is that the first contains the second latent within it; that we can turn the insights of post-modernism onto itself: it too was itself a difference and deferral of meaning waiting to be seen. From the viewpoint of classical psychoanalytical ideology, the Oedipal story of heterosexual identification was challenged by the pre-Oedipal possibilities of polymorphous sexuality; heterosexuality had repressed these various sexualities which had been latent within the oppressive constraints of the normative.

Reproduction and sexuality: social Darwinism again

When the inevitable backlash to sexual freedom and to political feminism arose, unsurprisingly it came with a virulent return to a version of social Darwinism: today's evolutionary psychology asserts the essential difference between the sexes based on their diverse roles of female investment in offspring and the male's sexual selection of the best female/s to house his genes, and all the different character traits that are said to follow. Reproduction for women and sexuality for men: indeed an 'essential difference' – and one that is made to account not only for all the diverse mating patterns but also for the psychosocial characteristics of humankind in its complex history. The concept of 'essential difference' is both universalistic and welded to origins; it is a parody of modernism. In the beginning ... Abortion becomes once again a focal point of struggle; 'right-to-life' arguments offer a painful mockery of the inevitability of infant mortality for most of the world's population.

The division of reproduction for women and sexuality for men haunts all contemporary western discourse, making evolutionary psychology an intellectual *huis clos* – finding in its object of study exactly the same terms it uses to analyse it. As the hegemonic attributions of male/female difference, both sexuality and reproduction have also been the objects of feminist inquiry and protest. The demographic transition to non-replacement populations invites a radical questioning of this duality. In itself it also offers another salience: the economically rich or becoming rapidly rich countries or the economically successful within poorer societies are opting for one-child or child-free status per two adults; the condemned of the earth continue to have children, which means the wealthy can replace their children from elsewhere. However, the fertility decline is debated largely in terms not of economics but of sexual difference.

Psychoanalysis: reproduction and sexuality

Classical psychoanalysis tries to account for the internalisation of sexual difference, not confronting but posing as a question how women come to be the reproducers and men the sexual beings. Its answers are radical in that it does not see that females are necessarily the occupants of the woman side, or males of the man side of the equation – both have 'male' sexuality and both can, in the psychic reality of fantasy, give birth. However, against the grain of received common-sense wisdoms as it undoubtedly is, psychoanalysis still retains the framework it is seeking to understand: a vertical framework of descent, a modernist grand narrative of the child as father to the man. I suggest that there is a different trajectory than that of the Oedipal child and pre-Oedipal infant – that another route is also taken by the helpless neonate, not only its dependence and subsequent conflict with parents, but its interaction with lateral groups, with siblings and peers. In such a trajectory, polymorphous sexuality is not banished and rendered forever infantile (the pre-Oedipal) but developed equally (and indifferently) into same-sex or different-sex (heterosex) possibilities. I suggest that there is both Oedipal reproductive sexuality (and its repression of perversity) and lateral non-reproductive sexuality with its own prohibitions and permissions which produces non-sexual sisterhood and brotherhood, or sexual but non-reproductive partnership, same gender or not the same gender; the chastity or the ecstasy of the group.

Vertical paradigms

The paradigms of meta-narratives, Darwin, Marx, Freud, were stories of descent: the *origin* of species necessitated the *descent* of man; history read forwards for Marx, backwards for Freud, was a vertical line: feudalism to capitalism to socialism to communism, adulthood to childhood to infancy – father to child, mother to infant. Within this vertical paradigm, the horizontal was suppressed. Sisters and brothers epitomise difference within sameness: categorically the same kin, same generation; categorically different genders and different ages (even twins are older/younger; Indonesian has only words which indicate older/younger sibling). Within kin, sister–brother differentiates gender no less than father–mother but we've paid scant attention:[6] we consider it is a derivative and thus that it is modelled on the child–parent relationship. Thus Freud claims that the vertical Oedipus complex in which the infant desires the mother extends to a 'family complex' when siblings come on the scene, and that the boy's incestuous wishes are for his mother and/or his sister, as though this relationship and this love-object were at most variations of the same, or the lateral were merely a repetition of the vertical. Yet if for the moment we stay with the Oedipus legend, it may be instructive that

---

[6] Melanie Mauthner's *Sistering* (2002) is one rare account. She offers a sociological description of sister relationships, claiming: 'Sistering influences the way gender identity is formed as we grow up' (1).

this is far from being the case. In Sophocles' play, only once does Oedipus refer to his being the brother as well as the father of his four children.[7] (Jocasta is, of course, not both mother and sister, she is mother and grandmother – to be mother and sister she would have had to marry her father). The play *Antigone*, chronologically later but written first, focuses on lateral relations, showing how different these are from vertical ones. The brothers Polyneices and Eteocles fight to the death (of both); the sisters, Antigone and Ismene, close friends, differ as to the necessity of giving all due funeral rites to their abused brother. Though betrothed and aware of forfeiting the joys of motherhood, in this play Antigone dies a *sister*, insisting that it is a sister's responsibility to recognise the equal claims of all brothers – in *Oedipus at Colonnus* she is primarily a daughter. Although aspects of the same person, daughter and sister are not only different roles, they are different places – one occupies a vertical, the other a horizontal position.

Horizontal possibilities

Work on horizontality is more honoured in the breach than in the observance. Since the 1980s there has been some attention from developmental psychologists[8] but more typical are the frustrated hopes of anthropologists such as Weissner and Gallimore who in 1977 opened their introduction to their article 'My Brother's Keeper: Sibling and Child Child-care Taking' thus:

The Handbook of Socialisation Theory and Research ... includes virtually no reference to caretaking of children by anyone other than parents. What cross-cultural evidence we can find indicates that non-parental caretaking is either the norm or a significant form of caretaking in most societies. Yet socialisation research rarely takes it into account. (169)

They conclude their article:

There are few topics in socialisation that can match child caretaking for number of hypotheses and problems to be explored. We hope the next

---

[7] See my 'Did Oedipus Have a Sister?', in Mitchell (2003).
[8] In the UK this is largely associated with Judy Dunn and her colleagues.

review of this area will have less occasion to report that data are sparse or nonexistent. (180)

Unfortunately there has been no subsequent review.

There are (at least) two possible strands for research into horizontal sibling relations: the sibling–sibling as in developmental psychology, 'theory of mind' and some sociology (e.g. Mauthner 2002), and investigation into structural caretaking roles. Because of the almost absolute domination of the vertical model, the western assumption of mother–infant care has left what little work there is to anthropologists aware of other cultural models. If we are to have a richer under-standing of the significance of the horizontal axis, the two approaches will need to come together. What follow are some speculative thoughts in response to this need. Why and how are feminists sisters? What does it imply?

Siblings: a rite de passage

I suggest that the birth, or expected birth, of the next sibling constitutes for the small child what is in our culture a largely unrecognised *rite de passage*. For the older child who was previously 'the baby', it constitutes a trauma of non-existence and thus, as in all such *rites*, this trauma is its centre point. One loses who one was in order to become someone new. Among the Tallensii of West Africa a child is not regarded as a social being until it has siblings. I suggest it is the new baby (actual or expected) who turns the previous baby at around the age of two to three into a girl or a boy – a social being, unlike the pre- or asocial infant. The point of transition is marked by traumatic absence of the older child's immature ego. We can imagine the toddler narcissistically looking forward, excited by the imminent arrival of the baby which will, so-to-speak, be more of itself. When it arrives, it claims all the title – it is the baby whom the toddler was yesterday. Yesterday's baby is baby no longer – she must become girl or boy, sister or brother.

Such a transition is sometimes claimed by parents and professional experts alike to be non-traumatic, or not even difficult in some instances: we are reassured that the older child has always loved and only loved the new one. Yet however happily and easily the child adapts, I believe that the newcomer's arrival technically constitutes the trauma which is at the centre of all *rites de passage*, whether these are marked and respected, or whether they are ignored as mostly happens in the western world. An older post-Oedipal child encountering an actual sibling for the first time is, of course, already a speaking, social being; we speak of such a child as an 'only child', until this point (no child under three is considered an 'only child', whatever the parents' or society's intention). An 'only child' is one who has had to use the fantasy of the sibling, and the reasons for its absence, for its socialisation. Whether or not this will change after decades of one-child family policies as in urban China, so far in human history, in reality or fantasy, there is always a sibling, a replication of oneself who has to become other than oneself. For the 'lonely only', the *fils unique*, or for the youngest child, no-sibling signifies the sibling's importance. One important meaning of becoming a social being is the recognition that there are others like oneself – a sibling is a primary and exemplary instance of this hard-to-swallow but so relieving ordinariness. At whatever age a sibling may arrive, there will be some repetition of the earlier experience. Yvonne Kapp was the second and last child when, at age ten, she thought her mother was pregnant:

All this time, some unborn brother or sister of mine had been lying under my mother's heart, and she never told me. I felt betrayed, and at the same time, a feeling I had never before experienced, an emotion so powerful and so violent swept over me that I thought it must destroy me. There was a strange tightening in my belly and a dreadful weight of terror and hatred of I knew not what. This anguish now fastened upon me like some gnawing animal from which ... like pain, there was no escape. What I went through then concentrated into little more than a few days was a lifetime savage and unforgettable jealousy of a younger sibling. That torment remains, in essence, indescribable, but it poisoned every waking moment. I did not know, of course, that it was jealousy, but I did know that in some horrible way my feelings were shameful and this attitude caused an overwhelming sense of guilt to my broken spirit. (Kapp 2001: 38–9)

The sibling (actual or always a possibility) is an essential but traumatic realisation. A psychological trauma is quantitatively a blow so strong that it breaks through the protective barriers of the psyche, releasing thereby an unbounded energy within the organism. Following a trauma, an effort is made by the all-but-destroyed ego, to bind the energy and convert the newly bound energy into a type of anxiety which will signal when danger threatens another time. For the development of this warning anxiety, there must be some ego: this will be the new ego of the child – "I'm a big girl/boy now; she/he is just a baby." What will be warned against is someone taking one's place. One can thus ask if both later tolerance of others who are both alike and different from the subject and intolerance of those who seem too close are not informed by this primary lateral experience?

In a novel that traces the borderland between a portrait of schizophrenia (1960s anti-psychiatry style) and political motivation to heal the divided self, heroine Jane Wild probably murders those who occupy her psychic territory; the novel by Emma Tennant is called *The Bad Sister*. May not all jealousy, murderous or within bounds, be informed by the first inevitable replacement of the subject by a sibling or sibling substitute? May not tolerance of others be informed by an ability to look after the one who no longer threatens one's own existence because she or he needs one's care? We think of mothers as all-important caretakers, forgetting that they were sisters first.

Child childcare

In 1971 Barry and Paxson examined the ethnographic material available for 186 societies. They found that 46.2 per cent of infants were cared for by their mothers, but almost 40 per cent were cared for fully or for more than half the time by other carers (Weissner and Gallimore 1977). After infancy, fewer than 20 per cent of children were cared for primarily by their mothers. In another study, reported by Weissner and Gallimore (1977), only in the case of New England was a mother more often present than a sibling during the researchers' observations. Girls are twice as often caretakers as boys, but no stigma is attached to boy child-caretaking in cultures where such child-caretaking is the norm. Western ethnographies often see other cultures behaving in a rejecting manner towards the toddler when a new baby is born. However, once we take on board the importance of child-caretaking, another explanation becomes possible: mothers regard some behaviour as intrusive if done by an adult and thus more appropriately left to siblings, especially as the baby gets older. The toddlers are being pushed out of babyhood into caretaking childhood by helping to socialise the new baby. Looking laterally, socialisation is, among other concerns, in itself about caretaking – by both genders.

If an older child does caretake, what sort of relationship between older and younger child might be implied? Various ethnographies suggest that the child may imitate the mother or both parents, or develop a different mode altogether. There is general agreement that the older child is taught the relevant aspects of childcare, is expected to perform well and is reprimanded or punished if she/he fails to do so. It is also agreed that child-caretakers take their role seriously and are proud of doing well. So the older child, often as young as three or four years, has moved into a new position. Could it not be that the narcissistic love with which she awaits the new baby's birth after the shock of otherness and the realization that this is not-me, through parental approval but *also* through lateral success, turns into self-esteem? The narcissist approves himself; for self-esteem we need to have internalised the affirmation of others. The helpless baby is proud to have become the helpful child; she has traversed her *rite de passage* successfully. She has won not only her parents', but her own and her younger sibling's respect.

Mirroring from mother to child, or self-reflection, has been noted and theorised. Jacques Lacan most fully formulated and named this 'mirror-stage'. In his thesis, the uncoordinated body of the baby finds a whole, coherent gestalt image in the mirror. This is the origin of the ego – in a split between an 'I' who looks and the 'me' who is seen, inverted as a mirroring must, and referred to from elsewhere (the mother): 'that's Jane'/'that's Johnny'. This is the origin of the ego which is thus always and necessarily constructed in alienation. Personalising Lacan's structural account, Winnicott saw the mother as reflecting the baby's true self to itself, or failing to do so, in which case the unrecognised infant is forced into compliance and false-self modes of behaviour. In both of these very different observations of the formation of the ego (Lacan) or self (Winnicott), the explanation rests as always on the vertical paradigm.

However, any observer can notice that any baby is far more interested in an older child than it is in either of its parents. It may be more attached to the mother, although this has not been tested for control with sibling caretakers. A young evacuee in London in World

War II caused no surprise when he refused to leave, clinging to a post-box and yelling for his older sister. So what of child mirroring? Uncoordinated movements of the baby would find a satisfactory containing echo in the controlled liveliness of the movements and expressions of the older child. This is a gestalt that is neither alienated, true nor false – it is relational. A baby of a few months will respond differently to different older children according to how they behave, and the older child when still very young will try to understand the mind of the baby. It is a mixture of projection, identification and observation. It is a two-way mirror: older child is adored, relied on, feared; baby is adored, admonished, found an irritant, provided with 'itself' as the child sees it and simultaneously offered a place of identification. The joys and awful scars of this mirroring perception can last a lifetime: an old man may still blench at the big ears an older brother ascribed to him in infancy.

The structural role of lateral relations would thus seem to involve establishing some degree of verticality, of dominance due to age and position. But this age and position are not generational. They are thus predominantly socially prescribed; they are more to do with human socialisation processes than with biological destinies. The biological referent of oldest and strongest often does not survive beyond infancy, when a six year old may start to compete successfully with an eight year old, nor does a gender hierarchy of 'might is right' pertain in infancy nor oftentimes even before puberty. Custom makes more girls than boys into caretakers but boys are equally accepted and equally competent.

The most significant feature of this lateral scenario is the transition from asocial or pre-social infancy to social childhood. Although this is achieved in interaction with vertical prohibitions, it is also independent of these. Children go through this *rite de passage* themselves: growing older biologically is one thing; moving from human animal to social human being, becoming a walking-talking Dombey (Dickens) another. At least in part this transition is contained within the parameters of lateral relationships. This is a potent underpinning of law and order; its presence and its breakdown can be witnessed when the same human being becomes the 'other' race or sex, or 'unfit', and is denigrated once more as the infantile, the not yet human.

Lateral equalities

Lateral, horizontal relations, however, also have egalitarian possibilities in a way that vertical relationships do not. Liberty, equality and fraternity point to a different concept of social organisation from that of totalitarian or dynastic regimes which are predicated on structural inequalities based on intergenerational hierarchy – the father of his people. There may be a Mother Superior, but the sisterhood is equal – sisters may shift and change power positions but there is no inherent hierarchy. It is this potentiality for equality that inspires the sisterhood of feminism, as it inspires feminism's aim: equality of sisters with brothers.

Carol Pateman and others have argued that the various modes of male domination, which in particular shifted from ruling fathers to ruling brothers in the English seventeenth century, are all versions of patriarchy. Despite the excellent analysis of the different forms, this conflation is, I believe, importantly inaccurate.

All societies have models both of vertical parenting and of horizontal siblinghood (both of which always extend beyond the biological), but the two are not the same and one should not be assimilated to the other. For example, the patriarchalism of early modern England (invoked by Pateman) when it was transformed into a fraternal contract society had emphasised the responsibility of brothers for sisters; however, according to Ruth Perry (2004), this responsibility gradually withered away in the eighteenth century to make room for the growing all-importance of the conjugal couple. The contribution of the notion of 'sister' to that of 'wife' in modern society has not, I believe, been considered. Here surely is a source of the idea that partners in a bourgeois marriage are lateral and equal? If this is the case, histories of shifts in family forms which accompany the rise of capitalism (a veritable academic industry) need to factor in changing sibling relations: the sister becomes less important for the brother because she becomes the wife of the husband – a change in affinal relations along the horizontal line.

Although many societies have had advocates for greater rights and powers, for lesser oppression of women, feminism as a political movement which puts politics in command of socio-economic change will arise in democracies which are predicated on the equality of man (why not woman?). Such a vision comes from the potential equality of siblings and sibling gender differences as these are variously constructed.

The demographic transition of declining reproduction to non-replacement populations, itself an effect of the move from kin to class society and an economy of surplus profit in which capital not people increases, obviously throws up a shift from the importance of giving birth to the importance of caring for offspring. There has always been child-caretaking but this becomes considerably less as children are taken out of the economy and into education. But the potential of gender equality of lateral relations means that, just as uncared-for sisters become cared-for wives, so fathers care for children when mothers are not available – just as when they were brothers, they cared for their younger siblings. Caring not procreation is the hegemonic task of 'advanced' economies or ones moving in that direction, from China to the corporate capitalists of India and West Africa via Europe and America.

Yet social Darwinism, and its contemporary vogue as evolutionary psychology, sees caring as only derivative of reproduction. It has to be blind therefore to the fact that throughout human history sibling care is predicated on the fact that children cannot reproduce: you cannot be a mummy or daddy, but you can look after the baby. Even in the great scale of things, sideways relationships, no less but certainly differently from descent, must have contributed to the survival of the fittest.

In the course of human history, descent and reproduction have become relatively less important; survival of the present is salient: equality, wars, caring, persecution are modalities also formed along a horizontal axis. A mother of small twins was pleasantly touched when she saw her eighteenth-month son bring his distressed sister a toy for comfort. She had not witnessed this apparently frequent behaviour before. It seemed to be the case that neither child needed to care for the other if the mother was present but that in her absence at playschool there was the expression of genuine concern along child–child lines; likewise the twins could bite, scratch and snatch each other's possessions. There is evidence that children, even if left to their own devices, can work out a form of governance as they socialise themselves; this can also turn to warfare.

'Theory of mind' analysts are now recognising the importance of child–child interaction for the development of cognition and reflexivity; other disciplines need to follow suit. The area is crucial for gender studies. A backlash of mother-caring Jane versus hunter father Tarzan calls on only half the story. Second-wave feminism added to first-wave the slogan 'Anything a woman can do, a man can do too', with particular reference to childcare. This plea for justice was surely rather an expression of historical development: boys, like girls, do not give birth, but they can and do caretake. Feminism is the practice of sisterhood and its claim to equality within siblinghood. It is not organised around procreation; this the backlash seizes upon.

Sexual difference around reproduction is the only important specialism within *Homo sapiens*; simpler organisms have more. Difference and divergence indicate adaptation. Reproductive technologies are changing the modes of procreation but not, anyway as yet, eradicating sexual difference in this sphere. Surely all one can say, however, is that the evolutionary advantage of sexual difference adheres to procreation. Human history suggests that caretaking is not dependent on procreation, nor therefore on sexual difference. How long it takes for history to become evolution is anyone's guess. But does it matter? Within evolution, difference is an interactive dependency; it is only within history that oppression or suppression has meaning. Although of course there are biological or neurological underpinnings of both caretaking and its obverse, aggression, these come into play with human socialisation. As such they do not have origins, but come and go in relationship to others. Child-caretaking is simply an example of the presence of this social behaviour.

UNICEF is currently drawing attention to the increasing prevalence of child-caretaking among the sick and wretched of the earth. It is deleterious for women as it curtails or prevents education which could in its turn lead not only to economic growth but to the greater independence and higher status of women. In fact in certain historical periods child-caretaking featured within the school system, with older children in huge classes taking care of and teaching smaller groups or individuals, either younger or less able in particular fields. Might the chronic state of indiscipline in education in the 'advanced' world reflect the absence of this lateral responsibility?

The point is not to recommend or dis-recommend child-caretaking. What matters is that we see that caretaking itself, like its absence and its opposites, is part of a social process which takes place along a horizontal axis and, of importance in the context of my argument here, is only secondarily gendered. It is gendered because it has been assimilated to the vertical process of parenting, which in its turn has been monolithically welded to procreation, to the exclusion or relegation of the many forms of non-reproductive child-caretaking which have always existed. In procreation sexual division pertains, and difference is a modality on which inequity comfortably rests.

The post-modern attack on modernism's concern with universality and with the origins of social forms can also be seen as an aspect of the coming out from under the dominance of the vertical model, of the horizontal in all its various forms of lateral relations, of a social with nothing but its origin in its own coming into being, whenever and wherever. Part, too, of the historical move that reflects the demographic transition in which caring takes precedence over procreation. The wonders (or pains) of conceiving and giving birth are themselves informed by the joy of the socially caring boy and girl. Feminism – caring, a new meaning to equality, sisterhood – could be a future for both women and men.

References

Banks, J. A. and Banks, O. (1964) *Feminism and Family Planning in Victorian England* (Liverpool: Liverpool University Press).

Barry, H., III and Paxson, L. M. (1971) 'Infancy and early child-hood: cross-cultural codes', *Ethnology* 10: 466–508.

Butler, J. and Scott, J. (1992/2003) *Feminists Theorize the Political* (London: Routledge).

Chodorow, N. (1978) *The Reproduction of Mothering* (Berkeley: University of California Press).

de Beauvoir, S. (1947) *Le Deuxième Sexe* (Paris: Gallimard); (1952) *The Second Sex* (New York: Knopf).

Dunn, Judy (1985) *Sisters and Brothers* (London: Fontana Paperbacks).

Firestone, S. (1971) *The Dialectics of Sex: The Case for Feminist Revolution* (London: Jonathan Cape).

Friedan, B. (1964) *The Feminine Mystique* (Harmondsworth: Penguin Books).

Hoare, B. (1967) 'On Juliet Mitchell's "Women: The Longest Revolution"', *New Left Review* 41: 78–81.

Jardine, L. and Swindells, J. (1989) *What's Left?* (London: Routledge).

Kapp, Yvonne (2001) *Time Will Tell* (London: Verso).

Kiernan, K., Lewis, J. and Land, H. (1998) *Lone Motherhood in Twentieth-Century Britain: From Footnote to Front Page* (Oxford and New York: Oxford University Press).

Lacan, J. (1949) 'Le stade du miroir comme formateur de la fonction de jeu', in *Ecrits* (Paris: Editions du Seuil), 93–101.

Mauthner, Melanie (2002) *Sistering* (London: Palgrave Macmillan).

Mitchell, J. (2003) *Siblings: Sex and Violence* (Cambridge: Polity Press).

Mitchell, J. and Oakley, A. (1986) *What is Feminism?* (Oxford: Blackwells).

Pateman, Carol (1989) *The Social Contract* (Stamford: Stamford University Press).

(1990) *The Disorder of Women: Democracy, Feminism and Political Theory* (Cambridge: Polity Press).

Perry, Ruth (2004) *Novel Relations* (Cambridge: Cambridge University Press).

Rowbotham, S. (1977) *Hidden from History: 300 Years of Women's Oppression and the Fight against It* (London: Pluto Press).

Scott, J. (1996) 'Gender as a Category of Analysis', in Scott (ed.), *Feminism and History* (Oxford: Oxford University Press), 152–82.

Seccombe, W. (1995) *Weathering the Storm: Working-Class Families from the Industrial Revolution to the Fertility Decline* (London: Verso).

Sophocles (1978) *The Theban Plays* (Harmondsworth: Penguin Books).

Steedman, C. (1987) *Landscape of a Good Woman* (Piscataway, NJ: Rutgers University Press).

Strathern, M. (2000) Talk to 'Women's Education Study Day' conference, Gender Studies, University of Cambridge, 25 November 2000.

Szreter, S. (1996) *Fertility, Class and Gender in Britain, 1860–1940* (Cambridge: Cambridge University Press).

Weissner, T. S. and Gallimore, R. (1977) 'My Brother's Keeper: Child and Sibling Caretaking', *Current Anthropology* 18, 2: 169–73.

Winnicott, D. W. (1967) 'Mirror-role of Mother and Family in Child Development', in *Playing and Reality* (Harmondsworth: Penguin Books), 130–9.

9 The politics of female diversity in the twenty-first century

CATHERINE HAKIM

T
HERE IS STILL no consensus on what the goals of feminism should be. This is largely because women themselves differ in their life-goals, needs and aspirations. Until recently, there has been rather more consensus on the key indicators of women's position in society, and the pace of change – which is glacial. However there is again little agreement on explanations for the slow pace of change, and what should be done about it. This chapter presents a new theory for explaining the lack of any fundamental change after the equal opportunities revolution of the late twentieth century; preference theory also shows that some women are benefiting greatly from recent changes while others are not, and predicts a continuing polarisation of the female workforce. Perhaps most important, preference theory predicts that sex and gender are ceasing to be key dividing factors in the workforce and in society; instead, it is lifestyle preferences, personally chosen values and life-goals that segment society and determine patterns of work and employment over the lifecycle.

New feminist myths

The pay gap (the difference in average hourly earnings between men and women) has long been used as a simple but telling indicator of sex discrimination in the labour market and, by implication, other areas of life. It is published annually in Britain, and is scrutinised closely every year by gender specialists. Is it up? Or down? Until recently, this was appropriate.

Historically, women's pay in Britain was around half that of men. From the mid-nineteenth century, and long before that, men were paid twice as much as women, even for identical jobs (Middleton 1988: 36–9). Similarly in the USA, employers paid women less than half, sometimes only one third or one quarter, of what they paid men (Pinchbeck 1930: 193–4, quoted in Padavic and Reskin 2002: 122).

191

Some part of this was due to the fact that physical strength was valued when jobs were mostly manual and often involved hard labour. However, overt and explicit sex discrimination was the main factor, and was only eliminated after the introduction of legislation prohibiting sex discrimination in the 1960s (USA) and 1970s (Britain). These laws had an immediate and sharp effect in Britain. The pay gap fell from 36 per cent to 20 per cent by 1995, then remained fairly stable. The American Equal Pay Act had a more gradual impact, and the pay gap fell from 40 per cent to 28 per cent by 2000 (Hakim 2004a: 168–9). Other European countries have similar pay gaps, and a similar lack of recent change, despite the introduction of laws prohibiting sex discrimination in the labour market (Hakim 2004a: 172). In Sweden, the pay gap even increased in the 1990s, to 18 per cent (Thörnqvist 2006: 314).

The European Commission has made closing the pay gap and the elimination of the gender segregation of jobs the two key indicators of progress on equality for women in the labour market, and believes that encouraging more women into employment helps to achieve this (Lewis and Giullari 2005). The fact that the pay gap has remained relatively stable for almost a decade in Britain, and shows little change in most other countries, prompts calls for more aggressive social engineering, stronger legislation to combat covert or indirect sex discrimination, more family-friendly policies to help more women into jobs, more training for women in sex-atypical occupations, and so on. The theories, explanations and policies that served us well in the twentieth century are reiterated, with demands for stronger policies of the same sort, a tougher approach until the unenlightened give way to progress.

The alternative perspective is that social and economic changes have made these twentieth-century theories, explanations and policies out-of-date and redundant, even counter-productive, in the twenty-first century. In addition, recent research has shown that some of our theories were wrong in the first place. But once policies have been agreed and implemented, often after protracted negotiation, it becomes difficult to admit that the theories they rest on are faulty. Few specialists in gender studies have the necessary expertise in labour market analysis to appreciate the implications of recent studies for gender theory.

Cross-national comparative studies by the ILO, OECD and EC (Anker 1998; Melkas and Anker 1998; OECD 2002; European

Commission 2002: 18–45), and by academic scholars (see the reviews in McCall 2001; Hakim 2004a: 170–82; Charles and Grusky 2004), have been overturning some well-established assumptions that turn out to be myths rather than fact. First, we now know that there is no direct link between occupational segregation and the pay gap; the association is coincidental rather than causal, and the two processes are independently socially constructed. Second, there is no direct causal link between economic and social development and occupational segregation, or the pay gap; modern and egalitarian societies do not necessarily have lower scores on these two indicators of gender equality in the workforce. The country with the lowest level of occupational segregation in the world is China, not Sweden, as so many believe. Many countries in the Far East have lower levels of occupational segregation than in Western Europe. The lowest pay gap in the world is not found in Sweden, as so many claim, but in Swaziland, where women earn more than men on average, followed closely by Sri Lanka. Third, higher levels of female employment produce higher levels of occupational segregation and a larger pay gap; they do not serve to improve gender equality in the workforce, as previously claimed. Even within Western Europe, countries with the lowest female employment rates tend to have the smallest pay gaps, as illustrated by Portugal and Spain compared to Finland and Germany (Hakim 2004a: 172).

Even more disconcerting is the evidence that family friendly policies generally *reduce* gender equality in the workforce, rather than raising it, as everyone has assumed until now. This conclusion has now been drawn simultaneously by several scholars working independently (Charles and Grusky 2004: 5–6, 10–11, 37, 297, 302–4; Hakim 2004a: 183; Hunt 2002; Jacobs and Gerson 2004: 7, 177; Thörnqvist 2006). In particular, Sweden's generous family friendly policies have created a larger glass-ceiling problem than exists in the USA, where there is a general lack of such policies (Albrecht, Björklund and Vroman 2003). Women are more likely to achieve senior management jobs in the USA than in Sweden: 11 per cent versus 1.5 per cent respectively in the 1980s (Rosenfeld and Kalleberg 1990: 88–9; see also Wright, Baxter and Birkelund 1995). Another study found that women held 11 per cent of all executive positions in Sweden compared to 14 per cent in Norway, 16 per cent in France, 17 per cent in West Germany, 19 per cent in Britain and 24 per cent in the USA

(Asplund 1984, quoted in Henrekson and Dreber 2004). The pay gap increased to 18 per cent in Sweden by 2001, and Swedish men still earn more than women in 90 per cent of all occupations (Thörnqvist 2006: 314). The most recent studies show women holding one third of managerial and professional positions in all public companies in Sweden, compared to slightly over half (51 per cent) of managerial and professional positions in the Fortune 500 companies in the USA; women's shares of CEO and vice-president positions were around 4 per cent in Sweden and 8 per cent in the USA (Henrekson and Dreber 2004). There is no doubt that family friendly policies help women to combine paid jobs with family work. What they do not do is solve the problem of gender inequality in the workforce.

Any serious consideration of the reasons for the relatively stable pay gap in Europe and the USA (which do not include job segregation) must now address continuing sex differences in work orientations and personal preferences regarding family roles. The research evidence is already to hand (Babcock and Laschever 2003; Hakim 1995, 1996, 2000a, 2003a, 2004a; Henrekson and Dreber 2004) and is accepted by many scholars (Thornqvist 2006; Blyton et al. 2006).

Only preference theory is consistent with the latest research findings, as well as historical research. Preference theory provides a more evidence-based theoretical framework for understanding current trends, as well as future developments in the twenty-first century in modern societies.

Preference theory

Preference theory is a new approach to explaining and predicting women's choices between market work and family work, a theory that is historically informed, empirically based, multidisciplinary, prospective rather than retrospective in orientation, and applicable in all rich modern societies (Hakim 2000a). Lifestyle preferences are defined as causal factors which thus need to be monitored in modern societies. In contrast, other social attitudes (such as patriarchal values and sex-role ideology) are either unimportant as predictors of behaviour, or else have only a very small marginal impact in creating a particular climate of public opinion on women's roles (Hakim 2003b, 2004b). Preference theory has been operationalised, and tested in two contrasting societies – Britain and Spain – with most predictions being supported (Hakim 2003a), and is being applied in other surveys.

Preference theory specifies the historical context in which core values become important predictors of behaviour. It notes that five historical changes collectively produce a qualitatively new scenario for women in rich modern societies in the twenty-first century, giving them options that were not previously available (Table 9.1). Small elites of women born into wealthy families, or prosperous families with liberal ideas, sometimes had real choices in the past, just as their brothers did. Today, genuine choices are open to the vast majority of women, not only particular subgroups. The five social and economic changes started in the late twentieth century and are now producing a qualitatively different scenario of options and opportunities for women at the start of the twenty-first century. The five conditions that create a new scenario are:

- The contraceptive revolution which, from the 1960s onwards, gave sexually active women reliable and *independent* control over their own fertility for the first time in history.
- The equal opportunities revolution, which ensured that for the first time in history women obtained the right to enter all positions, occupations and careers in the labour market.
- The expansion of white-collar occupations, which are far more attractive to women than most blue-collar occupations.
- The creation of jobs for secondary earners, people who do not want to give priority to paid work at the expense of other life interests.
- The increasing importance of attitudes, values and personal preferences in the lifestyle choices of people in prosperous, liberal modern societies.

The five changes are historically specific developments in any society. They are not automatic, and do not necessarily occur in all modern societies. They may not occur together, at a single point in time in a country. The timing of the five changes varies greatly between countries. The effects of the five changes are cumulative. The two revolutions are essential and constitute the core of the social revolution for women. The five changes collectively are necessary to create a new scenario in which women have genuine choices and female heterogeneity is revealed to its full extent.

Table 9.1 The four central tenets of preference theory

---

1 Five separate historical changes in society and in the labour market which started in the late twentieth century are producing a qualitatively different and new scenario of options and opportunities for women. The five changes do not necessarily occur in all modern societies, and do not always occur together. Their effects are cumulative. The five causes of a new scenario are:

- the contraceptive revolution which, from about 1965 onwards, gave sexually active women reliable control over their own fertility for the first time in history;
- the equal opportunities revolution, which ensured that for the first time in history women had equal access to all positions, occupations and careers in the labour market. In some countries, legislation prohibiting sex discrimination went further, to give women equal access to housing, financial services, public services, and public posts;
- the expansion of white-collar occupations, which are far more attractive to women than most blue-collar occupations;
- the creation of jobs for secondary earners, people who do not want to give priority to paid work at the expense of other life interests; and
- the increasing importance of attitudes, values and personal preferences in the lifestyle choices of affluent modern societies.

2 Women are heterogeneous in their preferences and priorities on the conflict between family and employment. In the new scenario they are therefore heterogeneous also in their employment patterns and work histories. These preferences are set out, as ideal types, in Table 9.2. The size of the three groups varies in rich modern societies because public policies usually favour one or another group.

3 The heterogeneity of women's preferences and priorities creates conflicting interests between groups of women: sometimes between home-centred women and work-centred women, sometimes between the middle group of adaptive women and women who have one firm priority (whether for family work or employment). The conflicting interests of women have given a great advantage to men, whose interests are comparatively homogeneous; this is one cause of patriarchy and its disproportionate success.

4 Women's heterogeneity is the main cause of women's variable responses to social engineering policies in the new scenario of modern societies. This variability of response has been less evident in the past, but it has still impeded attempts to predict women's fertility and employment patterns. Policy research and future predictions of women's choices will be more successful in future if they adopt the preference theory perspective and first establish the distribution of preferences between family work and employment in each society.

Source: Hakim 2000a.

With rare exceptions (Cleland 1985; Murphy 1993), male demographers have generally overlooked the social and psychological significance *for women* of what Westoff and Ryder (1977) call the contraceptive revolution. Demographers discuss the use of contraception without distinguishing between the methods controlled by men and those controlled by women. Modern forms of contraception (the pill, the IUD and female sterilisation) are thus defined primarily by their greater reliability, overlooking the crucial fact that they transfer control over reproduction from men to women. Control over their fertility produces a change of perspective among women, even a psychological change, creating a sense of autonomy, responsibility and personal freedom that is not achieved with contraception controlled by men. The contraceptive revolution is thus an essential precondition for the equal opportunities revolution and other changes to have any substantial effect on women's lives.

The contraceptive revolution also opens the door to voluntary childlessness: women who give priority to their career, leisure interests or other activities rather than to child-bearing and childrearing as a central life activity. In many modern societies, up to 20 per cent of women are now remaining childless, far beyond the 2–3 per cent of women affected by primary infertility (Hakim 2000a: 50–6). For this group of women, conflicts between the demands of family work and careers are effectively eliminated. One consequence is that the pay gap between men and women has effectively been replaced by what is called the 'family gap': the difference in average earnings between women who do, or do not, have children (Harkness and Waldfogel 1999). This development alone alerts us to the fact that it is no longer gender or sex per se that predicts lifestyles and careers in affluent modern societies.

Feminists complain that the equal opportunities revolution of the second half of the twentieth century failed to deliver equality of outcomes (Phillips 2004; Crompton and Browne in this volume). This complaint overlooks the fact that legislation is only one of several tools for social engineering, a tool that changes the basic rules of the game, but not the game itself, nor the players (Hakim 2004a: 185–98). In some countries, fiscal policy, institutional change and moral exhortation have achieved as much, or more, than legislation alone. Abolition of the marriage bar is one of the most significant achievements of the equal opportunities revolution – one that is often overlooked because it is now taken for granted that married women, and mothers, can have jobs, just like anyone else. The second achievement was the sharp narrowing of the pay gap between men and women once sex discrimination in pay rates was made unlawful. The third is the opening up of the educational system, at all levels, to girls and women. Once women gained an incentive to obtain qualifications, because they were able to use them in the labour market, long term, even after marriage and motherhood, they flooded into higher education, and then on into professional and managerial occupations. The feminisation of the workforce, at professional and managerial levels as well as in routine white-collar and service work, has created a fundamental change in the occupational structure. Fully integrated occupations, with women and men working side by side, instead of in separate work teams, are a new development (Hakim 1998). At the same time, these new desegregated professions provide the most trenchant proof that equal opportunities and non-discrimination in the labour market do not necessarily produce equal outcomes, because men and women often use their opportunities differently, owing to differing life-goals and identities (Hakim 1998: 221–34; 2000a: 39; 2004a: 180–2). Babcock and Laschever (2003) summarise this as the problem of women who fail to ask – for promotion or a pay rise, or a better deal in any aspect of life. But the real problem is that women often ask for different things – such as convenient hours and family friendly schemes instead of higher pay.

The equal opportunities revolution and the contraceptive revolution are the two most important social and economic changes because they give women a genuine choice between family work and employment. The two changes in the labour market make paid jobs far more attractive to women. The final change factor is the one that is most easily overlooked, because attitudes and values have generally been regarded as outcomes rather than as causal factors by sociologists (but not by social psychologists). Longitudinal studies in the USA and Britain have now been run for long enough for the causal impact of values, life-goals and aspirations to emerge clearly, for both men and women (Pilling 1990; Szekelyi and Tardos 1993; Duncan and Dunifon 1998; Schoon and Parsons 2002). In fact, analyses of longitudinal databases have shown that the long-term effects of attitudes are stronger than the short-term effects. This could be the reason why so many studies in the past concluded that attitudes and values did not predict behaviour. In any event, there is now little doubt that people in affluent liberal democratic societies regard themselves as having lifestyle choices to make. There is no longer a single model of the good life, and increasing cultural diversity underlines the point.[1]

In Western Europe, North America and other modern societies, these five changes only took place from the 1960s onwards. The timing and pace of change has varied, even between countries in Europe. However, the strong social, cultural, economic and political links between modern countries suggest that no country will lag behind on any of the changes indefinitely. All five changes were completed early in the USA and Britain, so that the new scenario was well established by the last two decades of the twentieth century in these two countries. Thus they provide the main illustration of the consequences of the new scenario for women.

Three lifestyle preference groups

Reviews of recent research evidence (Hakim 2000a, 2004a) show that, once genuine choices are open to them, women choose among three different lifestyles: home-centred, work-centred or adaptive (Table 9.2). These divergent lifestyle preferences are found at all levels of education and income, in all social classes and religious and ethnic groups (Hakim 2000a, 2003a). They are qualitatively different from the forms of diversity that have so far been recognised in feminist theory, essentially class, race or ethnicity, and sexual orientation (West and Fenstermaker 1995).

Adaptive women prefer to combine employment and family work without giving a fixed priority to either. They want to enjoy the best of both worlds. Adaptive women are generally the largest group among women (40–70 per cent), and will be found in substantial numbers in most occupations. Certain occupations, such as school-teaching, are attractive to women because they facilitate a more even work–family balance. The great majority of women who transfer to

---

[1] For example, research in Britain and Australia shows that 20–25 per cent of adults have downshifted in some way in the last decade (Blyton et al. 2006: 10). While some insist that long hours of work are a financial necessity, others choose to replace higher incomes with more free time.

Table 9.2 Classification of women's work–lifestyle preferences in the twenty-first century

Home-centred 20 per cent of women varies 10–30 per cent	*Adaptive* 60 per cent of women varies 40–80 per cent	*Work-centred* 20 per cent of women varies 10–30 per cent
Family life and children are the main priorities throughout life.	This group is most diverse and includes women who want to combine work and family, plus drifters and unplanned careers.	Childless women are concentrated here. Main priority in life is employment or equivalent activities in the public arena: politics, sport, art, etc.
Prefer *not* to work.	Want to work, but *not* totally committed to work career.	Committed to work or equivalent activities.
Qualifications obtained as cultural capital.	Qualifications obtained with the intention of working.	Large investment in qualifications/ training for employment/other activities.

Number of children is affected by government social policy, family wealth, etc. Not responsive to employment policy.

This group is *very* responsive to government social policy, employment policy, equal opportunities policy/propaganda, economic cycle/recession/growth, etc. Including: income tax and social welfare benefits, educational policies, school timetables, childcare services, public attitude towards working women, legislation promoting female employment, trade union attitudes to working women, availability of part-time work and similar work flexibility, economic growth and prosperity, and institutional factors generally.

Responsive to economic opportunity, political opportunity, artistic opportunity, etc. Not responsive to social/family policy.

Family values: caring, sharing non-competitive communal, focus on cohesion.

Compromise between two conflicting sets of values.

Marketplace values: competitive rivalry, achievement orientation, individualism, excellence.

Source: Hakim 2000a.

part-time work after they have children are adaptive women, who seek to devote as much time and effort to their family work as to their paid jobs. In some countries (such as the USA and southern European countries), and in certain occupations, part-time jobs are still rare, so other types of job are chosen. For example seasonal jobs, temporary work or school-term-time jobs all offer a better work–family balance than the typical full-time job, especially if commuting is also involved. *Faute de mieux*, adaptive women take ordinary full-time jobs – as illustrated by the USA, where there is a large literature setting out women's dissatisfactions with their 'double shift' (Hochschild 1990; Presser 2003; Jacobs and Gerson 2004).

Work-centred women constitute a minority, despite the massive influx of women into higher education and into professional and managerial occupations in the last three decades. Work-centred people (men and women) are focused on competitive activities in the public sphere – in careers, sport, politics or the arts. Family life is fitted around their work, and many of these women remain childless, even when married. Qualifications and training are obtained as a career investment rather than as an insurance policy, as in the adaptive group. Between half and three-quarters of men are work-centred, compared to a minority of women (10–30 per cent), except in professional and managerial occupations where women may form half the total (Hakim 1998: 221–34; 2003a: 183–4; Corijn and Hakim forthcoming).

The third group, *home-centred or family-centred women*, is also a minority, and a relatively invisible one in the western world, given the current political and media focus on working women and high achievers. Home-centred women prefer to give priority to private life and family life after they marry. This group tends to have larger families, with fertility rates twice as high as among work-centred women (Hakim 2003c: 365). These women avoid paid work after marriage except in a financial crisis. They do not necessarily invest less in qualifications, because the educational system functions as a marriage market as well as a training institution (Hakim 2000a: 193–222). Despite the elimination of the sex differential in educational attainment, an increasing proportion of all wives in the USA and Europe are now marrying a man with substantially better qualifications, and the likelihood of marrying a graduate spouse is hugely increased if the woman herself has obtained a degree

(Hakim 2000a: 216). This may be why women remain less likely to choose vocational courses with a direct economic value, and are more likely to take courses in the arts, humanities or languages, which have lower earnings potential but provide cultural capital that is valuable in the marriage market.

The three preference groups are set out, as sociological ideal-types, in Table 9.2, with estimates of the relative sizes of the three groups in societies, such as Britain and the USA, where public policy does not bias the distribution. In this case, the distribution of women across the three groups corresponds to a 'normal' statistical distribution of responses to the family–work conflict. In practice, in most societies, public policy is biased towards one group or another, by accident or by design, so that the exact percentages vary between modern societies, typically with a bias towards careerist women or towards family-centred women.

Each of the three lifestyle preference groups has a substantively different value system, as well as differing life-goals. Home-centred women have what can loosely be called family values, with an emphasis on the caring, sharing and non-competitive values of private family life. Work-centred people have marketplace values, with an emphasis on competitive rivalry, achievement orientation, and individualism rather than collectivism. These differences can bring women into conflict with each other – for example on whether public childcare services are necessary or not, whether positive discrimination in favour of women for promotion to top jobs is a good thing or not. As a result, there is no single, representative group of women in modern society, but three contrasting, even conflicting groups with sharply differentiated work and lifestyle preferences. In the USA, the conflict between work-centred and home-centred women has been expressed through the two women's movements: the feminist 'women's liberation' movement and the maternalist movement, with conflict often focused on the issues of abortion and the proposed Equal Rights Amendment. These fundamental conflicts of interest within the female population help to explain why women have never become a dominant political power, and why male hegemony was easily established and maintained.

Preference theory was developed with a focus on women's choices, but it is also applicable to men. However there is far less research available on men's lifestyle preferences – which is itself an indication that men have fewer choices to make, because continuous full-time lifelong employment is imposed on them, whether or not they have families to support. Survey questions that allow us to identify women's lifestyle preferences always work less well for men. For example it is hard to ask a man whether he is home-centred without being facetious. Nonetheless, some of the surveys investigating women's preferences have covered men as well, with moderate success. The results in Table 9.3 show a large degree of consistency, across countries, in the distribution of women's lifestyle preferences. This consistency is all the more remarkable given variations between the surveys in the questions asked, the sample designs, and the age groups covered. It is impossible to obtain survey data on preferences in Sweden (because of political correctness constraints), so information on actual career patterns from age 16 to 43 is used instead.[2] This shows that even in the most propitious circumstances, a minority one third of women are work-centred.

There is less consistency in the results for men. A British survey found a small majority of men to be careerist. A similar survey in Spain found a small majority of men to be adaptive. Neither of these surveys was able to identify a home-centred group separately from adaptive men. A more recent survey in Belgium-Flanders, using slightly different questions, showed three quarters of men to be work-centred, with a tiny fraction (2 per cent) being family-centred. Surveys in the Czech Republic and Japan, and a Swedish study, all covered women only.

The evidence to date is of substantial differences between women in the three lifestyle preference groups, but few or no differences between adaptive and careerist men in terms of activities and outcomes, reflecting the greater social constraints on men's lives than on women's lives (Hakim 2005: 69–70). Men are at least twice as likely as women to be work-centred, although the precise size of the difference is uncertain and could be much larger. Even in Sweden, in the most favourable social conditions, only one third of women are careerist, and 10–20 per cent is more typical. In contrast the majority of men are careerist, possibly up to three quarters (Table 9.3).

---

[2] The family-centred group is underestimated for Sweden, as it is defined as women who have never worked at all, thus excluding those who work until marriage or the first child, who are included in the adaptive group instead.

Table 9.3 National distributions of lifestyle preferences among women and men

	Family-centred	Adaptive	Work-centred
Britain			
all women aged 16+	17	69	14
women in full-time work	14	62	24
women in part-time work	8	84	8
all men aged 16+	?	<48	52
men in full-time work	?	<50	50
men in part-time work	?	<66	34
Spain			
all women aged 18+	17	70	13
women in full-time work	4	63	33
women in part-time work	7	79	14
all men aged 18+	?	<60	40
men in full-time work	?	<56	44
Belgium-Flanders			
all women	10	75	15
women with partners	12	75	13
all men	2	23	75
men with partners	1	22	77
Germany			
women	14	65	21
men	33		67
Czech Republic			
all women aged 20–40	17	70	13
women in employment	14	69	17
wives aged 20–40	14	75	11
Sweden			
women in 1955 birth cohort: actual lifestyle choices by age 43 (1998)	4	64	32
Japan Ideal lifecourse of unmarried women			
1987	37	55	8
2002	21	69	10

Table 9.3 (continued)

Sources: Data for Britain and Spain, 1999, extracted from Tables 3.14 and 3.15 in Hakim (2003a: 85, 87). Data for Belgium-Flanders extracted from Corijn and Hakim (forthcoming) based on a 2002/3 survey. Data for Germany extracted from Bertram et al. (2005). Data for Czech Republic from personal communication from Beatrice Manea, based on a November 2005 survey. Data for Sweden extracted from Huang et al. (2006) reporting analysis of a longitudinal dataset. Data for Japan from National Institute of Population and Social Security regular surveys of Views of the Unmarried about Marriage and Family in Japan.

Preference theory predicts that men will retain their dominance in the labour market, politics and other competitive activities, because only a minority of women are prepared to prioritise their jobs (or other activities in the public sphere) in the same way as men. This is unwelcome news to many feminists, who have assumed that women would be just as likely as men to be work-centred once opportunities were opened to them, and that sex discrimination alone has so far held women back from the top jobs in any society. It is this conclusion that makes preference theory unacceptable to feminists. Female heterogeneity and male heterogeneity invalidate the feminist assumption that the key conflict is between women's interests and men's interests.

Contextual factors

The USA, Britain and probably also the Netherlands currently provide the prime examples of societies that have achieved the new scenario for women. This does not mean that sex discrimination has been entirely eliminated in these countries. As definitions of sex discrimination keep expanding, from direct discrimination to increasingly arcane forms of indirect discrimination, this battle is arguably never won. However, these countries have trenchant equal opportunities legislation, backed up and enforced by a system of tribunals, equal opportunities commissions, and other tangible public and political support for converting the letter of the law into reality. Most European countries still have little or nothing actively to enforce equal opportunities legislation, so that little has changed, in practice. For example, in Greece, Italy and Spain, there is evidence of informal barriers to women's access to the labour market: female unemployment rates are more than double male unemployment rates, and there is some evidence of the disparity widening in recent years rather than falling. Within the European Union, only Britain, Ireland and the Netherlands have a public body responsible for enforcing equal pay and equal opportunities laws similar to the Equal Employment Opportunity Commission in the USA (Gregory, Sales and Hegewisch 1999). Equally important, Britain and the USA both have large and diverse populations, ensuring that cultural diversity and differences in values become accepted and even welcomed. Some European countries (notably the Scandinavian countries) have not yet come to terms with the ethnic, religious and cultural diversity that generally ensues from decades of immigration, and they have low acceptance of diversity in values and lifestyles.

Identifying Britain and the USA as two countries that have achieved the new scenario for women does not mean we expect convergence in work rates and lifestyle choices in these countries. Even the most liberal society and laissez-faire polity still has institutions, laws, customs, national policies and cultures that shape and structure behaviour. Choices are not made in a vacuum. Social and economic factors still matter, and will produce national variations in employment patterns and lifestyle choices, as illustrated by the contrasts between Britain and Spain (Hakim 2003a) or between Sweden and Japan (Table 9.3). In addition, the choices people make are moulded by an unpredictable constellation of events: economic recessions and booms, wars, changes of government, as well as events in private lives, individual ability, accidents or ill health, 'disastrous' marriages and 'brilliant' marriages. For example, Britain and the USA differ in the size and character of their part-time workforce. Universal and free access to health care in Britain means that people are free to choose their job and working hours, and even whether to work at all, without regard to any health benefits offered by employers. In the USA, health insurance benefits are a key feature of full-time jobs that biases choices away from part-time work or non-work. As a result of these differences, some adaptive women in Britain will choose permanent part-time jobs, or decide not to be employed at all, while some of their counterparts in the USA will choose full-time jobs. Jobless single mothers and their children receive exactly the same health care as everyone else in Britain. Such social and economic factors guarantee that there will always be differences between the new scenario countries in patterns of fertility and female employment.

In sum, in countries that have delivered the new scenario for women, lifestyle preferences determine:

- women's employment pattern over the lifecycle: choices between careers and jobs, full-time and part-time work, and associated job values;
- women's fertility: the incidence of childlessness and, for the majority who do have children, family sizes;
- women's responsiveness to public policies, employer policies, economic and social circumstances – including pro-natalist policies.

Preferences cannot predict outcomes with complete certainty, even when women have genuine choices, because of variations in individual abilities and factors in the social and economic environment. However, in prosperous modern societies preferences become a much more important determinant, maybe even the central determinant of women's behaviour.

The three lifestyle preference groups differ in values, goals and aspirations. That is, they are defined by their contrasting lifestyle preferences rather than by behavioural outcomes, which depend in part on the social and economic environment (Hakim 2003a). People who argue that women's choices are always shaped by external events and the situation around them are typically describing adaptive women, who are in the majority, and who are especially responsive to all types of social and economic policy, as shown in Table 9.2. The distinctive feature of the two polar groups of women (and equivalent men) is that they do *not* waver in their goals, even when they fail to achieve them. Work-centred people are defined by prioritising market work (or other competitive activities in the public sphere) over family work and family life, *not* by exceptional success in the public sphere, which is the result of many factors in combination. Given the much larger size of the adaptive group, it produces the largest absolute numbers of high achievers. The much smaller group of careerists has the highest percentage of high achievers, but this still translates into a smaller absolute number compared to the adaptive group.

Theoretical implications of female diversity

The diversity of women's lifestyle preferences, more precisely female heterogeneity, has three implications that are inconvenient for contemporary feminist theory, which is essentially twentieth-century theory. First, it produces conflict between the three groups of women on the proper goals of social policy. As Bryson (1992: 263) recognises, there is no consensus among women as to what the goals of feminism should be; but this insight is readily put aside by academics who offer recommendations for greater social engineering by the state. Second, because women collectively are more heterogeneous than men collectively, and because men include a much higher proportion of work-centred people (a clear majority), preference theory predicts that men will continue to outnumber women in positions that are attained through competitive rivalry. Third, sex and gender become redundant social categories, as lifestyle preferences now define the dominant interest groups.

A fundamental assumption of all feminist theory (at least Anglo-Saxon theory) is that the interests of men, and of women, are relatively homogeneous, and are often mutually incompatible (even if the categories of 'male' and 'female' are artificial social constructions).[3] This is the source of the continuing focus on gender inequalities, and the social policies required to achieve equality of outcomes (Phillips 2004). Bryson claims that feminists still believe men have a wide array of interests in maintaining women's subordination: emotional, psychological, sexual, domestic and economic vested interests (Bryson 1992: 156). She argues that the concept of patriarchy is central to modern radical feminism: the idea of men and women having conflicting interests, and that male power enables men to ensure that their interests take priority over women's interests (Bryson 1992: 181–8). Similarly, Phillips (2004) insists that differences in aspirations and dispositions between individuals, between men and women, cannot be an acceptable reason for any differences in outcomes,

---

[3] French feminist theory pre-dates Anglo-Saxon theory, starting with de Beauvoir's *The Second Sex* in 1949, and has taken a rather different path. In particular, French feminists accept that men and women relate to each other differently in France than in English-speaking countries; the sexes are seen as complementary rather than competing; and there tends to be more celebration of seduction and sexuality. Sexual difference in the private sphere is not seen as an impediment to formal legal equality in the public sphere (Allwood 1998).

particularly in incomes, occupations, responsibilities and time-use. Any inequality of outcomes is thus interpreted automatically as proving inequality of opportunity, and is noxious.

All these theories rest on research evidence for the twentieth century and earlier periods. There is a profound absence of historical sensitivity in current feminist theory. There is also an unwillingness to set out the social and economic conditions required to create a situation of genuine choice about lifestyles for women – or for men. In contrast, preference theory is historically informed: it sets out the five social and economic conditions required to create the 'new scenario' in which women can make genuine choices, and claims that these conditions are met in the USA, Britain and the Netherlands but not, as yet, in all European countries. Given the evidence that men are even less able to implement their lifestyle preferences than are women (Hakim 2003a: 141; 2005), the theory clearly needs to be extended to address male choices as well. However, the theory has been shown to work in relation to women, even though social and economic factors continue to play a part in outcomes (Hakim 2000a: 168–70; 2003a: 140).

Phillips (2004) is right to point out that outcomes do not invariably reflect preferences. Economists have traditionally made this assumption or, more accurately, used this shorthand. Outcomes were treated as 'revealed preferences' by economists. However sociological research has taken a different approach, treating preferences as something to be studied empirically. One of the major innovations of preference theory is that it underlines the distinction, in attitude research, between choice and approval, between personal preference and societal norms. The two are not synonymous. For example, many people believe it would be better if everyone used public transport and no one smoked; however they may still prefer to drive a car and smoke themselves. Social attitude surveys concentrate on measuring societal norms, not personal preferences, despite the fact that views on the public good have little or no impact on individual behaviour – as illustrated by patriarchal attitudes. In contrast, personal lifestyle preferences do determine behaviour, to a large extent (Hakim 2003a, 2003b, 2004b), and this is especially clear in longitudinal studies (Hakim 2000a: 128–56). Once again, feminist theory remains embedded in twentieth-century knowledge and ideas, uninformed by new evidence on twenty-first-century developments. What is especially useful about recent tests of preference theory is that they demonstrate the *relative* impact of preferences, patriarchal values, and social and economic factors (Hakim 2003a: 140), and how the impact of social and economic factors differs between the three preference groups. The most common failure of recent critiques of preference theory is that they rely on existing social attitude data and questions, and hence analyse data on societal norms, *not* data on personal preferences. It is thus predictable that there would be a weak link between societal norms and individual behaviour (McRae 2003; Hakim 2003b, 2007; Crompton and Lyonette 2005).[4]

However, the most troublesome contribution of preference theory is to show that the increasing heterogeneity of women's lifestyle preferences demolishes the central idea in what might be called victim feminism – the thesis that the most important dividing line is between the interests of men and women, and that men are to blame for women's position in the labour market and in society. On the contrary, careerist men and women share the same values and aspirations as regards public lives. Spouses who prefer a family model based on role segregation also share common values and interests, certainly as regards fiscal and social policy, despite their different (complementary) contributions to the household economy. There is more scope for conflicting interests between careerist women and family-centred women than between men and women collectively, as Gerson (1985) recognised decades ago. This could be one reason why professional women and academics deny the very existence of all groups other than the careerist group they belong to. Further, as so many people have invested their intellectual careers in twentieth-century victim feminism, this perspective will not easily fade from use. But the evidence is already overwhelming.

If feminist theory does not adapt and change to recognise the new realities, the chances are that it will become marginalised. There is some evidence of this already, in generational differences: many younger women, especially the well educated, regard feminism as an anachronistic relic of twentieth-century ideas. Many gender studies

---

[4] Unlike Crompton and Lyonette (2005), an analysis of ISSP data by Reed and Blunsden (2006) does make the distinction between societal norms and preferences, and finds surprisingly strong correlations between sex-role beliefs and women's employment decisions.

courses appeal more strongly to young women from non-European and non-modern countries rather than to young Europeans. They recognise that active sex discrimination persists in their own societies. But young Europeans already perceive sex discrimination to be the less important factor in current developments. The story is more complicated than that, and they see the need for gender neutral theories and perspectives.

Some argue that gender neutrality was already present in twentieth-century feminist theory. A good example of twentieth-century theorising is offered by Zaretsky's (1986) brilliant essay that attempts to synthesise Marxist historical analysis, psychoanalysis, and feminist writing on the family and personal life to explain the dichotomy between public and private life, male and female. Zaretsky argues that these are false dichotomies, artificial and socially constructed within capitalist economies. The evidence goes against him, as the distinctions are recognised in all societies, whether or not women are involved in both spheres. Similarly, the 'cult of domesticity' is neither unique to capitalist societies, nor universal within them, as he claims. Zaretsky dismisses the male/female distinction as unfounded but, like many feminists, he goes on to reinvent it. Following Chodorow (1978) and later writers, he presents the male/female distinction as the product of (universal) psychological processes in childhood which create similarity and difference, female relatedness and male separateness. A complex argument then leads to universal male patriarchal authority, which socialism and capitalism both failed to eliminate – at least up to the mid-1980s. Zaretsky's need to return to, and underline, the male/female distinction after a ritual denunciation of the concepts is fairly typical of current feminist theory. In contrast, preference theory is gender neutral and unisex in its perspective and predictions.

Research already shows that sex/gender is redundant in explaining the pay gap; the key dividing line is between women who choose to become mothers and childless women. This has now become a real choice for women, even in countries like Sweden with vigorous pro-natalist policies, where childlessness is stigmatised as much as the full-time homemaker role. Preference theory argues that this choice reflects fundamental values and life-goals, which differ between people. New tests of preference theory (Hakim 2003a) confirm that the three preference groups can be identified among men as well as women, even in societies such as Spain, where social and economic conditions are not conducive to female careerists or male home-makers. We can now move beyond sex and gender to focus instead on the social roles that women and men prefer, and adopt for their own lives. Preference theory is unisex. Lifestyle preferences cut across sex/ gender as well as class, income, ethnic group or race, age and education levels (Hakim 2003a).

The polarisation process that differentiates two-earner, one-earner and no-earner households is already recognised. Preference theory predicts the polarisation of family models – between families with, and without, a clear separation of sex roles. In future, this will be a far more important political, economic and social dividing line than the sex/gender issue that academic feminists still cling to, and that seems increasingly irrelevant to large numbers of young people.

The essentialist critique

The most common perspective on preference theory has been to classify it as a development of neoclassical economics and rational choice theory (Devine 1994; Crompton 1997: 16–19; Crompton and Harris 1998; Goulding and Reed 2006: 216–25), and then to offer the usual sociological critiques of these economic theories. More recently, Crompton has renewed her attack on preference theory by claiming that it is gender essentialist (Crompton and Lyonette 2005; Crompton, chapter 10 in this volume). This claim is without foundation, and rests on Crompton's total misrepresentation of preference theory. More important, essentialist critiques fail to understand the complexity of causal processes and the ecological fallacy.

Preference theory is not gender essentialist, and there is nothing to support such a claim in any of my publications. On the contrary, preference theory is an explicitly unisex theory which shows that sex and gender are now redundant concepts, which cease to be important factors and are already being replaced by lifestyle preferences as the crucial differentiating characteristic in labour supply (Hakim 2000a: 280; 2003a: 261) and even that lifestyle preferences are replacing sex and gender as the central determinant of social activities and social roles more generally (Hakim 2004a: 202). Normal logic indicates that preference theory is totally incompatible with the essentialist idea of important and unalterable differences between men and women.

Indeed it has been argued that victim feminism is essentialist in its emphasis on sex/gender, and is thus flawed.[5]

Crompton categorically mischaracterises preference theory. First, she asserts that, in contrast to men, the *majority* of women are home-centred and family-orientated (Crompton and Lyonette 2005: 605). In fact, preference theory states very clearly that a *minority* of women, 10–30 per cent, are family-centred, as shown in Table 9.2. This empirically based observation has been further supported by all recent studies, as shown in Table 9.3.

Second, Crompton claims that preference theory draws upon Goldberg's (1993) theory that testosterone is a major source of sex differences in motivation, ambition and behaviour (Crompton and Lyonette 2005: 604; Crompton, chapter 10 in this volume). In fact, his work is a trivial element in the book on preference theory (Hakim 2000a), and does not feature in the four main tenets of the theory shown in Table 9.1.[6] In *Key Issues in Women's Work* (2004a), I treat socio-physiological theories (including Goldberg's thesis) as one of *four competing explanations* for women's position in the labour market – the other three being feminist theories (Hartmann, Walby), rational choice theory (Becker, Polachek, Mincer) and preference theory (Hakim). There is no suggestion, here or anywhere else, that preference theory rests on Goldberg; they are presented as *competing* theories! Furthermore, I cite chaos theory as the main intellectual influence, and explicitly reject biological and evolutionary explanations, noting that Goldberg's thesis has yet to be proven as an explanation of women's position in the labour market (Hakim 2004a: 16, 208).

---

[5] Western bloc countries exported victim feminism to Eastern Europe after 1989. However Eastern European women viewed western feminism as cultural feminism (as distinct from socialist feminism), and they also saw it as essentialist in character (Ghodsee 2004: 732, 748) because of the insistence on gender and the conflicting interests of men and women, rather than on class and conflicting class interests. This underlines the ambivalent nature of western victim feminism.

[6] In *Preference Theory*, Goldberg is only one among more than 900 references cited in the Bibliography. The data on testosterone available at that time are stated to be misleading in their implications for sex differences in behaviour (Hakim 2000a: 260). In *Key Issues in Women's Work* more recent research results on the similar effects of testosterone on women (as well as men) are reported, and Goldberg's work is set in the context of related feminist theories (Hakim 2004a: 7–8).

Crompton's essentialist critique of preference theory is erroneous and unjustified. However, essentialist critiques are theoretically inadequate in any case, and are also out of touch with the latest research results.

Currently, the most popular conception of essentialism[7] is the social Darwinism/evolutionary psychology perspective which asserts an essential and ineradicable difference between men and women owing to differential roles in reproduction: women invest more heavily in their offspring, while men focus on attracting numerous sexual partners to spread their genes widely. Reproduction thus becomes women's priority and sexuality is the male priority, with consequences for the differential development of social characteristics and values. Preference theory contradicts this thesis, pointing out that a substantial minority of women in modern societies (up to 20 per cent) choose not to have children at all, give priority to their activities in the public sphere and remain voluntarily childless. Studies of the childless make it clear that voluntary childlessness occurs in all three lifestyle preference groups (Hakim 2003d). Furthermore, most women nowadays have only two children, on average. Childrearing ceases to be a full-time lifelong activity, as it frequently was in the past, and adaptive women seek to combine family work with paid jobs. It is clear that the two revolutions produce a fundamental change in women's life-choices and values.

Another problem is that gender essentialism no longer exists as conceived (or caricatured) by feminists. Even committed evolutionists insist that the debate over causes is not about culture (or social structure) versus biology, but about culture and social structure *alone* as the dominant cause of sex differences versus culture and biology *jointly* playing important roles (Browne 2006: 151). The debate is about the *relative* importance of different factors, and this requires solid research evidence rather than theoretical debate. For example, research evidence might well show that the influence of the factors covered under the umbrella term 'biology' account for only 1–3 per cent of behaviour in modern societies, in which case they can be disregarded for all practical purposes.

---

[7] It is probably fair to say that the term essentialism is used by feminist scholars more often as a vague but pejorative value-judgement to justify rejecting a theory than as a precise thesis open to investigation and testing, as illustrated by Walby (1990).

The most desperate final argument of feminists is the claim that any report of statistical differences in the attitudes and behaviour of men and women is 'essentialist'. This is nonsense. Statistical differences between groups, their size and importance, are the essence of modern social science research. Crompton and others adopting this position reveal themselves as ideologues rather than objective social scientists.[8] Social scientists cannot discard rules of evidence and proof in research on the social world. Unfortunately this does happen, periodically, even in respectable academic journals, because of the intrusion of political advocacy and political correctness into the social sciences. For example, there has been a long-running debate in the *American Psychologist* on research that seeks to establish which sex differences in personality, ability and social behaviour are vanishing, and which remain important. Some scholars argue that research on sex differences should never be published, in case the results support stereotypes and thus, it is claimed, support essentialist ideas and women's subordination (Walsh 1997: 15–31). However reports regularly conclude that sex differences remain – in attitudes, values and behaviour – and confirm popular stereotypes (Burke and Weir 1976; Swim 1994; Beutel and Marini 1995; Eagly 1995; Hakim 1995, 1996; Baron-Cohen, this volume). The most recent meta-analysis underlines that *most* sex differences are very small, with moderate or large differences only on motor ability, aggression and sexuality, especially attitudes to casual sex (Hyde 2005). Aggression is of particular importance because it is linked to drive and determination, motivation to succeed, risk-taking and ambition as well as verbal and physical aggression, and because the sex differences are largest in real-world settings (Archer 2005; Baron-Cohen, this volume). For example, for a variety of reasons, wives continue to treat their husband's job as more important than their own,[9] and this is reflected in different work orientations.

What everyone forgets is the ecological fallacy, which means that causal processes can look totally different at the macro-level and the micro-level (Robinson 1950; Hakim 2000b: 98, 162, 213). Data

---

[8] It is also inconsistent to accept research on sex differences in earnings as valid, while rejecting research on other sex differences as politically suspicious.

[9] This is most clear in situations where there is a genuine (and private) choice, and no practical constraints, such as class identity. Data for 1985–91 for Britain show that women still attach more weight to their husband's occupation than to their own when defining their class identity (Sobel et al. 2004).

at one level of analysis cannot necessarily be read across to the other level. As chaos theory points out, even tornadoes have tiny beginnings. Similarly, tiny differences at the aggregate level can have large consequences at the micro-level of individual lives. There are two reasons why even small sex differences in average scores on characteristics may translate into substantial cumulative sex differences in the workplace and other real-world contexts. First, it has long been known that the variability in male distributions is larger than for females. There are more male than female geniuses, and also more males among the mentally retarded. Even when average scores on a characteristic are identical, there will be more high-scoring men than women, more exceptionally talented men than women on that feature (Hyde 2005: 587). Second, in the real world, it is individuals who are selected for jobs or for promotion, not groups. The individual who displays a marginal advantage on some characteristic, such as numerical ability or motivation, will be selected over others, even if all the candidates score high on the relevant characteristics. Small or tiny group differences still leave some individuals whose success in the labour market is significantly boosted by marginally higher scores on certain characteristics. This marginal advantage at each level of the occupational hierarchy can cumulate into important sex differentials at the top of the hierarchy. In sum, even in the absence of sex discrimination, small average sex differences at the aggregate level can have large, practical importance in the real world, at the micro-level where individuals compete for the top jobs. This 'structural' feature of causal processes is invariably misunderstood and overlooked by feminist scholars who focus on 'gender inequality'.

The problem of genuine choices

Feminist theorists often focus on the problematic nature of 'choice'. For example, they point out that many social roles are socially constructed, and conclude that the choice of a particular role must also be socially constructed. But this is a non sequitur. Social roles are public, and require socially coordinated behaviour, and consensus about their central features. Choices are ultimately private decisions, even if other people are consulted and influence them. Few people would choose a physician who made entirely personal, idiosyncratic decisions as to what his role was, whether to cure or kill patients. Public roles are subject to public controls. But the decision to become a doctor, or not, remains entirely personal, even if others seek to influence the choice. The choice of spouse is the most personal of all, and is generally especially important for career patterns and lifestyles.

It is self-evident that choices always take place within the context of a particular society, historical time, and the particular talents and abilities of the individual. I cannot 'choose' to be the first President of the USA, or the next Maria Callas. We can accept that contextual social factors and individual abilities remain important, while still underlining the fact that women in liberal modern societies in the twenty-first century have lifestyle choices that were unimaginable even fifty years ago.[10] In addition, women now have more choices than men, for whom the main breadwinner role is an unavoidable social obligation, whether they like it or not.[11]

Similarly, it will not do for feminists and others to argue that women cannot make 'free' choices unless everyone else, especially men, makes choices that are convenient for the first person. At worst, this is logical nonsense. At best, it replaces male hegemony (or patriarchy) by female hegemony (or matriarchy). The argument also ignores the fact that women's lifestyle preferences are now too diverse for this to be a realistic and feasible goal.

Fourth, there is the argument that choices are socially embedded, or socially determined, so do not reflect women's 'true' desires and interests. One variant of this argument leads to the writer claiming superior knowledge of what women (should) want, and demanding

[10] Some go further to argue that in affluent modern societies economic and social constraints and resources are largely perceptual and essentially bounded by a person's world-view (Goulding and Reed 2006: 216, 229).

[11] The modern male perspective on many of these issues is presented by a sociologist who is only too aware of the conventional social structural perspective (Giddens 1992). He points out that men seek status among other men, the status conferred by material rewards in the context of rituals of male solidarity. The male world entails instrumental values and economic individualism. Male self-identity is sought primarily in work. He also suggests that male anger and sexual violence constitute a new, modern phenomenon, the result of male resentment of women's intrusion into public settings. Giddens points out that men are still imprisoned in the role of breadwinner, even though the economic benefits men provide for women are now resented rather than appreciated.

that her views form the basis for public policy development. The classic example of this is found in Sweden. Interview surveys with new mothers showed that almost all did *not* want to share parental leave with the father; they preferred to use *all* parental leave themselves. This clear-cut citizen vote was ignored by the Swedish government in favour of social engineering. A new policy of compulsory paternal leave was imposed, with 'Daddy months' reserved exclusively for fathers, with the aim of re-educating Swedish citizens on what they *should* want.

The second variant of this argument claims that choices are, in practice, determined by social class, ethnicity, and other factors. This argument does at least accept that research evidence is relevant and cannot be tossed aside. Unfortunately, the research evidence does not support the conclusion. Political theorists are rarely experts in sociological empirical research. They are never up-to-date with the latest findings, which are the best indicator of future trends. Over twenty years ago, Davis (1982) showed that social class has very little impact on social and political values; education has a stronger impact. But education beyond the compulsory level is itself chosen and actively pursued; it is not an accident of birth, an ascribed characteristic. More important, none of these factors *wholly determines* attitudes; they are only subsidiary influences, the ones we can easily identify and measure, but not the main causes or sources.

However the main problem with the argument that choices are simply class determined is that it is demonstrably false. As noted above, there is a fundamental difference between *personal preferences* and *societal norms*. Social class and related factors have no influence on the former, but do have an impact on the latter. Lifestyle preferences and ideals regarding the family division of labour cut across social status and economic groups, and across ethnic groups as well. In contrast, there are marked differences between socio-economic groups, and ethnic groups, in societal norms, such as the acceptance of patriarchal values (Hakim 2003a: 100–1, 143–7). It is only personal preferences that shape behaviour, and preferences are *not* class determined. Feminist theory has become out of touch with current trends and the research evidence for the twenty-first century.[12]

[12] Similarly, feminist critiques of preference theory are routinely out-of-date and uninformed by the latest research evidence. For example, several of the

Implications for state policy

What are the implications of these research findings, and preference theory, for state policy?

First, female diversity means that no single group can speak for all women, any more than a single group can speak for all men. This means that governments should stop listening exclusively to feminists, because they offer a biased and one-sided presentation of women's interests. Virtually all feminists, whether academics, activists or politicians, will be full-time workers and work-centred careerists, who have little personal appreciation of the competing interests of home-centred women, and only a fuzzy understanding of the interests of adaptive women. I have yet to attend any feminist conference or seminar where a spokesperson for pressure groups representing full-time mothers was invited to speak. Most meetings of this sort claim that women choosing full-time motherhood do not, cannot exist – unless they are the victims of patriarchal brainwashing. It is essential that governments and social policy-makers start listening to representatives of all groups of women, rather than feminists who represent the interests of careerist women in the main.

Second, social and family policy needs to be diversified to offer benefits to all groups of women. At present, most countries tend to favour just one of the three lifestyle preference groups, especially in places where a single party has been in power a long time, as in Sweden. In countries with a wide spread of political opinion, and regular changes of government, such as France, social policy is more likely to be diversified to take account of all groups of women. Diversification of social policies is difficult, and requires far more imagination than in the past, when policies were aimed at an assumed homogenous collectivity of women-in-general. However designing policies that are neutral between the three lifestyle preference groups is feasible, as I have shown elsewhere (Hakim 2000a: 223–53), and some social scientists are taking up the challenge (Blyton et al. 2006). The first, essential, step is to analyse existing policies to identify the

contributors in El-Sawad and Cohen (2006) offer critiques of preference theory that only address publications in the 1990s, up to the main Preference Theory statement (Hakim 2000a), and ignore subsequent publications that provide extensive new empirical evidence on the interplay of preferences and contextual factors (Hakim 2003a, 2003c, 2005).

biases they contain, overt or covert, in prioritising one model of the family and women's role over others. The second is to adopt a policy of neutrality between the lifestyle preference groups. For the labour market, this means that there are two very different types of career: the full-time lifelong work-centred career (usually labelled as the male stereotype) and the adaptive career that demands a large degree of work–life balance, and may include long spells of part-time work, or absence from the labour market (Hakim 2006).

Many current problems and debates are due to black/white zero-sum game thinking: *either* social and employment policies are based exclusively on the work-centred career model, *or* policy is based exclusively on the second model, which is currently championed by the European Commission. In reality, one-size-fits-all policies are too rigid and fail to recognise the real diversity of lifestyle preferences in the workforce. Diversity thinking says let a hundred flowers bloom, and we can certainly operate with at least two models of careers.

There are already examples of social policies that are sufficiently open ended and neutral to offer benefits to people in both types of career, as well as to people who want to be full-time homemakers and parents. One example is the hugely successful homecare allowance in Finland, Norway, France and Germany. Employers' policies can also be diversified, as illustrated by 'cafeteria benefits' and 'flexible benefits'. New, flexible work–life balance arrangements for time off paid work (paid or unpaid) and reduced hours are also important. However it is unrealistic to expect that someone who spends a large part of adult life engaged in other activities would not be penalised at all in his/her employment career. This does not mean that top jobs should be reserved for work-centred careerists exclusively, simply that it is a reasonable prediction that their probability of success will be higher than for adaptives collectively.

Will policies that recognise diversity produce substantive similarity (equality of outcomes rather than equal opportunities) between people in the two types of career? Of course not. You cannot square the circle. The chances of reaching the top jobs are higher among work-centred careerists. However, even at the top of each profession, work-centred people may be outnumbered by people in the adaptive group, simply because this group is so much larger. Unfortunately, media interest focuses on the more glamorous careerists, typified by pop stars, rather than the more numerous but nameless, invisible government officials who typify the balanced adaptive career. We need more realistic role models.

Conclusions

Feminist theories, and the evidence they rest on, are out-of-date. Theorists and their evidence are backward-looking, and remain stuck in the twentieth century. There have been dramatic social and economic changes in the latter part of the twentieth century that are creating a qualitatively new scenario for women in the twenty-first century. Feminist theory needs to take account of preference theory, new research evidence and changing social trends. Young women do not see the world the same way as their mothers did – mainly because the world has actually changed, and young women feel they are making real choices as to how they live their lives today. In the near future, men will start to demand the same flexibility and diversity of choices.

References

Albrecht, J., Björklund, A. and Vroman, S. (2003) 'Is There a Glass Ceiling in Sweden?', *Journal of Labor Economics* 21: 145–77.

Allwood, G. (1998) *French Feminisms* (London: UCL Press).

Anker, R. (1998) *Gender and Jobs: Sex Segregation of Occupations in the World* (Geneva: ILO).

Archer, J. (2005) 'Sex differences in aggression in real-world settings: a meta-analytic review', *Review of General Psychology* 8: 291–322.

Asplund, G. (1984) *Karriärens Vilkor: Män Kvinnor och Ledarskap* (Stockholm: Trevi).

Babcock, L. and Laschever, S. (2003) *Women Don't Ask: Negotiation and the Gender Divide* (Princeton: Princeton University Press).

Bertram, H., Rosler, W. and Ehlert, N. (2005) Nachhaltige Familienpolitik (Berlin: Bundesministerium fur Familie, Senioren, Frauen und Jugend).

Beutel, A. M. and Marini, M. M. (1995) 'Gender and Values', *American Sociological Review* 60: 436–48.

Blyton, P., Blunsdon, B., Reed, K. and Dastmalchian, A. (eds.) (2006) *Work–Life Integration: International Perspectives on the Balancing of Multiple Roles* (New York: Palgrave Macmillan).

Browne, K. R. (2006) 'Evolved Sex Differences and Occupational Segregation', *Journal of Organizational Behaviour* 27: 143–62.

Bryson, V. (1992) *Feminist Political Theory* (London: Macmillan).

Burke, R. J. and Weir, T. (1976) 'Some Personality Differences between Members of One-Career and Two-Career Families', *Journal of Marriage and the Family* 38: 453–9.

Charles, M. and Grusky, D. B. (2004) *Occupational Ghettos: The Worldwide Segregation of Women and Men* (Stanford, CA: Stanford University Press).

Chodorow, N. (1978) *The Reproduction of Mothering: Psychoanalysis and the Sociology of Gender* (Berkeley, CA: University of California Press).

Cleland, J. (1985) 'Marital Fertility Decline in Developing Countries: Theories and the Evidence', in J. Cleland and J. Hobcraft (eds.), *Reproductive Change in Developing Countries: Insights from the World Fertility Survey* (Oxford: Oxford University Press), 223–52.

Corijn, M. and Hakim, C. (forthcoming) 'Lifestyle Preferences in Belgium-Flanders'.

Crompton, R. (1997) *Women and Work in Modern Britain* (Oxford: Oxford University Press).

Crompton, R. and Lyonette, C. (2005) 'The New Gender Essentialism – Domestic and Family Choices and Their Relation to Attitudes', *British Journal of Sociology*, 56: 601–20.

Davis, J. A. (1982) 'Achievement Variables and Class Cultures: Family, Schooling, Job and Forty-Nine Dependent Variables in the Cumulative GSS', *American Sociological Review* 47: 569–86.

Devine, F. (1994) 'Segregation and Supply', *Gender, Work, and Organization* 1: 94–109.

Duncan, Gregg J. and Dunifon, R. (1998) 'Soft Skills and Long Run Labor Market Success', *Research in Labor Economics* 17: 123–49.

Eagly, A. H. (1995) 'The Science and Politics of Comparing Women and Men', *American Psychologist* 50: 145–58 (with comments by Hyde and Plant, Marecek, and Buss, and response by Eagly, 159–71).

El-Sawad, A. and Cohen, L. (eds.) (2006) 'Symposium on Careers and Family-Friendly Policies', *British Journal of Guidance and Counselling* 34: 273–379.

European Commission (2002) *Employment in Europe* (Luxemburg: OOPEC).

Gerson, K. (1985) *Hard Choices: How Women Decide about Work, Career and Motherhood* (Berkeley and Los Angeles: University of California Press).

Ghodsee, K. (2004) 'Feminism-by-Design: Emerging Capitalisms, Cultural Feminism, and Women's Nongovernmental Organisations in Postsocialist Eastern Europe', *Signs* 29: 727–53.

Giddens, A. (1992) *Intimacy* (Cambridge: Polity Press).

Glass, J. (2004) 'Blessing or Curse? Work–Family Policies and Mothers' Wage Growth over Time', *Work and Occupations* 31: 367–94.

Goldberg, S. (1993) *Why Men Rule: A Theory of Male Dominance* (Chicago: Open Court).

Goulding, C. and Reed, K. (2006) 'Commitment, Community and Happiness: A Theoretical Framework for Understanding Lifestyle and Work', in Blyton et al. (eds.), *Work–Life Integration: International Perspectives on the Balancing of Multiple Roles* (New York: Palgrave Macmillan), 216–33.

Gregory, J., Sales, R. and Hegewisch, A. (1999) *Women, Work and Inequality: The Challenge of Equal Pay in a Deregulated Labour Market* (London: Macmillan).

Hakim, C. (1995) 'Five Feminist Myths about Women's Employment', *British Journal of Sociology* 46: 429–55.

(1996) 'Labour Mobility and Employment Stability: Rhetoric and Reality on the Sex Differential in Labour Market Behaviour', *European Sociological Review* 12: 1–31.

(1998) *Social Change and Innovation in the Labour Market* (Oxford: Oxford University Press).

(2000a) *Work–Lifestyle Choices in the 21st Century: Preference Theory* (Oxford: Oxford University Press).

(2000b) *Research Design* (London: Routledge).

(2003a) *Models of the Family in Modern Societies: Ideals and Realities* (Aldershot: Ashgate).

(2003b) 'Public Morality versus Personal Choice: The Failure of Social Attitude Surveys', *British Journal of Sociology* 54: 339–45.

(2003c) 'A New Approach to Explaining Fertility Patterns: Preference Theory', *Population and Development Review* 29: 349–74.

(2003d) *Childlessness in Europe*, Report to the Economic and Social Research Council (London: London School of Economics).

(2004a) *Key Issues in Women's Work: Female Diversity and the Polarisation of Women's Employment* (London: GlassHouse Press).

(2004b) 'Lifestyle Preferences and Patriarchal Values: Causal and Non-causal Attitudes', in Janet Z. Giele and Elke Holst (eds.), *Changing Life Patterns in Western Industrial Societies* (New York: Elsevier), 69–91.

(2005) 'Sex Differences in Work–Life Balance Goals', in D. Houston (ed.), *Work–Life Balance in the Twenty-First Century* (London: Palgrave Macmillan), 55–79.

(2006) 'Women, Careers, and Work–Life Preferences', *British Journal of Guidance and Counselling*, special issue ed. Amal Al-Sawad and Laurie Cohen, 34: 281–94.

(2007) 'Dancing with the Devil? Essentialism and Other Feminist Heresies', *British Journal of Sociology* 58: 123–32.

Harkness, S. and Waldfogel, J. (1999) *The Family Gap in Pay: Evidence from Seven Industrialised Countries* (London: London School of Economics, Centre for Analysis of Social Exclusion).

Henrekson, M. and Dreber, A. (2004) 'Female Career Choice and Career Success: Institutions, Path Dependence and Psychological Feed-back Effects', Stockholm School of Economics, Department of Economics.

Hochschild, A. (1990) *The Second Shift: Working Parents and the Revolution at Home* (London: Piatkus).

Huang Qinghai, El-Khouri, B. M., Johansson, G., Lindroth, S. and Sverke, M. (2006) 'Women's Career Patterns: A Study of Swedish Women Born in the 1950s', *Journal of Occupational and Organizational Psychology*.

Hunt, J. (2002) 'The Transition in East Germany: When Is a Ten-point Fall in the Gender Wage Gap Bad News?', *Journal of Labor Economics* 20: 148–69.

Hyde, Janet S. (2005) 'The Gender Similarities Hypothesis', *American Psychologist* 60: 581–92.

Jacobs, J. A. and Gerson, K. (2004) *The Time Divide: Work, Family and Gender Inequality* (Cambridge, MA: Harvard University Press).

Lewis, J. and Giullari, S. (2005) 'The Adult Worker Model Family, Gender Equality and Care: The Search for New Policy Principles and the Possibilities and Problems of a Capabilities Approach', *Economy and Society* 34: 76–104.

McCall, L. (2001) *Complex Inequality: Gender, Class and Race in the New Economy* (New York: Routledge).

McRae, S. (2003) 'Constraints and Choices in Mothers' Employment Careers: A Consideration of Hakim's Preference Theory', *British Journal of Sociology* 54: 317–38.

Melkas, H. and Anker, R. (1998) *Gender Equality and Occupational Segregation in Nordic Labour Markets* (Geneva: International Labour Office).

Middleton, C. (1988) 'The Familiar Fate of the *Famulae*: Gender Divisions in the History of Wage Labour', in R. Pahl (ed.), *On Work* (Oxford: Blackwell), 21–47.

Moen, P. (ed.) (2003) *It's About Time: Couples and Careers* (Ithaca, NY and London: ILR Press).

Murphy, M. (1993) 'The Contraceptive Pill and Women's Employment as Factors in Fertility Change in Britain 1963–1980: A Challenge to the Conventional View', *Population Studies* 47: 221–43.

OECD (2002) 'Women at Work', in *Employment Outlook*, (Paris: OECD), 61–125.

Padavic, I. and Reskin, B. (2002) *Women and Men at Work*, 2nd edn (Thousand Oaks, CA: Pine Forge Press).

Phillips, A. (2004) 'Defending Equality of Outcome', *Journal of Political Philosophy* 12: 1–19.

Pilling, D. (1990) *Escape from Disadvantage* (London: Falmer).

Pinchbeck, I. (1930/1990) *Women Workers and the Industrial Revolution, 1750–1850* (London: Virago).

Presser, H. B. (2003) *Working in a 24/7 Economy: Challenges for American Families* (New York: Russell Sage Foundation).

Reed, K. and Blunsden, B. (2006) 'Should Mothers Work? An International Comparison of the Effect of Religion on Women's Work and Family Roles', in P. Blyton et al. (eds.), *Work–Life Integration: International Perspectives on the Balancing of Multiple Roles* (New York: Palgrave Macmillan), 135–49.

Robinson, W. S. (1950) 'Ecological Correlations and the Behaviour of Individuals', *American Sociological Review* 15: 351–7.

Rosenfeld, R. A. and Kalleberg, A. L. (1990) 'A Cross-national Comparison of the Gender Gap in Income', *American Journal of Sociology* 96: 69–106.

Schoon, I. and Parsons, S. (2002) 'Teenage Aspirations for Future Careers and Occupational Outcomes', *Journal of Vocational Behaviour* 60: 262–88.

Sobel, M. E., De Graaf, N. D., Heath, A. and Zou Ying (2004) 'Men Matter More: The Social Class Identity of Married British Women, 1985–1991', *Journal of the Royal Statistical Society A* 167: 37–52.

Swim, J. K. (1994) 'Perceived versus Meta-analytic Effect Sizes: An Assessment of the Accuracy of Gender Stereotypes', *Journal of Personality and Social Psychology* 66: 21–36.

Szekelyi, M. and Tardos, R. (1993) Attitudes That Make a Difference: Expectancies and Economic Progress, Discussion papers of the Institute for Research on Poverty, University of Wisconsin.

Thörnqvist, C. (2006) 'Family-Friendly Labour Market Policies and Careers in Sweden – and the Lack of Them', *British Journal of Guidance and Counselling* 34: 309–26.

Walby, S. (1990) *Theorizing Patriarchy* (Oxford: Blackwell).

Walsh, M. R. (ed.) (1997) *Women, Men, and Gender: Ongoing Debates* (New Haven and London: Yale University Press).

West, C. and Fenstermaker, S. (1995) 'Doing Difference', *Gender and Society* 9: 8–37.

Westoff, C.F. and Ryder, N.B. (1977) *The Contraceptive Revolution* (Princeton: Princeton University Press).

Wright, E.O., Baxter, J. and Birkelund, G.E. (1995) 'The Gender Gap in Workplace Authority: A Cross-national Study', *American Sociological Review* 60: 407–35.

Zaretsky, E. (1986) *Capitalism, the Family and Personal Life* (New York: Harper & Row).

10 Gender inequality and the gendered division of labour

ROSEMARY CROMPTON

THE DIVISION OF LABOUR between men and women makes a major contribution to the material and social inequalities associated with gender. It has a dual aspect in that, first, most women still retain the primary responsibility for caring and domestic work (which is usually unpaid), and second, women (in aggregate) do not gain the same level of reward from participation in paid employment as do men (in aggregate). Up to the middle of the twentieth century, the 'male breadwinner' model of employment and family articulation was underpinned by extensive gender segregation in both the 'public' and 'private' spheres of work. Men in full-time employment received a 'family wage' and related benefits; women gained benefits, often indirectly, as wives and mothers. Since the 1950s and 1960s, however, technological change has brought with it the transformation of production systems, as well as developments in areas such as communications and financial intermediation that have contributed to the 'globalisation' of markets and cultures. Thus the world of paid work is in the process of being transformed. In parallel, the 'feudal' (Beck 1992) allocation of market work to men and domesticity to women has begun to break down as more women (particularly married women) have entered and remained in employment. Thus the 'male breadwinner' model began to unravel.[1] Efficient and widely available contraception led to widespread family limitation, and an increasing number of women found themselves 'available' for employment by their late thirties and early forties. From the 1960s onwards, 'second-wave' feminism began to have a

[1] There were, of course, variations in both the extent and nature of the 'breadwinner'model as between different countries and amongst different class groupings. Many working-class women have continued to 'work' to support their families, often through homeworking or casual work (Glucksmann 2000). Women without a male provider were, perforce, constrained to find employment of some kind.

growing impact, both on women as individuals and on social policy and legislation.

Women in the United States, Europe, Scandinavia and most other advanced industrial countries had secured rights to equal treatment in the sphere of employment by the 1970s. Nevertheless, despite this formal equality between men and women in relation to the market, major inequalities in employment between men and women still persist in practice. The structure of employment is still characterised by occupational segregation (that is, the concentration of men and women into different occupations), and there remains a substantial gap between men's and women's pay and incomes. Women (in the USA) pay a wage penalty for motherhood that has been estimated at between 5 and 7 per cent per child (Waldfogel 1997; Budig and England 2001). In part, the income gap is itself a consequence of occupational segregation, as 'women's' jobs – such as nursing, care and secretarial work – tend to be not as well paid as 'men's' jobs, such as skilled craft occupations. Women are also more likely to work part-time, and are more likely to take employment breaks, than men. Another contributory factor to women's inequality in the sphere of paid work lies in the fact that, even when women enter the same occupations as men, more often than not they fail to rise through organisational and professional hierarchies.

Any explanation of women's persisting inequalities in the sphere of employment is bound to be complex. In this chapter, one of our aims will be critically to examine explanations that assert that these inequalities are an outcome of individual and family choices or 'preferences'. It will be argued that preference-based explanations rest upon an essentialist view of gender, despite an overt embrace of 'change'. Changes in gender relations have indeed taken place, and it is important that they are recognised. Most importantly, institutions that were developed on the basis of 'male breadwinner' assumptions require modification. Amongst the most important of these institutions are state welfare regimes, which are widely seen to be in need of modification and reform. An influential recent contribution (Esping-Andersen 2002) has placed the issue of women's employment at the centre of suggested policy reforms. However, this commentary also assumes that the majority of women will 'choose' to give priority to family care, and as a consequence a modified breadwinner model is effectively endorsed.

In this chapter, it is argued that such a model would be associated with continuing gender inequality. However, the answer is not to reject the importance of preference and/or choice as a consequence of this conclusion, but rather to continue with the task of addressing the context within which choices are made and preferences exercised. This will require an examination of the outcomes of recent changes in the employment relationship itself.

Choice and 'preference'

As 'preference theory' is the subject of another chapter of this book (see Hakim, chapter 9), only the briefest of outlines will be given here. Hakim argues that the equal opportunities and contraceptive revolutions have made women able to choose between the alternatives of family work and employment. As a consequence of these 'genuine choices' that are open to them, three groups of women, characterised by different 'lifestyle preferences', may be identified. These are work-centred women, for whom employment is a priority, adaptive women, who combine employment and family work without giving a fixed priority to either, and home- or family-centred women, who give priority to home and family life. These categories are also to be found amongst the male population, but fewer men are 'home-centred' or 'adaptive'. 'Preference theory' rests upon the identification of 'preference categories' that vary in their distribution between men in aggregate and women in aggregate. Thus the explanation of these variations is key to the theory.

Here Hakim draws upon the work of Goldberg (1993), who argues that male hormones such as testosterone are a major source of sex differences in motivation, ambition and behaviour (Hakim 2004: 4; see also Hakim 2000: 258–62).[2] Thus men (in aggregate) are more aggressive and competitive than women in the world of employment, and: 'Women accept hierarchy so long as it is men who are in positions of power and authority. Male dominance is accepted, as Goldberg argued; female dominance goes contrary to sex-role stereotypes and is unwelcome, uncomfortable, and frequently rejected'

---

[2] Hakim also refers to theories of patriarchy (see Walby 1990; Hartmann 1976), as well as to neoclassical economic theories (e.g. Becker 1991) in developing her arguments.

(Hakim 2004: 110). Hakim argues that her theory is 'unisex', and thus not biologically essentialist (Hakim 2004: 16) in that a minority of men are 'home-centred'. However, this argument is not persuasive. As biological gender essentialists are careful to argue, they do not claim that their theories identify characteristics that apply to 'all women' or 'all men' (Baron-Cohen 2004; see also chapter 4), but they do not seek to reject the 'essentialist' label.[3] However, this chapter is not primarily concerned to explore gender essentialism as such, but rather to focus on the issue of 'choice'. Hakim argues that in societies that have achieved the new 'choice' scenario for women (the USA, Britain and the Netherlands), the pattern of women's employment (and its attendant inequalities) is primarily determined by the choices that they have made (Hakim 2004).

'Preference theory' has been extensively criticised (Ginn et al. 1996; Crompton and Harris 1998). These criticisms fall into two broad categories: (a) a failure conclusively to establish stable categories of different 'types' of women (Procter and Padfield 1998; McRae 2003), and (b) the priority given to 'choice' over contextual constraints in Hakim's theory (Devine 1994). Here we will not directly engage with these wider criticisms, but rather we will examine some of the underlying assumptions of 'preference theory', as well as the consequences of accepting these assumptions.

As we have seen, it can be argued that 'preference theory' is essentialist in that aggregate differences between men and women are seen as being, to a considerable extent, the outcome of sex differences in levels of testosterone. These biochemical differences between males and females are then linked to sex-related behavioural characteristics in employment. Whether women and men are 'really' the same or different is a topic that has been endlessly debated, both by feminists and by others. Gender essentialists argue that the attributes specific to each sex are of an intrinsic nature closely associated with physical, physiological or psychological differences. Thus the perceived differences between men and women are 'natural' (Crompton and

---

[3] 'I would weep with disappointment if a reader took home from this book the message that "all men have lower empathy" or "all women have lower systematising skills". Hopefully, I have made clear that when we talk about the female brain or the male brain, these terms are short for psychological profiles based upon the average scores obtained when testing women as a group, or the average scores obtained when testing men as a group' (Baron-Cohen 2004: 183).

Lyonette 2005). For millennia, women were regarded as the 'natural' inferiors of men: 'It is thus clear that there are *by nature* free men and slaves, and that servitude is agreeable and just for the latter … Equally, the relation of the male to the female is *by nature* such that one is superior and the other inferior, one dominates and the other is dominated' (Aristotle, cited in Dahrendorf 1969). As Dahrendorf argues, this kind of argument renders impossible a sociological treatment of inequality, as that which exists 'by nature' does not have to be explained or challenged.

Early feminists contested this notion of women's 'natural' inferiority, but found themselves faced with what Pateman (1989) has described as 'Wollstonecraft's dilemma'. That is, whilst demanding equal rights to citizenship with men, women also insisted that *as women* they had specific needs and talents, linked to their capacity for reproduction, and that these should be recognised. As ever, sexual difference was immediately elided into gender stereotypes, and during the nineteenth century women (or rather, wives and mothers) were increasingly seen as representing the societal embodiment of humane and communal values, as uniquely moral and selfless beings, devoted to the welfare of their families (Williams 1991). In the twentieth century, 'difference' feminists argued that, in contrast to men, women are characterised by a superior 'ethic of care', undervalued in a 'masculine' world but nevertheless necessary for human survival (Gilligan 1982; Tronto 1993).

However, as feminists have always realised (hence Wollstonecraft's dilemma), an emphasis on 'difference' can serve to undermine claims to gender equality. If women claim to be the equals of men, then, so the argument goes, they are constrained to be 'like men'. If women claim special treatment on the grounds that they are *women*, then they cannot claim to be the equals of men. Thus the pairing of 'equality' and 'difference' might seem to present an impossible choice: 'If one opts for equality, one is forced to accept the notion that difference is antithetical to it. If one opts for difference, one admits that equality is unattainable' (Scott cited in Pateman 1992: 17). However, as Lister (1997: 12) has argued, the juxtaposition of 'equality' and 'difference' is neither logical nor legitimate: 'Equality and difference are not incompatible; they only become so if equality is understood to mean sameness.' The opposite of equality is not difference, but inequality. Furthermore, as Williams (2000) has argued, two logically separate issues have often been conflated in these discussions. First, whether men and women are *really* 'the same' or 'different', and second, whether the biological differences between men and women mean that they should be treated differently in policy terms (for example, in respect of maternity leave). Thus one might not hold to the view that women alone are uniquely nurturing, but nevertheless support policies specific to women's maternity-related needs.

Although Hakim is certainly not engaging in the debates relating to 'difference' feminism, her argument has some similarities with the issues it generates in that she suggests that the majority (that is, 'home-centred' together with 'adaptives') of women are innately programmed to give priority to their families (rather than employment) in some way or another. Hakim's work is therefore open to interpretations similar to those faced by 'difference' feminists. If, because of their nature, women choose to behave in a manner different from men in respect of employment, then can the outcomes of this behaviour be described as 'unfair' even if they are unequal? We should not be surprised, therefore, to find that gender essentialism is often found linked to neoliberal economic and political thinking, as it neatly resolves a potential logical contradiction. It might be argued that if all individuals are to be seen as free to make choices (a basic tenet of neoliberal thinking), then why should a particular category of individuals (i.e. women) be constrained in their choices (i.e. traditionalism in gender roles would limit 'choice' in employment). However, this contradiction is resolved if it is asserted that the differences between men and women are 'natural' and that the choices made by women are in accordance with this 'nature' and therefore not constrained by dominant (male) norms and/or inequalities of condition.

Recent developments in both politics and social theory would also give broad support to the development of policies responding to 'preferences' that allow for individual 'choices'. Social theorists have argued that contemporary societies are increasingly 'individualised', and that 'choice' has assumed a greater significance than hitherto: 'The contemporary individual ... is characterised by choice, where previous generations had no such choices ... he or she must choose fast as in a reflex' (Beck and Beck-Gernsheim 2002; Lash 2002: ix). Political neoliberalism argues for market deregulation and the supremacy of untrammelled 'choice' in the conduct of human affairs. Thus, as O'Neill (1999: 85) has argued, there has been something of a 'convergence of a postmodern leftism with neoliberal defences of the market'. An emphasis on the reflexive individual and a focus on individual identities rather than collective actions and outcomes has many resonances with neoliberalism, and the promotion of individual rights and recognition meshes well with the arguments of those who have criticised the way in which collective provision has 'disempowered' individuals. As others have argued, however, there are powerful arguments against the development of policies that primarily rest on individual 'choice' (Nussbaum 2000). In particular, individual preferences (and thus choices) are always socially embedded and constrained, and may be shaped by unjust background conditions, as well as by habit and engrained normative assumptions. As Robeyns argues in chapter 3 of this book, normative gender stereotypes may be seen as making a major contribution to gender injustice. 'Preference deformation' may result in individuals making the 'wrong' choices as far as their own welfare is concerned (e.g. a dutiful wife who chooses to remain with a physically abusive husband). However, as noted above, the problem of preference deformation is sidestepped if it can be assumed that 'preferences' are innately associated with a particular category, or sex, of person.

There are a number of reasons, therefore, for treating Hakim's 'preference theory' with considerable caution. In developing 'preference theory', she makes a number of other claims that should also be addressed. Her criticisms of the use of indices of occupational segregation as a measure of gender inequality are well taken; it is not a particularly appropriate measure (Blackburn, Jarman and Brooks 2000).[4] However, rather more care should be exercised in making cross-national comparisons (see Crompton and Lyonette 2006). For example, it is likely that women earn more than men in Swaziland because able-bodied Swazi men are employed outside Swazi borders, rather than because Swazi women are out-performing Swazi men in competition for the same jobs (see Hakim, chapter 9). Her argument that family friendly policies generally *reduce* gender equality in the

---

[4] Blackburn et al. (2000) argue that segregation indices are not adequate as measures of gender inequality, and that gender pay equality may best be achieved via the implementation of policies that would reduce wage differentials in society as a whole. The Scandinavian example, where the gender wage gap is low but indices of segregation are high, provides an empirical demonstration of this argument.

workforce raises the continuing problem of deciding on appropriate cross-national measures of gender inequality. For example, the proportion of women in managerial occupations is likely to be higher in countries where the proportion of jobs classified as 'managerial' is also high (such as the USA), and lower where the proportion of jobs classified as 'managerial' is relatively low (such as Germany). Thus would a comparison of proportions between the two countries really be comparing like with like? As Hakim herself has acknowledged (2004: 172), we should not be particularly surprised if a nationally low level of female labour-force participation is associated with a smaller gender pay gap, as these smaller female workforces are likely, on average, to be better educated and qualified than the male workforce in the countries concerned.

These kinds of problems suggest that single-item measures should be used with caution in discussions of gender inequality. Korpi (2000) has employed a number of different measures in his comparative assessment of the impact of state policies on both class and gender inequalities. He found that levels of gender inequality are lowest in 'encompassing' welfare states providing high levels of dual earner family supports (the Nordic states). These states are also characterised by high levels of women's employment. Conservative (or corporatist) welfare regimes providing general family supports, directed at the nuclear family, tend to be associated with relatively high levels of gender inequality, and low levels of women's employment (given that social and employment protections are directed at the male breadwinner/provider in such regimes; see Esping-Andersen 2002). Basic security or 'liberal' regimes (lacking in either dual earner or general family supports) tend to be associated with moderate levels of gender inequality, and relatively high levels of women's employment (although high levels of class inequality), given that there are relatively few barriers to women's employment in the labour markets of such regimes.

There is, therefore, evidence available that suggests that 'dual earner' or 'family friendly' policies can serve to enhance gender equality. Nevertheless, as Korpi's analysis also suggests, family supportive policies directed at women within the nuclear family context may not contribute to women's equality as they will tend to reinforce a gender traditional division of labour, even if they are ostensibly gender neutral. In a similar vein, if it is mainly women who take up 'family friendly' employment options then this, too, is likely to perpetuate gender inequality in employment, as 'family friendly' career options are not usually associated with career progression or success (Crompton, Dennett and Wigfield 2003). These kinds of considerations, of course, are at the core of 'equality' feminism's ambivalence in respect of 'difference' or 'welfare' feminism. We will return to this issue at the end of this chapter.

Women's employment and welfare states

State policies, therefore, have been demonstrated to have a considerable impact on gender inequality. An influential text (Esping-Andersen 1990) exploring the impact of state policies was initially subject to extensive feminist criticisms, largely because Esping-Andersen's original analysis did not include the unpaid 'welfare' provided by women in the home (Lewis 1992). However, his most recent work (Esping-Andersen 2002) does address the topic of women's equality. Esping-Andersen has argued for the need for a 'new gender contract' in the building of 'new welfare states' that will reflect new social realities. Modern (European) welfare states, he argues, are in crisis because of a series of exogenous 'shocks' – including an ageing population, economic globalisation that brings with it the reduction of social benefits and pressure on wages in order to enhance competitiveness, and growing family instability. As he argues, it would seem that, therefore, 'if, as in most of Europe, welfare states are committed to uphold existing standards of equality and social justice, the price is mass unemployment; to reduce unemployment, Europe appears compelled to embrace American-style deregulation' (Esping-Andersen 1999: 3).

Thus Esping-Andersen argues that women's employment is the most important element in any attempt to address the crisis of the modern welfare state and indeed 'women are the vanguard force of change in the new economy' (Esping-Andersen 2000: 759). If women's employment increases, then the demand for services (no longer supplied by the stay-at-home woman) will rise, thus creating more employment. Rising employment will increase or maintain levels of taxation, allowing for the long-term maintenance of benefit levels. In order for this 'win–win' scenario to be successful, he argues, it is important that services are no longer provided within the family, as in, for example, conservative (or 'familialist') welfare states such as Germany or Spain. In order to make services more affordable, there will have to be some downward pressure on wages ('Conservative' job protections make the cost of services in continental Europe high; see Esping-Andersen 1999: 113). Moreover, Esping-Andersen argues that modern welfare states must refocus their priorities away from the protections associated with the breadwinner model (such as employment status protection and pension maintenance) and towards those most in need. Those most in need are dual earner families with young children (on whom the future of welfare ultimately depends) and the young (poorly educated) unemployed. This refocusing of priorities, he argues, must also address the problems of entrapment that are found in liberal regimes – notably because of poverty in childhood and low-wage, low-skill jobs in adulthood (or no jobs at all). 'Guarantees against immobility' need to be introduced by the removal of risks associated with marital instability and low skills. These include support for families of all kinds, including universally available childcare provision, and enhanced training and educational provision.

'Gender equality', therefore, has become 'the lynchpin of any post-industrial equilibrium' (Esping-Andersen 2002: 6). Some of Esping-Andersen's prescriptions, for example the provision of universal and affordable childcare, have been a central aim of feminist struggles for many years. However, in a number of other respects, it may be suggested that Esping-Andersen's analysis and prescriptions for economic regeneration and welfare state reform will serve to perpetuate gender inequality as well as being antithetical to work–life articulation. For example, he argues that an increase in the sharing of domestic work by men (particularly childcare) would simply encourage family-based service provision and therefore not make a contribution to employment generation. For similar reasons, any reductions in working hours would also increase the likelihood of family self-servicing, and therefore a reduced hours or employment sharing strategy (such as the 35 hour week in France) is not necessarily positive as far as job creation is concerned (Esping-Andersen 2000, but see Bishop 2004). However, long hours of employment work within dual earner households do not make a positive contribution to work–life 'balance'. Moreover, as women predominate in the kinds of service sector jobs for which wage reductions are being advocated by Esping-Andersen, any such reductions would reinforce material inequalities between men and women (thus reinforcing the 'rational' choice made by men in partnerships to put their efforts into market work rather than care work).

A further questionable assumption made by Esping-Andersen is that policy may be guided by *women's* (not men's) 'preferences', as Hakim has argued (Esping-Andersen 2002: 72–3). Most women, he argues, aim for a dual role combination of employment and motherhood (Hakim's 'adaptives'). Thus equity – or fairness – will be achieved by a combination of institutional supports (most particularly, universal childcare) that facilitate this combination, together with the availability of 'mother' (note not 'father') 'friendly' employment. He draws on the example of the Nordic countries, which have been extremely successful in drawing mothers into employment as a consequence of high levels of childcare provision as well as the creation of 'mother-friendly' job opportunities in the public sector (Esping-Andersen 2002: 76). One consequence of this combination, however, is high levels of occupational segregation in the Nordic countries, where women as employees are concentrated in the 'public ghetto'.[5] Therefore, as Esping-Andersen notes, gender neutrality or equality in employment has not been achieved (although the gender wage gap in the Nordic countries is relatively low).

As we have seen, whether or not indexes of occupational segregation are appropriate as measures of gender inequality is itself a debatable point. For the moment, however, we would note that this preference-based approach takes the gender division of labour between market and caring work as being an unproblematic 'given', and it is assumed that it is women who desire dual roles, not men. 'Preferences', as argued in the previous section of this chapter, are a dangerous guide to policy given that they are liable to be shaped by habit, low expectations and unjust background conditions. Women may often seek 'mother friendly' employment given their conventionally assigned

---

[5] Esping-Andersen's major preoccupation here is with the question of fertility. The supports provided for mothers' employment in the Nordic countries have resulted in the maintenance of fertility rates. In contrast, in the conservative, familialist, welfare states (e.g. Italy, Spain), where employed mothers have few supports, fertility rates have fallen dramatically, and people are having fewer children than they would prefer. During the 1990s recession, and cutbacks in 'mother friendly' public sector employment in Sweden, fertility rates fell, particularly amongst less educated women.

caring responsibilities and the enduring power of the ideology of domesticity. 'Mother friendly' employment may thus be 'preferred', but it is at least arguable that women might actually 'prefer' *not* to have to make a 'choice' between marginalised 'mother (or family) friendly' employment and 'standard worker' mother (or family) unfriendly employment. As Esping-Andersen (2002: 91) observes, the marginal preference of a competitively exposed firm would, if costs were equal, favour male workers over (protected) female employees. Moreover, 'Everywhere, the greater risk associated with female employees would spur a rational manager to favour men when promoting employees to higher echelon functions' (91).

Contemporary discussions of welfare state reform advocate a move away from a 'male breadwinner' and towards a 'citizen worker' model (Lewis 2002). However, as Lewis argues, the kind of change in welfare states that is being advocated by current reformers – that is, of 'recasting the central work/welfare relationship in order to promote labour market activation and "make work pay" ' (Lewis 2002: 333) is not, in practice, being accompanied by the kinds of changes needed to address properly the question of the work of care. Esping-Andersen does advocate universal childcare provision, but this is a necessary, but not sufficient, answer to the problem of gender inequality, as can be seen in the example of the Nordic countries discussed above. Children need to be delivered to and collected from day care, and day care schedules tend (unavoidably, as day care workers have homes and families too) to be rather rigid and not always responsive to the demands of new forms of flexible working. Unpaid caring suffers from Baumols' 'cost disease' (Esping-Anderson 1999: 56) for the same reasons as paid service employment, in that it often cannot be provided in a shorter time period without reducing the quality of the care.

Moreover, as we shall argue, the changes brought about by the development of 'high-commitment' (or 'high-performance') management strategies have brought about increases in work intensity and working hours that will have a negative impact on capacities for work–life articulation amongst both men and women, particularly in dual earner households. Gallie (2002: 97) has demonstrated that across Europe, there has been a 'sharp intensification of work effort, posing serious risks of work stress and tension between work and family life'. 'High-commitment' and 'high-performance' management strategies have come about in part because of the perceived need for social engineering in order to moderate workplace conflicts, as well as in order to increase organisational competitiveness and maximise employee integration. Co-operative, high-performance work systems have increased work intensity, particularly in competition-driven, private sector employment.

Addressing the question of care within a gender equality framework, therefore, means not only the provision of alternative (i.e. non-family) care arrangements, but also facing up to the realities of contemporary workplace developments that would seem to be making employment 'carer-unfriendly' for both men and women. Esping-Andersen, in his discussions of welfare state reform, has placed much emphasis on the need to create the circumstances in which individuals can avoid 'entrapment' in either poverty or low-level employment – or even no employment at all. However, policy proposals based on women's assumed 'preferences' for care – even via the 'dual roles' model – make it unlikely that women can avoid the 'entrapment' of responsibilities for caring work. The goal of gender equality is indeed an ambitious one, but our discussion will suggest that it is unlikely to be achieved unless something is done about the nature of employment itself. To continue to work with assumptions which are grounded in unconvincing theories about women's preferences is likely to perpetuate gender inequality.

Changes in employment

The 'standard' worker generated by the 'male breadwinner' model of employment and family articulation was available to work long hours, and give extra effort when required. The employment demands made of the 'standard worker' are not compatible with caring responsibilities. Capitalist organisational logic requires 'the abstract, bodiless worker, who occupies the abstract, gender neutral job (and) has no sexuality, no emotions, and does not procreate' (Acker 1990). Although the 'breadwinner' model may have been eroded, as Moen (2003: 3) has argued, there is increasingly a mismatch between the current reality, in which employees are increasingly likely to have caring responsibilities, and the work-hour and career policies and practices 'developed in response to the needs of the first (US) workforce of mostly young, mostly white working-class and middle-class men, located for the most part in (unionised) and white-collar jobs in the manufacturing sector in the first half of the twentieth century'. For not only has the gender composition of the workforce changed, but so has the nature of work itself. In 'western' countries, employment in manufacturing, that dominated employer–employee relations and their structuring for much of the twentieth century, has increasingly been replaced by employment in services of all kinds.

As argued above, developments in state welfare regimes can play a central role in facilitating adaptations to the new realities. States may also legislate in respect of employment relations, most particularly by introducing national controls on hours of work (Fagan 2002). Empirical research has demonstrated that working hours are one of the most significant factors affecting individual capacities successfully to combine paid employment and family life (White et al. 2003). However, many states, particularly those broadly embracing neoliberal economic policies (such as Britain and the USA), are reluctant to interfere in the employer's 'right to manage'. Britain, for example, negotiated a partial exemption from the EU Maastricht treaty, which introduced statutory maximum hours of work, and British men have amongst the longest hours of full-time work in Europe. Flexible working hours have obvious advantages in enabling individuals (usually women) to combine paid work and care work, and indeed are seen as a major strategy whereby the 'new realities' of the increased employment of women may be accommodated (COM 2001; DTI 2003). Flexible employment is also advantageous to employers, as it may be used to extend operating hours without paying an overtime premium. However, employment flexibility, which is concentrated amongst women, is not usually associated with individual success in the labour market, and flexible workers often tend to be in lower-level positions. As Purcell, Hogarth and Simm (1999) have argued, the 'uneasy reconciliation of work and family life in Britain has largely been achieved by means of a gender-segmented labour market and the part-time work of women'. Perrons' (1999) cross-national European study of flexible working in the retail industry demonstrated that in all of the countries studied (Britain, Sweden, France, Germany, Spain and Greece) it was women who worked flexibly, and took the major responsibility for caring work as well.

It is also the case that other recent developments in the world of employment are making paid employment rather more, not less, difficult to combine with family and caring responsibilities.

'High-commitment' (or 'high-performance') human resource practices, which seek to obtain a greater discretionary effort from employees, have been widely introduced in many contemporary organisations. These include the setting of targets, individual appraisals and training, and performance-related pay. Individualised career development is also central to high-commitment management practices. Rather than (as in the past) being sponsored through a fixed and stable bureaucratic hierarchy, individuals are encouraged to self-develop through what is often a fluid and changing organisational structure. However, considerable efforts are required in order to achieve a promoted position. The long hours working, and 'presenteeism', associated with managerial and professional jobs would be widely recognised. However, recent research has demonstrated that individuals who wish to be promoted even from relatively low-level jobs will also be faced with the requirement to work long hours in order to demonstrate 'promotability'. Promoted jobs, even at a relatively low level in the hierarchy, are rarely part-time (Grimshaw et al. 2002; Crompton et al. 2003). Even non-promoted employees (for example, in financial services), may find themselves constrained to work longer hours in order to meet their job targets. The 'employment in Britain' surveys (see Taylor 2001) demonstrate a sharp decline in satisfaction with working hours between 1992 and 2000. Satisfaction with working hours amongst managerial and professional men had declined from 36 to 16 per cent; and amongst unskilled men from 34 to 15 per cent (a similar decline was also found amongst women).

Neoliberal governments tend to rely on exhortation, rather than regulation, in their efforts to persuade employers to introduce positive 'family friendly' or 'work–life' policies. As has been noted above, flexible working can have many advantages for employers, is relatively costless to introduce, and indeed may be a source of saving (on pay for overtime, unsocial hours and break times). Other work–life policies, such as paid carers' days or parental leave, do apparently involve costs for employers. However, empirical research (Crompton et al. 2003) has demonstrated that parental and carers' absences (and indeed absences more generally) are not matched by the recruitment of extra staff, but rather are 'managed' by lower-level supervisors and managers. This means an increase in work intensity for those not taking leave (particularly supervisors – another feature making promotion an unattractive option for those with caring responsibilities). Particularly when workplaces are small, carers entitled to leave may be reluctant to take advantage of it, given their awareness of the likely impact of their absence on their colleagues at work.

Drago and Hyatt (2003: 143) have argued that the one type of work–family policy not found bundled with other work–family policies, or common in high-commitment workplaces, is childcare, because 'it is not profitable for employers to foot the bill for it'. Thus it is likely that 'markets will not induce an optimal mix of work–family policies in the absence of (government) intervention'. Employer-provided work–life policies will be of particular importance for employees in national contexts in which statutory protections and state supports for family life are relatively lacking, such as Britain and the United States (Canada, Australia and Japan are other examples of advanced and prosperous societies where statutory family supports are weak). However, cross-nationally, comparative data indicate that in countries with low levels of statutory support and regulation, 'voluntary' provision by employers of supportive work–life policies falls very far short of making up the 'deficit' in state supports (Evans 2001; OECD 2001). Countries with low levels of statutory supports, such as Britain, Ireland and the United States, also have relatively low levels of employer-provided supports as compared to countries such as Germany and Austria. The lowest incidence of extra-statutory employer-provided work–life policies is in fact found in the Nordic countries, where national provision is highest, and the state (as in, for example, the case of Sweden) has deliberately taken over a good deal of the caring role of the family. The highest level of employer support is found in countries where there are medium levels of statutory supports, such as Germany, Austria and the Netherlands.[6] Evans (2001: 30) has suggested that this pattern might indicate that 'national legislation tends to encourage private provision up to a point, and then tends to displace it'. Whatever the explanation of these trends, however, it remains the case that employees in countries with the lowest level of state supports – that is, countries broadly characterised by neoliberal labour market policies – appear to suffer

---

[6] France is a particular case here, lying around the middle of the distribution. Levels of childcare provision in France are historically high, as are state supports for working mothers, but France has not adopted the gender 'equality agenda' to the same extent as many other countries. (See Crompton and Le Feuvre 2000.)

a 'double disadvantage' as far as work–life policies are concerned. Universalistic national protections and provisions are weak, and governmental reluctance to interfere in the employers' 'right to manage' means that supportive policies remain at the discretion of employers.

Conclusions

In this chapter, it has been argued that the gendered division of labour in both the 'public' and the 'private' spheres remains central to the explanation and understanding of aggregate levels of material inequalities between men and women. As such, it resonates with Fraser's arguments that a politics of redistribution, as well as of recognition, is required in order to achieve gender equity, and a 'bifocal vision' (see Fraser, this volume) is required in order to address the problem. In this chapter, therefore, we have returned to the labour-centred problematic that characterised the earlier decades of second-wave feminist work. It has been insisted that the gender division of labour remains one of the major axes of gender inequality, and that the work of care, as necessary to human survival, is also 'work'. Women still remain largely responsible for the work of care, as Williams (2000) has put it: 'the ideology of domesticity did not die, it mutated'. As a consequence women find themselves at a disadvantage in the employment sphere. Moreover, a 'parity of esteem' for caring work in relation to market work has nowhere been established – indeed, this state of affairs may be seen as a persisting gendered inequality of recognition. Thus women continue to experience a double disadvantage in respect of the gendered division of labour.

However, as developed by Hakim, 'preference theory' sees this gendered division of labour as an outcome not of constraints but of 'choices', reflecting the existence of different types or categories of women characterised by different preferences for particular combinations of employment and family work. However, as Nussbaum (2000: 114) has argued, preference-based approaches may be:

rejected as a basis for fundamental political principles precisely because they [are] unable to conduct a critical scrutiny of preference and desire that would reveal the many ways in which habit, fear, low expectations and unjust background conditions deform people's choices and even their wishes for their own lives ... feminists who challenge entrenched satisfactions are frequently charged with being antidemocratic and totalitarian for just this way of proceeding.

'Preference theory', it has been argued in this chapter, supplies a powerful rationale for the gendered status quo and thus persisting material inequalities between men and women. A parallel has been drawn between 'preference theory' and 'difference' feminism, in that they face similar problems because an embrace of gender 'difference' might be seen as implying an implicit acceptance of unequal gender outcomes as a consequence of this 'difference'. The aim here is not to reignite, or continue with, arguments as to whether women are *really* different, or have different preferences, as compared to men. Rather, it has been argued that what is important is to re-examine and re-evaluate institutions and practices that were constructed on the basis of 'breadwinner' assumptions; that is, the contexts within which 'choices' are made. These institutions and practices need to be reconfigured in order to adapt to the changing realities of women's aspirations to equality, their employment patterns, and changes in the nature of employment itself.

In making these adaptations, the policies developed by nation-states will assume a major role. It has been demonstrated that those states that have developed the most supportive policies for dual earner families are also characterised by lower levels of gender and class inequality (Korpi 2000; see also Gornick and Meyers 2003). However, to the extent that state policies incorporate assumptions as to women's 'normal' preferences for care, these policies will also contribute to the perpetuation of gender inequality.[7]

Neoliberal states (such as the USA and Britain) are characterised by a relatively low level of dual earner family supports, as well as a marked reluctance to intervene in the employer–employee relationship. Recent empirical evidence suggests that contemporary developments in the management of employees, including the introduction of individualised, high-performance, high-commitment managerial strategies, are increasing levels of work intensity, thus making employment more

---

[7] Historically, conservative or 'corporatist' welfare states have made this assumption, and as Korpi (2000) demonstrates, gender inequality is relatively extensive in such countries (e.g. Germany).

family 'unfriendly', particularly for people who wish to be promoted. In these kinds of circumstances, it is not surprising that many women (and some men) with family responsibilities should 'choose' not to pursue promotion opportunities. It might be argued that what is required is for men to make a greater contribution to domestic work and caring – women still carry out more than twice as much domestic work as men, and much more than this in some countries (Crompton 2006). However, increasing employment intensity for men is not likely to enhance the amount of time and energy they have available to devote to caring and domestic work. 'Letting the market decide' is not likely to result in an increase in the time and resources directed at unpaid caring and family work, and as Gornick and Meyers (2003: 107) have argued: 'The results of the American experiment with market-based solutions (to the needs of dual earner families) have been calamitous for many American parents and children.' Individuals, of course, are 'free' to make their own arrangements, but the evidence reviewed in this chapter suggests that state supports for dual earner families, which would include interventions in the employment relationship such as controls over working-time practices, will be required in order to adapt both to the new realities of women's employment patterns and to women's aspirations to equality with men.

References

Acker, J. (1990) 'Hierarchies, Jobs, Bodies: A Theory of Gendered Organisations', *Gender and Society* 4, 2: 139–58.

Baron-Cohen, S. (2004) *The Essential Difference* (New York: Basic Books).

Beck, U. (1992) *Risk Society* (London: Sage).

Beck, U. and Beck-Gernsheim, E. (2002) *Individualization* (London: Sage).

Becker, G. (1991) *A Treatise on the Family* (Cambridge, MA: Harvard University Press).

Bishop, K. (2004) 'Working Time Patterns in the UK, France, Denmark and Sweden', *Labour Market Trends* March: 113–22.

Blackburn, R. M., Jarman, J. and Brooks, B. (2000) 'The Puzzle of Gender Segregation and Inequality: A Cross-National Analysis', *European Sociological Review* 16, 2: 119–35.

Budig, Michelle J. and England, Paula (2001) 'The Wage Penalty for Motherhood', *American Sociological Review* 66: 204–25.

COM (2001) 'Employment and Social Policies: A Framework for Investing in Quality' Brussels 20.6.2001.

Crompton, R. (2006) *Employment and the Family* (Cambridge: Cambridge University Press).

Crompton, R., Dennett, J. and Wigfield, A. (2003) *Organisations, Careers and Caring* (Bristol: Policy Press).

Crompton, R. and Harris, F. (1998) 'Explaining Women's Employment Patterns: "Orientations to Work" Revisited', *British Journal of Sociology* 49, 1: 118–36.

Crompton, R. and Le Feuvre, N. (2000) 'Gender, Family and Employment in Comparative Perspective: The Realities and Representations of Equal Opportunities in Britain and France', *Journal of European Social Policy* 10, 4: 334–48.

Crompton, R. and Lyonette, C. (2005) 'The New Gender Essentialism: Domestic and Family "Choices" and Their Relation to Attitudes', *British Journal of Sociology* 56, 4: 601–20.

(2006) 'Some Issues in Cross-national Comparative Research Methods: A Comparison of Attitudes to Promotion, and Women's Employment, in Britain and Portugal', *Work, Employment and Society* 20, 2: 389–400.

Dahrendorf, R. (1969) 'On the Origin of Inequality among Men', in A. Beteille (ed.), *Social Inequality* (Harmondsworth: Penguin), 17–44.

Department for Trade and Industry/HM Treasury (2003) *Balancing Work and Family Life: Enhancing Choice and Support for Parents* (London: HMSO).

Devine, F. (1994) 'Segregation and Supply: Preferences and Plans among "Self-Made" Women', *Gender, Work and Organization* 1, 2: 94–109.

Drago, R. and Hyatt, D. (2003) 'Symposium: The Effect of Work–Family Policies on Employees and Employers', *Industrial Relations* 42, 2: 139–43.

Esping-Andersen, G. (1990) *The Three Worlds of Welfare Capitalism* (Cambridge: Polity Press).

(1999) *Social Foundations of Postindustrial Economies* (Oxford: Oxford University Press).

(2000) 'Interview on Post-industrialism and the Future of the Welfare State', *Work Employment and Society* 14, 4: 757–69.

(2002) (with D. Gallie, A. Hemerijck and J. Myles) *Why We Need a New Welfare State* (Oxford: Oxford University Press).

Evans, J. (2001) *Firms' Contribution to the Reconciliation between Work and Family Life* (Paris: OECD Labour Market and Social Policy Occasional Papers).

Fagan, C. (2002) 'How Many Hours? Work-Time Regimes and Preferences in European Countries', in G. Crow and S. Heath (eds.), *Social Conceptions of Time: Structure and Process in Work and Everyday Life* (London: Palgrave Macmillan), 69–87.

Gallie, D. (2002) 'The Quality of Working Life in Welfare Strategy', in G. Esping-Andersen et al., *Why We Need a New Welfare State* (Oxford: Oxford University Press), 96–129.

Gilligan, C. (1982) *In a Different Voice* (Cambridge, MA: Harvard University Press).

Ginn, J., Arber, S., Brannen, J., Dale, A., Dex, S., Elias, P., Moss, P., Pahl, J., Roberts, C. and Rubery, J. (1996) 'Feminist Fallacies: A Reply to Hakim on Women's Employment', *British Journal of Sociology* 7, 1: 167–74.

Glucksmann, M. (1995) 'Why "work"? Gender and the "Total Social Organisation of Labour" ', *Gender Work and Organisation* 2, 2: 63–75.

Goldberg, S. (1993) *Why Men Rule: A Theory of Male Dominance* (Chicago: Open Court).

Gornick, J. C. and Meyers, M. K. (2003) *Families That Work* (New York: Russell Sage Foundation).

Grimshaw, D., Beynon, H., Rubery, J. and Ward, K. (2002) 'The Restructuring of Career Paths in Large Service Sector Organisations: "Delayering", Upskilling and Polarization', *Sociological Review* 50, 1: 89–115.

Hakim, C. (2000) *Work–Lifestyle Choices in the 21st Century* (Oxford: Oxford University Press).

(2004) *Key Issues in Women's Work* (London: GlassHouse Press).

Hartmann, H. (1976) '*Capitalism, Patriarchy and Job Segregation by Sex*', in M. Blaxall and B. Reagan (eds.), *Women and the Workplace* (Chicago: University of Chicago Press), 137–69.

Korpi, W. (2000) 'Faces of Inequality', *Social Politics* 7, 2: 127–91.

Lash, S. (2002) 'Introduction' to U. Beck and E. Beck-Gernsheim, Individualization (London: Sage).

Lewis, J. (1992) 'Gender and the Development of Welfare Regimes', *Journal of European Social Policy* 2, 3: 159–73.

(2002) 'Gender and Welfare State Change', *European Societies* 4, 4: 331–57.

Lister, R. (1997) 'Dialectics of Citizenship', *Hypatia* 12, 4: 1–21.

McRae, S. (2003) 'Constraints and Choices in Mothers' Employment Careers', *British Journal of Sociology* 53, 3: 317–38.

Moen, P. (ed.) (2003) *It's About Time: Couples and Careers* (Ithaca, NY and London: Cornell University Press).

Nussbaum, M. C. (2000) *Women and Human Development* (Cambridge: Cambridge University Press).

O'Neill, J. (1999) 'Economy, Equality and Recognition', in L. Ray and A. Sayer (eds.), *Culture and Economy after the Cultural Turn* (London: Sage), 76–91.

OECD (2001) 'Balancing Work and Family Life: Helping Parents into Paid Employment' Chapter 4, *Employment Outlook* (Paris: OECD).

Pateman, C. (1989) 'The Patriarchal Welfare State', in C. Pateman (ed.), *The Disorder of Women* (Cambridge: Polity Press), 179–209.

(1992) 'Equality, Difference, Subordination: the Politics of Motherhood and Women's Citizenship', in G. Bock and S. James (eds.), *Beyond Equality and Difference: Citizenship, Feminist Politics, and Female Subjectivity* (London and New York: Routledge), 17–31.

Perrons, D. (1999) 'Flexible Working Patterns and Equal Opportunities in the European Union', *European Journal of Women's Studies* 6: 391–418.

Procter, I. and Padfield, M. (1998) *Young Adult Women, Work, and Family: Living a Contradiction* (London and Washington, DC: Mansell).

Purcell, K., Hogarth, T. and Simm, C. (1999) *Whose Flexibility?* (York: Joseph Rowntree Foundation).

Taylor, R. (2000) 'The Future of Employment Relations'. www./eeds.ac.uk/esrcfutureofwork/

Tronto, J. (1993) *Moral Boundaries: A Political Argument for an Ethic of Care* (London and New York: Routledge).

Walby, S. (1990) *Theorizing Patriarchy* (Oxford: Basil Blackwell).

Waldfogel, J. (1997) 'The Effect of Children on Women's Wages', *American Sociological Review* 62: 209–17.

White, M., Hill, S., McGovern, P., Mills, C. and Smeaton, D. (2003) ' "High-Performance" Management Practices, Working Hours and Work–Life Balance', *British Journal of Industrial Relations* 41, 2: 175–95.

Williams, J. C. (1991) 'Domesticity as the Dangerous Supplement of Liberalism', *Journal of Women's History* 2, 3: 69–88.

(2000) *Unbending Gender* (New York: Oxford University Press).

11 | *The principle of equal treatment and gender*

Theory and practice

JUDE BROWNE

HERE IS A TROUBLING theoretical–empirical divide in contemporary approaches to equality and justice. All too often guiding principles prescribed by normative social and political theorists are divorced from the workable mechanisms available to political reformers. In turn, reformers are themselves all too often unclear as to what precisely should be held up as guiding objectives if they are to accomplish their purpose. The result is unsurprisingly often disappointing. Social equality between men and women, more commonly termed 'gender equality', is one such case and will be the general theme of this chapter.

Central to any account of equality is the principle of equal treatment, and it is this principle's translation into practice that I wish to consider specifically. The principle of equal treatment is a constitutive feature of justice and a minimum political standard throughout mainstream western political culture (Habermas 1983; Kymlicka 1990; Nagel 1991). It is understood as prescribing treatment of individuals as equals, i.e. with equal concern and respect (Dworkin 1977: 370) and not the often unacceptable notion that all individuals are indistinguishable and thus should be treated uniformly. To treat people *equally*, in this latter sense, might of course be appropriate according to the principle of equal treatment but is not necessarily so. This subtlety allows us to create institutions and structures which can administer the equal treatment of individuals who are alike in 'relevant and specified respects' in a way that is constructive and just. This is the understanding upon which the European Union has construed its particular 'Principle of Equal Treatment' (ETP) which is the bedrock of Community Law and all member states' equality and anti-discrimination laws.

Over the following pages, I will focus on the ways in which the ETP has been interpreted and implemented to ill effect, particularly in the context of British sex discrimination law. In so doing, I argue that, irrespective of establishing grand principles of justice and equality as intended objectives, the operational details of institutional attempts to implement those principles more often than not dilute our social and political goals to such an extent that they render them ineffective. By emphasizing the pervasive lack of fit between theory and practice, this chapter seeks to remind us that we should not rely solely on normative prescriptions in seeking solutions to problems, but also consider the all too often counter-productive details of implementation.

The first section of the chapter briefly calls into question the usage of the term 'gender' when thinking about how social and political goals of equality between men and women should be articulated. This is an ostensibly pedantic point but one which rewards closer scrutiny. The second section explains how the ETP underpins Britain's two major pieces of sex discrimination law, the Equal Pay Act and the Sex Discrimination Act. Despite their being orientated towards a seemingly straightforward objective – the equal treatment of men and women in relevant and specified respects – we can see that both Acts are far from effective agents of equality. The explicit claim here is that 'the devil is in the detail' of exactly how the principle of equal treatment is implemented. Following on from that, the third section points to perhaps a more fundamental problem with the interpretation of the principle of equal treatment, and this brings us to the question of what exactly should be considered 'relevant' in terms of which individuals should be treated equally. In focusing on 'specific rights' I illustrate how men and women are treated differently, and in the particular case of paid parental leave, I argue, treated unjustly on the basis of tacit assumptions about the respective capabilities of each sex. Furthermore, the spirit of the principle has probably been polluted with political and economic considerations, the ramifications of which are a major source of substantive inequality between men and women and one which is harmful to society both socially and economically. Thus, legislation designed to increase the well-being of relevant individuals has, somewhat ironically, delivered in part at least the opposite effect. This, as we shall see, is certainly true in the case of Herr Hofmann. (*Ulrich Hofmann v Barmer Ersatzkasse. Landessozialgericht Hamburg – Germany. Equal treatment for men. Case 184/83*).

A note on 'gender'

In thinking about the question of which people should be treated equally and in what relevant respect, I wish to make a point about the concept of gender itself. I suggest that to use 'gender' for the purposes of constructing particular social and political *goals*, such as equality and justice, is confusing. If we think back to the Introduction of this book where the concepts of sex and gender were set out, what would it really mean to pursue 'gender equality' or 'gender justice', or to eradicate the 'gendered pay gap'? To offer 'equality of gender' would presumably be to equalize the conditions of those pertaining to differing cultural codifications; to eradicate the 'gendered pay gap' would be to eradicate income differences between people who identify with, or are identified by, varying degrees of femininity or masculinity. This would be neither possible nor particularly desirable in the pursuit of any practical notion of societal justice. 'Gender' is not the relevant respect in which individuals should be rendered equal. 'Gender' is a description of people's characteristics and behaviours which may or may not be determined by their sex. Surely, our focus is better articulated as the eradication of *discrimination* based on a range of differences (sex, sexuality, gender characteristics, etc.) rather than, in effect, to suggest the actual pursuit of the equalization of socially constructed gender traits. This is not to deny the importance of 'gender' as a descriptive concept, nor should it be understood as a return to outdated crude categories of analysis; this corrective is only possible in the wake of the last three decades of gender analysis. The concept's merits are clear when we consider the prejudiced assumptions made about one's abilities and capabilities according to sex or sexuality. Indisputably, one can have culturally identified 'feminine' or 'masculine' traits, or differing sexual preferences irrespective of one's biology – and in this sense, the concept of gender is vitally different from traditional views on what it means in behavioural terms to be of a particular sex. But still, 'gender equality' as a societal goal is a problematic term and, given the ambiguity which surrounds it, I suggest that in prescribing policy designed to combat empirical problems such as the durable pay gap between men and women, we should abandon 'gender' as a way of labelling objectives of equality.

With this in mind, I hope to show, as a secondary observation, that those who discriminate, personally or institutionally, wittingly or unwittingly, base their judgements on stereotypes of sex, and it is on this view that I claim we should address the use of negative stereotypes rather than aim for 'gender equality'. The following sections incorporate this position in a demonstration of the systematically defective implementation of the principle of equal treatment.

The Equal Treatment Principle translated into practice: sex equality and sex discrimination laws

Closely refereed by the European Union, the evolution of sex equality legislation in Britain has long been a tumultuous process (see, for example, Fredman 1997; Deakin and Morris 1998; Meehan 1985; and on development of European Law, Hepple 1995, 2002). Nevertheless, we now have laws specifically designed to equalize the conditions and pay of men and women since the early 1970s. As British law currently stands, the primary approach to combating inequality in employment is determined by the Equal Treatment Principle (ETP), as defined by the European Union's Equal Treatment Directive (ETD) 2002/73/EC.[1]

The ETD's (Article 2) definition of the ETP is 'that there shall be no discrimination whatsoever on the grounds of sex either directly or indirectly by reference in particular to marital or family status'. Thus, under the Directive, discrimination is divided into two concepts: *direct discrimination*, 'where one person is treated less favourably on grounds of sex than another is, has been or would be treated in a comparable situation'; and *indirect discrimination*, 'where an

---

[1] All Member States of the EU are bound by Article 141 (formerly 119) of the EC which stipulates that 'each Member State shall ensure that the principle of equal pay for male and female workers for equal work or work of equal value is applied'. This directly applicable provision has been supplemented by directives on pay, employment and vocational training, and statutory social security, self-employment, and the burden of proof. UK law frequently has had to be amended so as to comply with EU law and with ECJ interpretations of EU law. Thus the previous ETD (76/207/EEC) was amended in 2002 and is relabelled as 2002/73/EC, and now also covers pay discrimination in addition to selection criteria, recruitment, promotion and training, working conditions, and dismissals, and brings sex discrimination law in line with that relating to race, religion or belief, sexual orientation and disability. See Equal Opportunities Review (2002) for detailed discussion of the implications relating to the amended Directive.

apparently neutral provision, criterion or practice would put persons of one sex at a particular disadvantage compared with persons of the other sex, unless that provision, criterion or practice is objectively justified by a legitimate aim, and the means of achieving that aim are appropriate and necessary'.

The original intent of this approach was to enforce 'blindness' to certain basic characteristics such as race or sex, so that one could not be discriminated against merely on these grounds. For example, since the 1990 Dekker case (*Elisabeth Johanna Pacifica Dekker v Stichting Vormingscentrum voor Jong Volwassenen (VJV-Centrum) Plus. Case C-177/88*), an employer is deemed to be in direct contravention of the ETP 'if he refuses access to employment, vocational training, promotion, or working conditions [or] ... refuses to enter into a contract with a female candidate whom he considers to be suitable for the job where such refusal is based on the possible adverse consequences for him of employing a pregnant woman'. The ETP, as defined by the ETD, underpins the two primary pieces of sex discrimination law in Britain: the Equal Pay Act and the Sex Discrimination Act.

'The devil is in the detail'

The following examples illustrate in detail how seemingly progressive pieces of legislation, designed to enact the ETP, are bogged down in counter-productive clauses which render them highly ineffective as agents of equality. Only through examining the details of enforcement can we really detect the problems of employing abstract theory without paying sufficient attention to practical mechanisms.

1970 Equal Pay Act (EqPA)[2]

To contextualize the function of this particular Act it is useful to note that the pay gap between men and women in Britain has stood at approximately 18 per cent for full-time workers for over twenty years and a staggering 40 per cent for part-time workers[3] (EOC 2005a: 1).

---

[2] As amended of 2005.

[3] Some 46 per cent of the workers in the British labour market are women and 44 per cent of these work part-time (EOC 2005a: 1).

The EqPA was designed to eradicate unequal rates of pay and contractual conditions between individual men and women in comparable employment. Any person bringing forward a complaint (the complainant) of unequal pay under the Act is required to find an *actual* comparator of the opposite sex in the same employing institution. When the Act was introduced in 1970,[4] it required 'equal treatment' for men and women only in two distinct situations: either when employed in 'like work' which is defined as 'the same' or 'broadly similar', or when employed in work that had been rated as equivalent by a job evaluation conducted by the employer (EqPA 1970. s. 1(2) (a)). However, employers were not obligated to undertake such evaluations. With little incentive to monitor the inequities between men's and women's pay, comparisons of individuals' terms of employment were less than reliable (Hepple 1984). In response to a ruling by the EU, the UK enacted the 'Equal Value Amendment' (EVA) in 1983 so that, since then, the Act applies to a situation where there is work of 'equal value', thereby widening the interpretative scope of comparability.

However, despite the 1983 amendment, the problem of how to motivate less than willing employers to investigate pay differentials remained unsolved. Indicative of this difficulty are the unsavoury results revealed by extensive research by the Equal Opportunities Commission (EOC), which investigated the usage of internal pay audits within British organizations (see Neathey, Dench and Thomson 2003). While the majority of employers (54 per cent of large and 67 per cent of medium-sized employers) maintained they had comprehensive measures in place to ensure that women and men received equal pay, they had no plans to conduct pay audits. (One can only wonder what were considered 'comprehensive measures'.) Only 18 per cent of large employers and 10 per cent of medium-sized employers have actually carried out any sort of pay review and, where pay gaps were found, they were often considerable, in some cases as much as 40 per cent. Even armed with the relevant information, a complainant can only hope to establish 'work rated equivalence' under the EqPA if both her job and the job of her comparator were

---

[4] Although the EqPA was ratified in 1970, it was not implemented until 1975, primarily in order 'to give employers time to adjust' (Deakin and Morris 1998: 546).

rated as equivalent under the *same* employer review (IRS Employment Review 2004a).[5] Perhaps the most objectionable finding, however, was that a fifth of all employers (22 per cent) explicitly prohibited employees from sharing with each other any information relating to the details of their earnings. This not only means that it is extremely difficult to ascertain whether one is being paid a lower rate than the 'going market rate', but also precludes the possibility of formally identifying a comparator, even if relevant information has been shared 'illicitly'.[6] It seems a little ironic, then, that even Patricia Hewitt (Secretary of State for Trade and Industry and Minister for Women from 1999 to 2005) said of this particular EOC report, 'this research reveals a depressing snapshot that shows too many workplaces are still stacked against women fulfilling their true earning potential'.[7]

As I show elsewhere (Browne 2004, 2006), time after time, employers and in particular managers responsible for recruitment and promotion make a priori stereotypical assumptions about women's capacity for productive output. Repeatedly it was disclosed in anonymous interviews that there was a 'rational calculus' for recruiters to favour men for certain higher-status positions because

---

[5] The term 'same employer review' stretches to 'single source', that is, the same employer irrespective of out-sourcing, etc. See *A. G. Lawrence and Others* v *Regent Office Care Ltd, Commercial Catering Group and Mitie Secure Services Ltd* (Case C-320/00).

[6] Since 6 April 2003 individuals who believe that they may not have received equal pay are allowed to request information from their employers (see *Equal Opportunities Review* 117, May 2003, p. 13 and p. 22). Previously one had to initiate tribunal proceedings to get the employer to disclose pay data by way of discovery. However, under the new procedure the employer *is allowed to rely on confidentiality* as a ground for refusing to disclose. The new procedure is mainly intended to avoid unnecessary proceedings by allowing women to see whether there is a likely comparator. However, it does not avoid the need for mandatory pay audits which would compel the employer to initiate change.

What remains to be seen is whether applicants will be able to use the new ETD wording (2002/73/EC) to tackle pay discrimination that falls outside the scope of Article 141. That is, it is not yet clear whether it will allow claims using a hypothetical comparator rather than, as required by Article 141, an actual comparator. This is a problem exacerbated by high levels of horizontal segregation, whereby the majority of women tend to work in female dominated occupations.

[7] See EOC (2003) Employers must tackle complacency and secrecy on equal pay: Embargo: 00.124 March 2003 www.eoc.org.uk/Default.aspx?page=15167& lang=en.

of the assumption that women, whether mothers or non-mothers, would behave according to their 'gender', i.e. stereotypical characteristics which were often less valued than those of men. Invariably, these were judgements made irrespective of employees' experience or education.[8]

In light of this 'rational calculus', used consciously or unconsciously to predict the behaviour of each sex, it is not altogether surprising that there is a lack of enthusiasm actively to engage with the issue of pay inequities between men and women. This view is advocated by the likes of Becker (1981, 1985, 1991) and Posner (1992), both of whom build their arguments on economic human-capital-based explanations of pay differentials. These perspectives I consider essentially counterproductive to the pursuit of substantive equality between men and women. This is best illustrated by elucidating the unhelpful circularity of human-capital-based claims: *Women have less human capital and thus must be less productive than men. How do we know this? Because women are paid less than men in a market that reflects productivity by level of remuneration. Why are they paid less than men? Because they have less human capital and thus must be less productive – how do we know this?*

And the cycle of logic goes on (see Browne 2006). On this view, there is little need for further investigation as to why women are paid on average lower wages than men. It is assumed that the market is perfect in that it remunerates according to productivity whilst not taking into account the many reasons why someone might be working part-time or in a lower-status occupation irrespective of their human-capital endowments (or if they do have lower human-capital levels why this is the case in practical terms). Certainly it is not a helpful logic by which to generate the will of employers to investigate the pay differentials in any depth (Browne 2006). Unfortunately, however, it is a predominant logic in the context of the labour market.

Overall, it would seem that the EqPA is far less effective than we might at first hope. But the EqPA's limitations do not end with failing to secure that investigative internal pay audits are carried out. Further

---

[8] See EOC (2005a) for contemporary educational statistics which show how girls are outperforming boys at school and represent 56 per cent of those in higher education for example.

procedural shortcomings of the EqPA, which diminish its impact on inequality, include the following:

1 The Act only establishes the right to contractual and pay equality with a specific comparator. Each case brought forward to tribunal is treated individually, and, if successful, does not technically apply to colleagues in the same position as the complainant.[9] Trade unions and the EOC are not able to take group or representative action on behalf of similarly affected individuals. Therefore, it can take years to achieve equal pay, and the wider impact of ensuring sex equality in this way may be seriously limited.

2 In cases where the tribunal has commissioned an investigation into a complainant's claims,[10] the independent panel appointed by the Advisory, Conciliation and Arbitration Service (ACAS) consists of only twelve part-time assessors. Thus it is not surprising that the assessment process is extremely lengthy and can take up to two years to complete. As Rubenstein poignantly remarks, 'Recent decisions of the European Court of Human Rights have made it clear that undue delay is a contravention of the right to a fair hearing under Article 6: justice delayed is justice denied. The government has been fortunate not to be taken to Strasbourg by an equal value complaint' (Rubenstein 2004: 23). This onerous procedure undoubtedly represents a significant disincentive for many potential complainants, particularly for those who are in low-paid, low-status positions and who also may feel insecure in their jobs.

---

[9] See note 6.

[10] Claims can be brought at any time during employment and within six months of leaving employment. As a result of the ECJ ruling on the *Preston v Wolverhampton Healthcare NHS Trust litigation* (Case C-78/98), the 1970 EqPA (Amendment) Regulations 2003 make it clear that, where there was a 'stable' employment relationship between the woman and her employer, the relevant limitation date for bringing an equal pay claim is six months after the end of the stable relationship. There are exceptions, such as when the woman 'is under a disability' or where the employer has deliberately concealed a relevant fact, in which case the six-month period will run from the date she discovered or could reasonably have discovered the fact. Also note that the 2003 Regulations limit the back pay that can be claimed, to six years in England and Wales and five years in Scotland (corresponding to the limits in each country for bringing contractual claims).

The EOC supports about 5 per cent of sex discrimination cases each year and trade unions have supported some major, high-profile cases. But there is no legal aid available to the majority of individual complainants who, even if successful in their claim, have to bear their own legal costs. Again, this will deter many individuals from bringing forward justified grievances, and this is an ironic characteristic of a justice system purportedly orientated towards those in lower-paid jobs.

The notion of 'proportional equality' is not currently recognized under the EqPA. To illustrate, while a complainant might be able to show that she was paid only 60 per cent of the comparator's wages, the tribunal could deem the complainant's job to be 'worth' 95 per cent of the comparator's job. Under the EqPA there would no grounds for awarding proportional compensation or for setting future proportional remuneration levels. The definition of equality under the EqPA must be *absolute*, irrespective of the degree to which someone is justifiably aggrieved. This form of injustice is a substantial contributor to the pay gap (vertical occupational sex segregation). Since the amendments to the ETD (2002/73), there has been some speculation as to whether the new wording might require that proportional equality be upheld in the future.[11] However, when translating the revised Directive into UK law, the Department of Trade and Industry (DTI) ignored this possibility, which, as Rubenstein notes, 'is rather disingenuous' (Rubenstein 2005: 23).

A defence mechanism available to the employer is that of 'material factors'. These factors may be legally accepted as 'justifiable', non-discriminatory causes of pay disparity between men and women. There are three types: 'labour market factors', 'organizational factors' and 'personal factors'. 'Labour market factors' may be invoked in the case of labour shortages, where higher wages may be offered and paid to employees in 'hard to fill' posts. An 'organizational factor' is 'a difference which is connected with economic factors affecting the efficient carrying on of the employer's business' (*Rainey* v *Glasgow Health Board*, 1987). For example, it may be within an employer's rights to restrict higher-paid shift work to full-time employees (the

---

[11] Article 3(1) of the amended Directive applies to 'employment and working conditions, including dismissals, as well as pay, as provided for in the Directive 75/117/EEC', which is the EPD. The EPD requires 'the elimination of all discrimination on grounds of sex with regard to all aspects and conditions of remuneration' for the same work or for work of equal value.

majority of whom might be male) as opposed to (predominantly female) part-time employees. Finally, 'personal factors' can be used to justify differential pay between the complainant and the comparator, based on the comparator's seniority, superior qualifications or greater productivity. In some cases, of course, these may well be useful ways of classifying acceptable exceptions to the rule. However, as several commentators have pointed out, 'material factors' (including 'personal factors') are open to wide and often dubious interpretations, which can become a fundamental stumbling block to many legitimate claims of injustice (see, for example, Hepple 1984; Rubenstein 1984; Fredman 1997; Deakin and Morris 1998). In a recent case,[12] the Employment Appeal Tribunal held that the employer was not required to produce specific justification for using 'length of service' as a criterion for paying a woman less than her longer-serving male comparators doing equivalent work. Jarman's (1992) research, echoed by the EOC (2005b), suggests that female complainants who have taken maternity leave face being ascribed lower 'merit of service', a factor invoked by the employer as a reason to pay women less than men.

There are problems of intelligibility. As Lord Denning pointed out, 'ordinary individuals who are affected by equal pay for work of equal value ought to be able to read and understand the Regulations. Not one of them would be able to do so. No ordinary lawyer would be able to understand them. The industrial tribunals would have the greatest difficulty and the Court of Appeal would probably be divided in opinion.'[13] Needless to say, it is inexcusable that an Act designed to protect the disadvantaged is unintelligible even to the advisors of those who need to rely upon it. Almost twenty years later, the EOC is still campaigning for the Government to implement changes to legislation making it more accessible.

The EqPA is retrospective rather than pre-emptive in its impact. Even where a complainant's case is successful, there is no legal mechanism in place to ensure that the employer ceases to engage in discriminatory practices. As we have seen, the motivation for employers to act pre-emptively is weak in the context of non-mandatory

[12] *Health & Safety Executive v Cadman* (IRS Employment Law Review, 2004a, pp 61–3).
[13] Lord Denning, House of Lords Debate (H.L. Deb.), vol. 445, cols. 901–2, December 5, 1983.

internal audits, and given the very small number of cases actually won by complainants and the low level of compensation that employers are forced to pay successful complainants. In 2003 the EqPA was amended, granting back-pay of up to six years, and in that year the median award for sex discrimination was £5677. While this is an improvement, it hardly serves as a stern warning to employers who contravene the law.

At first sight, then, the EqPA's intention and remit may *seem* logical and straightforward, and it may appear to represent an invaluable aid to those who experience the injustice of labour market exploitation. Yet, upon closer inspection, it is quite clearly infused with crude and unwarranted interpretations of 'equal treatment', and considerable disincentives to bring forward claims which render the Act's breadth of impact far from impressive. One need only refer to the pitiful success rate of complainants under the EqPA to bring home this point: between 1976 and 2000 a total of 12,934 complainant applications were made, but only 2540 managed to gain a hearing, and just 641 of these were successful. What is more, it is interesting to note that 25 per cent of tribunal claims end in complete victory for the employer (IRS Employment Review 2004b).

1975 Sex Discrimination Act (SDA)[14]

Unlike the remit of the EqPA (which only allows for claims of unequal pay and contractual terms), the SDA provides for a much more extensive assortment of claims against discrimination, including, for example, the areas of labour market recruitment, promotion and training, and termination of employment. Broadly speaking, the purpose of the SDA is to prohibit discrimination on the grounds of sex in employment, as well as in areas of education and the provisions of goods (facilities, services and premises to members of the public, and so forth). The Act is not all-embracing; for example, it does not cover those situations where it is considered essential that an employee should be of a particular sex in order to conserve decency or privacy in the workplace, or where one sex is eligible for a specific employment protective right, such as the right for female employees to claim maternity leave when pregnant.

---

[14] As amended of 2005.

Another problem is that of the burden of proof. Despite the EC Burden of Proof Directive (97/80) which shifts the burden of proof from the complainant to the employer when the complainant has, prima facie, a legitimate claim of unlawful discrimination, there is little evidence that it has become easier for complainants to win their cases of direct discrimination. In such cases, unreasonable behaviour by the employer (related to sex difference) should lead to a straightforward reversal of the burden of proof to the employer. However, proving indirect discrimination can still be very difficult, particularly since workplace statistics are held by the employer.[15]

In the end, therefore, the SDA contains many similar practical drawbacks to the EqPA, such as the lengthy assessment procedures and the lack of legal aid for complainants. Additionally, it is worth considering one further criticism of the SDA. Although complainants under the SDA, unlike the EqPA, are only required to provide a hypothetical comparator(s), the focus remains on individual disadvantage rather than group disadvantage. It does not automatically follow that a successful case secures the equal treatment of peers under the SDA.

Overall, it is evident that the effectiveness of the EqPA and the SDA as means with which to combat inequality is highly questionable. Furthermore, the sceptic might argue that their inept design appears to serve an altogether different purpose. It is plausible to claim that legislation equipped with more intrusive and coercive powers would prove intolerable to employers, who insist that such intervention unduly stifles the creative dynamics of the free market, which in turn is claimed to depress the national economy. Accordingly, the very best that can be expected from current arrangements is that the employer is called to award recompense, for it is rare that further punishment

---

[15] Note that under Section 7B of the 1970 EqPA the complainant has the right to ask his or her employer for information that would help to establish whether or not he or she had received equal pay for equal work in comparison to a worker of the opposite sex, and if not what the reasons are for this. See the Equal Pay Questionnaire introduced under the Employment Relations Act (2002) (the DTI website gives an example of the questionnaire at www.dti.gov.uk). In equal pay cases, once a difference in pay is shown between women and men doing work of equal value, the employer has to prove that the difference is genuinely due to 'material factors'. However, just how obligatory these questionnaires actually are and how effectively they are employed is debatable. See, for example, the case of *Sinclair Roche and Temperley and ors v Heard and anor.* EAT, 2004 IRLR 76.

will be administered, irrespective of the fact that such activities are unlawful. Consequently, it might be argued, the EOC's research on employer flexibility for parents indicates that over half the requests for changes to working arrangements were rejected and that around 30,000 working women who were refused alternative working arrangements were either dismissed, made redundant or forced to resign (EOC 2005b). (It is reported that only 2 per cent of employees who turned to their company's grievance procedures succeeded in getting their proposed working arrangements accepted.) In 2003, the government introduced the right to *request* flexible working arrangements for parents of children under the age of six (or eighteen if the child had a disability). There is no *automatic* right to flexible working arrangements under the new provision however, but it does serve as a reference point for those seeking to facilitate a work–life balance by changing their working arrangements. Whether or not this initiative provides sufficient incentive for employers to overcome their resistance to granting requests remains to be seen. I share therefore the sentiments of Fraser, Bryson and Crompton (see chapters 1, 2 and 10 of this volume) who all infer that the strength of one's claims to policy provisions should not be overestimated within legal systems servile to political and economic objectives.

The equal treatment principle translated into practice: specific rights

Moving beyond the two primary British sex discrimination Acts, we find more problems embedded within the interpretation of the ETP in relation to specific employment protection rights for parents ('specific rights'). Unlike either of the sex discrimination Acts, specific rights differ depending on the sex of the employee. It will be argued that despite being guided by normative objectives of equality and protection of individuals from discrimination, specific rights in Britain are accompanied by insufficient financial support and are thus rendered largely ineffective. Predominantly based on assumptions relating to gender roles, it is considered reasonable by the relevant adjudicating bodies to distinguish between men and women in terms of their apparent differing economic needs, as will be defined further on. This logic is obstructive, rather than a facilitation of relevant and justified sex equality.

The current array of 'specific rights' available in Britain relate to antenatal care[16] and to maternity leave, paternity leave and parental leave, accompanied with the right to return to one's original place of employment under protection against discrimination.

- Maternity Leave: Since 2003, state-provided standard (or 'ordinary') maternity leave in Britain stands at twenty-six weeks (including two weeks' compulsory protective leave).[17] This provision stipulates that mothers are entitled to 90 per cent of their usual employment earnings for the first six weeks, followed by twenty weeks at £106 (set in 2005), and a further twenty-six weeks of unpaid leave, eligibility pending.[18]
- Paternity Leave: Finally introduced in Britain in 2003 under EU pressure, this benefit provides two consecutive weeks of paid leave within fifty-six days of the birth of the child. The rate of statutory pay is akin to maternity leave *after* the first six weeks, £106 per week.[19]
- Parental Leave: In 1999, the EU Parental Leave Directive was implemented in Britain.[20] It offers parents of either sex thirteen weeks' leave for each child born after 15 December 1999, available until the child reaches the age of five.[21] As with maternity and

---

[16] Mothers have the right not to be refused paid leave on the grounds of keeping an appointment for antenatal care according to the ERA 1996 s.99. This specific right is not further considered here.

[17] Unless the woman works in a factory, in which case compulsory maternity leave is four weeks. See the Tailored Interactive Guidance on Employment Rights. See www.tiger.gov.uk.

[18] Those eligible for additional leave paid at £100 (or 90 per cent of earnings for the full twenty-six weeks if this is less than £106 a week) must have completed twenty-six weeks of continuous service with their employer by the beginning of the fourteenth week before the expected week of childbirth. Additional maternity leave starts immediately after ordinary maternity leave and continues for a further twenty-six weeks (unpaid). Under the Work and Family Bill 2006 there are plans to increase this period of leave from twenty-six to thirty-nine weeks.

[19] Or 90 per cent of earnings if less than £106. Fathers are entitled to paternity leave so long as they have been continuously employed with their employer for twenty-six weeks (ending the fifteenth week before the baby is due).

[20] Following Britain's eventual acceptance of the EU Social Chapter in 1999, after having rejected the Directive in 1994. The right to parental leave has been implemented in Britain under the Employment Rights Act 1999.

[21] The Directive advises that parents should be offered leave up to their child's *eighth* birthday, but includes a clause allowing Member States to adjust the length of provision.

paternity leave, the right to return to work after parental leave is guaranteed by law. However, Britain's adoption and interpretation of this Directive excluded the statutory provision of *paid* leave and bestowed employers with the power to decide exactly when leave should be taken.

The undoubted improvements introduced by the Labour Government notwithstanding, Britain still offers some of the lowest specific parenting benefits in Europe. In terms of maternity leave, for example, pregnant women in Luxemburg are entitled to sixteen weeks of maternity leave at full pay; in Denmark, twenty-eight weeks at 90 per cent of pay; in Italy twenty-eight weeks at 80 per cent of pay with an optional six months during the child's first year at 30 per cent of pay; in Germany, fifteen weeks at full pay; in France, sixteen weeks at 84 per cent of earnings; in Belgium, thirty days at 82 per cent and then 75 per cent for a further fifteen weeks. The assumption underlying the meagre British provision of six weeks at 90 per cent of average earnings is that women are able to depend on a second wage during the remaining twenty weeks of leave (paid at only £106).[22] It is worth mentioning here the ECJ ruling in the 1996 Gillespie case, which stipulated that maternity pay must not be 'set so low as to jeopardize the purpose of maternity leave' (*Joan Gillespie and others* v *Northern Health and Social Services Boards, Department of Health and Social Services Board*, 1996 [ECR], p I-00475 paragraph 25). The ruling in this case did make it clear that women on maternity leave were not entitled to full pay, but after the first six weeks of leave each mother is granted only £160 per week in Britain, which, if we calculate according to the average full-time worker's thirty-five-hour week, amounts to just £3.03 per hour, thus falling far short of the national minimum wage set at £5.05 per hour, as of October 2005. This means that the average worker, earning £430.93 per week, would lose a hefty £270 of her weekly earnings while on maternity leave. The problem also occurs with paternity leave, which is paid at the same rate but for only two weeks, amounting to a mere 25 per cent of the average paid holiday leave.

---

[22] Note that in the 1980s Britain became the only Member State in Europe to have *decreased* maternity rights.

These provisions, therefore, are not satisfactory, catering neither for low-income families in particular nor for the demands of modern family life in general. Now that dual earner and single-parent headed families are more prevalent than the traditional 'male breadwinner' model,[23] many families are simply unable to subsist on the meagre benefits available in Britain.[24] Moreover, these inadequate provisions serve to lessen the impact of attitudinal shifts towards more routine fathering (whether economically or psychosocially motivated). As much qualitative research of Britain's workers shows, the entitlement to unpaid parental leave is no more than a dead letter and, as it currently stands, statutorily provided paid leave relating to child-birth and subsequent care is primarily linked to an employee's physical and social function as 'mother' (Browne 2006).

Under the particular interpretation of the ETP as depicted by the ETD, special treatment in favour of pregnant workers is permitted on the view that such special treatment serves to protect them during a vulnerable time. Returning to the propositions with which this chapter began, this special treatment clause within the ETP is based upon the idea that individuals should only be treated equally in terms of specified relevant respects. The question is, of course, which respects are relevant? Bearing this question in mind, the ETP is particularly awkward in the context of pregnancy, where there is no male comparator, and in the context of primary childcare activities where it is *assumed* that there is no male comparator, i.e. primary childcare is not considered to be a relevant respect in which men and women should be treated equally in terms of financial provision. The 1984 ECJ ruling in the case of *Ulrich Hofmann v Barmer Ersatzkasse*, yet to be superseded, embodies this dilemma. Herr Hofmann (residing in Hamburg, Germany), the father of a new baby, claimed that he was being discriminated against on the grounds of sex, because he was denied access to paid benefits, only available to the mother, despite being his child's primary carer. Hofmann's circumstances were such that he had been granted unpaid leave by his employer after the compulsory maternity leave period of eight weeks ended, until the

---

[23] This relates to the Western European and the US context. See Hobson and Morgan (2002).

[24] Other provisions such as SureStart and Tax Credits are not discussed here but are of course relevant to the wider discussion (see Browne 2006).

child reached six months of age. During this period, Herr Hofmann was the primary carer of his child as the mother had returned to work. Had the mother availed herself of further statutory maternity leave until the child was six months, she would have been able to claim state-paid benefits of up to DM 25 per day. As this was available only to mothers, Hofmann was unable to claim such benefits (*Hofmann*, 1984, p. 03047). He argued, therefore, that the German maternity leave provision (*Mutterschutzgesetz*) was in breach of the ETP as defined by the ETD (26/207) and thus also of European Community Law as regards access to employment, vocational training and promotion, and working conditions.

In response, however, the ECJ ruled that the 'Directive 26/207 is not designed to settle questions concerning the organization of the family, or to alter the division of responsibility between parents' (*Hofmann*, 1984, p. 03047, summary paragraph 1). This is a stunning statement, since it clearly relies upon an a priori notion of what the division of responsibility between parents should be, i.e. that only mothers should be primary carers.

Moreover, the ECJ reserved the right of Member States to design their own provisions, which are;

intended to protect women in connection with 'pregnancy and maternity'. Directive 76/207 recognizes the legitimacy, in terms of the principle of equal treatment, of protecting a woman's need in two respects. First, it is legitimate to ensure the protection of a woman's biological condition during pregnancy and thereafter until such time as her physiological and mental functions have returned to normal after childbirth. Secondly, it is legitimate to protect the special relationship between a woman and her child over the period which follows pregnancy and childbirth, by preventing that relationship from being disturbed by the multiple burdens which would result from the simultaneous pursuit of employment. (*Hofmann*, 1984, p. 03047, summary paragraph 2)

Though the physical trauma of giving birth calls for a compulsory protective period of recovery and recuperation for the mother, it is important to draw attention to the ECJ's comments regarding the return to normal of the mother's 'mental functions', and the 'special relationship between a women and her child' – these are points to which we shall return in a moment.

The ECJ went on to justify its decision in the following terms:

such leave may legitimately be reserved to the mother to the exclusion of
any other person, in view of the fact that it is only the mother who may find
herself subject to undesirable pressures to return to work prematurely.
(*Hofmann*, 1984, p. 03047, summary paragraph 3)

As spelt out here, the ECJ considers that only mothers are 'subject to
undesirable pressures to return to work' soon after the arrival of a
new child. It is then at the discretion of the Member States to decide
the degree and the nature of protection to be offered to pregnant
women or new mothers in order 'to offset the disadvantages which
women, by comparison with men, suffer with regard to the retention
of employment' (*Hofmann*, 1984, p. 03047, summary paragraph 4).
The fact that fathers may experience the same difficulty in retaining a
close bond with the child because of financial and employment
obligations during the first few months is simply not considered.
Rather, it is stated that 'the Directive does not impose on member
states a requirement that they shall, as an alternative, allow such leave
to be granted to fathers, even where the parents so decide' (*Hofmann*,
1984, p. 03047, summary paragraph 5).

The details of Hofmann's complaint are pertinent. He argued,
against the interpretation of the ECJ, that the main objective of the
leave available to mothers *after* the compulsory maternity leave of
eight weeks (two weeks in Britain) until the baby is six months old
must be to secure the best interests of the *child* rather than of the
mother. If indeed this is the case, then there should be grounds upon
which the father (as well as the mother) may access paid leave
provisions, in accordance with the ETP. His claim is based upon the
following three observations;

1 'the fact that the leave is withdrawn in the event of the child's
   death ... demonstrates that the leave was created in the interests of
   the child and not of the mother' (*Hofmann*, 1984, p. 03047,
   objection paragraph 10). This is a particularly relevant point in the
   context of the ECJ's invocation of 'the protection of a woman's
   biological condition ... until such time as her physiological and
   mental functions have returned to normal after childbirth'. This
   rationale is used directly as a justification for excluding fathers

from access to paid 'maternity' leave beyond the mother's compulsory period of eight weeks in Germany.

2 'the optional nature of the leave [after the compulsory eight weeks] ... means that it cannot be said to have been introduced to meet imperative biological or medical needs' (*Hofmann*, 1984, p. 03047, objection paragraph 10). Again, this emphasizes the problems of invoking women's physiological and mental condition as rationale for denying paid leave to fathers post the compulsory period for mothers. Also we might add a criticism here of the ECJ's notion of the 'special relationship between a women and her child'. If such a special relationship with the child is only possible with the mother and is unquestionably vital to the child's well-being, then it does not make sense to make it optional to the mother. Moreover, in the event of the mother opting not to take advantage of this leave, as in the Hofmann case, the ETP would seem to promote the view that *no* parental care is better than paternal care!

3 'Lastly, the requirement that the woman should have been employed for a minimum period prior to childbirth; this indicates that it was not considered necessary to grant the leave in the interests of the mother, otherwise it ought to have been extended to all women in employment irrespective of the date on which their employment commenced' (*Hofmann*, 1984, p. 03047, objection paragraph 10). Even if, therefore, it cannot be shown that the policy was designed in the best interests of the child, Hofmann's contention is that the policy certainly was not intended to be in the best interests of the mother, and again if this is the case the rationale for excluding fathers from paid provision collapses.

According to Hofmann, the protection of the mother against the multiplicity of burdens imposed by motherhood and her employment could be achieved by non-discriminatory measures, such as permitting the father to enjoy the leave with pay, thereby creating a period of parental leave post the compulsory maternity leave.[25] That would release the mother from the responsibility of caring for the child, thereby enabling her to resume employment as soon as the compulsory

---

[25] As Ewing argues, 'If the law is to contribute to a genuine improvement of the position of women with children, it is crucial to ensure that parenting rights are extended to both parents' (Ewing 1996: 154).

protective maternity leave period had expired. Hofmann also maintained that the available options to parents should be in accordance with the ETP and the choice made in each case be the prerogative of the parents. In this way, moreover, men (as well as women) would be protected from being 'subject to undesirable pressures to return to work prematurely'.

Hofmann did not win his case in 1984. Yet the logic of his claim still stands up today, and it is imperative, I argue here, that we reconsider the dubious reasons for resisting Hofmann's compelling reinterpretation of the ETP. Judging by the comments contained within the European Court reports on Hofmann's case it seems that the final ruling was an uncomfortable one:

The Commission draws attention to the fact that, in a number of member states, social legislation is moving towards the grant of 'parental leave' or 'child-care leave' which is to be preferred to leave which is available to the mother alone. It is stated that it was considering whether to bring actions for failure to fulfil a treaty obligation against a number of member states which, in various forms, retained measures which were comparable to the maternity leave provided for by the German legislation. (*Hofmann*, 1984, p. 03047, grounds paragraph 13)

Certainly, one could argue that political considerations were decisive in this case, for to have fulfilled Hofmann his request would have been tantamount to forcing a Member State radically to reconfigure its domestic policy (and if it had, in this case in Germany, it would not have been long before all member states would have had to do the same). This aside, the only other justification for not considering 'paid leave for the purposes of primary child-care' as a relevant respect in which men and women should be treated equally is one based on stereotypical assumptions about what role men and women should respectively play in the lives of their children. Neither motivation nor justification is warranted. Also, here my previous comments on 'gender' at the beginning of the chapter are relevant. In the case of Hofmann, we are concerned with the fact that he should not be discriminated against purely because he is a man; we are not concerned with whether or not he has particular gender characteristics.

Clearly, gestation, parturition and breast-feeding are unique to women (and therefore rightfully protected by compulsory maternity leave), but the exclusive nature of these functions does not extend to 'parenting', which might more usefully be recognized as a shared responsibility of mothers and fathers. This view is echoed in a vast number of case studies. For instance, Burgess (1996, 1997), drawing upon extensive empirical research in conjunction with a wide-ranging review of numerous similar studies (such as those of Bell 1983; Colman and Colman 1988; and Pittmann 1993), asserts that 'what has been shown – and shown over and over again with almost painful ease – is how sex role *conditioning* drives a wedge between men and their parenting instincts' (Burgess 1997: 98, emphasis in the original; see also Gregg and Washbrook 2003).[26]

The biological function to procreate and breast-feed does not secure innately superior parenting skills. 'Parenting' demands a whole range of abilities (such as the ability to construct imaginative ways of playing, to communicate, to teach, to tend to sickness, to supervise, to dress, to bathe, to put to bed and simply to spend creative time with children), characteristics which, by any account, are not the sole preserve of one particular sex. This point is stressed by Burgess, who contends that parenting styles are determined by situation and not by sex. According to her, when fathers are exposed to the experience of being routine carer, their capacity for tending to children in different contexts is as varied as that of women, ranging from the model parent at one end of the spectrum to the hopelessly inept at the other. Moreover, there is mounting evidence that, given the opportunity, many fathers are in fact demanding to spend more time than ever with their children. This undoubtedly is the result of huge shifts in social attitudes of the new parenting generation and associated changing social norms (see Hatter 2002; Gregg and Washbrook 2003; O'Brien and Shemilt 2003; Browne 2006).

The likelihood of creating an environment in which parents are able to enact their duties or their express wishes, irrespective of their sex, is largely dependent on the dictates of societal ideals, organization and legal underpinnings. Unfortunately then, contemporary interpretations of the principle of equal treatment (particularly the

---

[26] In addition to incorporating contemporary sociological and psychological research in her work, Burgess draws from a large array of anthropological research stretching over many decades, ranging from classic studies, such as Malinowski (1927) and Mead (1935), through to more contemporary works such as Hewlett (1991).

way in which the ETD has prescribed the ETP) has shown itself to be limited in this respect by permitting the neglect of the 'male as parent' and in so doing directly perpetuating the stereotypes of 'gender' – a condition Fredman refers to as 'rigid role demarcation' (Fredman 1997: 206).

There has of course been a recent revolutionary moment in British social policy first referred to in the 2005 Labour Party Manifesto (LPM). There Blair's government set out proposals (which one would have to consider radical in the British context) to alter maternity leave provisions in order 'to give fathers more opportunities to spend time with their children ... including the option of sharing paid leave' (LPM, 2005, chapter 6). New policy proposals include the extension of statutory maternity pay to nine months[27] and the right for women to transfer up to six months of their paid maternity leave to fathers during the first year of the child's life from April 2007. These are extremely welcome developments in social policy terms, but once again they contain some serious limitations with unfortunate ramifications and are not in conformity with the principle of equal treatment argued for by Hofmann and advocated here.

First, even with the extension of leave for women, the low statutory pay is a deterrent to most dual income families. While all the details of this scheme are yet to be fleshed out, it looks likely that the new transferable leave will be available to the father *only* after three months of the mother's maternity leave. One feature which is certain, however, is that fathers will only be entitled to the statutory flat rate maternity pay (currently set at £106 per week), upon which it is extremely difficult for families to rely for any sustained period even as an income secondary to the average wage.

Second, the parents of a child are not allowed to take their leave simultaneously. The idea is that only when the mother returns to work will the father be able to begin his period of transferred leave (having exhausted his statutory paternity leave of two weeks), so that the total period of leave taken is continuous. For many parents, alternative arrangements might better suit their needs; for example, both might wish to take part-time leave simultaneously. This might be a much more reasonable financial arrangement for many families,

---

[27] There is also a pledge to extend maternity leave (paid at standard rate, currently £106 per week) to one year (Labour Party 2005: chapter 6).

where a pro-rata part-time wage in addition to half the statutory maternity pay would enable (and encourage) families to take the leave available to them without seriously jeopardizing their economic stability.[28] Furthermore, this arrangement would be more in line with an interpretation of the equal-treatment principle that would not be based on gender role stereotypes.

In addition, demographic changes and the ever growing concern that the next generation will not be financially self-sufficient in old age should be an economic motivator for politicians to promote the extension of paid parental/maternity leave to both parents (excluding the compulsory period only). Such provisions would invariably enable more women to remain in the labour market full time and, vitally, better to prepare for their old age in the form of occupational pensions. This is a long-term and very important concern for both individuals and the state when we consider that, even today, people aged eighty-five and over are the fastest-growing age group in the British population. There are now eighteen times as many 'over-eighty-fives – referred to by the Office for National Statistics (ONS) as the 'oldest old' – as there were in 1901 (1,104,000 compared with 61,000) and this figure is expected to more than double to 2,479,000 by 2031. What is more, for every man there are currently 257 women in this age group (ONS 2005a). In terms of the wider group of 11 million pensioners (those aged over sixty-five), 63 per cent (6.93 million) are women. The average income of women in retirement is just 57 per cent that of retired men. Only 13 per cent (1.43 million) of women pensioners receive a full basic state pension based on their own national insurance contributions.[29]

Only 56 per cent of working women are employed full-time, earning, as mentioned earlier, an average of 18 per cent less than men (and 40 per cent less for the 43 per cent who work part-time). Of these, only 38 per cent of working women are members of an occupational pension scheme. Consequently, according to the National Pensioners' Convention, one in four older women live below the poverty line and two out of every three of the pensioners who claim means-tested

---

[28] If the father, who has taken transferred leave, subsequently decides to return to work earlier than planned, the untaken leave is automatically lost to the family as a whole. This seems absurd, and it is not at all clear why it is part of the policy regulations.

[29] See National Pensioners' Convention www.npcuk.org for full discussion.

support are women. These alarming trends coincide with the fact that the first few years of the twenty-first century saw the lowest ever birth-rate in the history of Britain (ONS 2005b). Currently, the average income for a pension household is £12,400, which is less than half the national average wage, with 2.2 million pensioners living below the official poverty line (Brewer et al. 2005).

Indicative of the growing concern amongst European governments regarding top-heavy demographic trends, French prime minister (2005–7) Dominique de Villepin vouched to pay mothers £507 per month, up to a year, for every *third* child born, in order to provide an incentive for French parents to have more children – despite France already having the second-highest birth-rate in Europe. Similarly, demographic concerns provided the rationale behind Sweden's policy to encourage higher birth-rates. Generally regarded as having one of the most advanced, family friendly schemes in the world, Sweden pioneered paid maternity leave in 1955, which it later converted into paid parental leave in 1974. Given the extensions to the paid parental scheme since (currently paid at a high rate of income replacement by the state of 80 per cent of earnings and accompanied by the right to return to employment with protection against discrimination)[30], it is no surprise that Sweden has the highest female economic activity rates (82.6 per cent), has the third-highest fertility rate in Europe after Ireland[31] and France, and enjoys the highest male

[30] Current Swedish legislation provides the right to seven weeks of paid maternity leave prior to the birth and seven weeks after the birth for all women regardless of employment history. Both sexes are entitled to 480 days' (approx. thirteen months) leave up until the child's eighth birthday, if they have six months' employment history or twelve months over the previous two years. This is shared between the mother and the father, who can choose who will take the leave and when it will be taken. There are, however, sixty days that are tied specifically to each parent, i.e. thirty days each known as 'mamma month' and 'pappa month'. These distinct periods of leave are provided to encourage fathers to take leave. In a similar vein, in Norway parents are entitled to fifty-two weeks of parental leave at 80 per cent of their earnings or forty-two weeks of leave at 100 per cent of their earnings. Up to thirty-nine weeks of leave (at 80 per cent of earnings) or twenty-nine weeks leave (at 100 per cent of earnings) can be taken flexibly as reduced working hours. Where parental leave is taken in the form of reduced hours, the length of leave is extended correspondingly. Four weeks of the parental leave must be taken by the father, otherwise it will be lost.

[31] The high fertility rates in Ireland are related to low usage of contraception rather than comparatively generous state benefits.

take-up rates (77 per cent) for parental leave in Europe (see O'Brien and Shemilt 2003; Haas and Hwang 2005).

The gender stereotypes upon which British policy provision judgements are currently made not only deny men the plausible opportunity of becoming active routine parents (re the issue of pay) but also consequently designate the role of primary carer to women, regardless of the psychosocial preferences or economic needs of the individuals in question. Such judgements and the resulting character of state provision have had enormous impact on the general structure of society and the interrelated lifestyle choices that people have no option but to make vis-à-vis their employment trajectories and domestic arrangements. The particular interpretation of the principle of equal treatment discussed in this chapter has instigated misshapen policies which act to 'herd' individuals into self-fulfilling and self-perpetuating stereotypical roles. Though of course some people's choices indeed may coincide with expressed preferences which pertain to a binary understanding of 'gender', the 'herding effect' nevertheless sustains the robust nature of the status quo in contemporary society, replete with unnecessary demarcations along the lines of sex. This is perhaps a point to consider when assessing Hakim's preference theory (see chapter 9).

Conclusions

In this chapter, I have tried to illustrate in general that the common division of labour between normative social and political theory and policy design does not serve the contemporary objectives of relevant equality and justice well. To ignore the detail of social and institutional environments and structures into which normative principles are to be imported as political and legal objectives is in fact self-defeating. In a similar vein, we have seen the ways in which practitioners have unsuccessfully interpreted and implemented the principle of equal treatment and have thereby largely rendered counter-productive both sex discrimination Acts and specific rights designed to protect and financially sustain individuals. On the one hand, sociological, policy and economic analyses of inequality are predominantly concerned with how inequalities may be identified and measured, and with the nature of their causes and effects; on the other, normative theory is predominantly concerned with what kind of equality, if any, should be offered, and to whom. Yet the unfortunate lack of mutual engagement of the former and the latter all too frequently promotes an ineffective approach to the pursuit of social and political goals.

Specifically, using empirical examples, I have illustrated how patterns of inequality are based upon stereotypical assumptions about the capabilities of each sex, irrespective of normative and practical ambitions. The aim here has not been to prescribe how men and women, or each as parents, *should* act, but rather to show how the opportunity to fulfil various aspirations, preferences or needs is inhibited by the unjustified curtailment of choice. Such a curtailment is directly and systematically generated by the misguided widespread social and institutional assumptions that one sex necessarily commands superior parenting abilities. The majority of funded provisions for supporting the role of parents are available *only* to women, which leads to 'systemic dissonance' between the actual aspirations/ preferences of female *and* male workers and the structured environment in which their work–life balance choices are to be made. It is this inability to fulfil certain preferences, the resulting restrictions and the consequent social norms that lead to substantive inequality between men and women. Accordingly, we should critically interrogate the assumptions that underpin the purportedly sound interpretations of the principle of equal treatment and the stereotypes which they effectively uphold. In so doing, we should consider prising sex discrimination measures (specific protective measures excluded) away from the pursuit of an inadequately conceived pursuit of 'gender equality'. This, it is suggested here, would not only afford individuals far more freedom to explore and realize their preferences and needs, but also result in new social norms and institutional procedures which better lend themselves to the principle of equal treatment: the equal treatment of individuals who are alike in 'relevant respects' in such a way that is constructive and just. On the view presented here, a reinterpretation of what is 'relevant' for both men and women of the twenty-first century is well overdue.

References

Becker, G. (1981, 1991) *A Treatise on the Family* (Cambridge, MA: Harvard University Press).

(1985) 'Human Capital, Effort and the Sexual Division of Labour', *Journal of Labour Economics* 3: 33–58.

Bell, C. (1983) *Fathers, Childbirth and Work* (Manchester: Equal Opportunities Commission).

Brewer, M., Goodman, A., Shaw, J. and Shephard, A. (2005) *Poverty and Inequality in Britain 2005*. Commentary No. 99. FIS. London.

Browne, J. (2004) 'Resolving Gender Pay Inequality? Rationales, Enforcement and Policy', *Journal of Social Policy* 33, 4: 553–71.

(2006) *Gender Inequality and Sex Segregation in the Modern Labour Market* (Bristol: Policy Press).

Burgess, A. (1997) *Fatherhood Reclaimed: The Making of the Modern Father* (London: Vermillion).

Burgess, A. and Ruxton, S. (1996) *Men and Their Children: Proposals for Public Policy* (London: Institute for Public Policy Research).

Colman, A. and Colman, L. (1988) *The Father: Mythology and Changing Roles* (Wilmette, IL: Chiron).

Deakin, S. and Morris, G. (1998) *Labour Law* (London: Butterworths).

Dworkin, R. (1977) *Taking Rights Seriously* (Cambridge, MA: Harvard University Press).

EOC (2003) *Annual Report* (Manchester: EOC).

(2005a) *Facts about Men and Women in Great Britain* (Manchester: EOC).

(2005b) *Time to Deliver* (Manchester: EOC).

Equal Opportunities Review 117 (May 2003).

Equal Opportunities Review 106 (June 2002).

Ewing, K. (ed.) (1996) *Working Life: A New Perspective on Labour Law* (London: Lawrence and Wishart).

Fredman, S. (1997) *Women and the Law* (Oxford: Oxford University Press).

Gregg, P. and Washbrook, E. (2003) *The Effects of Early Maternal Employment on Understanding the Impact of Poverty on Children of the 90's*. CMPO Working Paper Series 03/070.

Haas, L. and Hwang, C. P. (2005) The Impact of Taking Parental Leave on Fathers' Participation in Childcare and Ties with Children: Lessons from Sweden Conference Paper. First International Conference – Community, Work and Family, 16–18 March 2005, Manchester, UK. See www.did.stu.mmu.ac.uk/cwf/Haas_HwangManchester.doc.

Habermas, J. (1983) 'Discourse Ethics: Notes on a Program of Philosophical Justification,' in J. Habermas, *Moral Consciousness and Communicative Action*, trans. C. Lenhardt and S. Weber Nicholsen, 1990 (Cambridge, MA: MIT Press), 43–115.

Hatter, W., Vinter, L. and Williams, R. (2002) *Dads on Dads: Needs and Expectations at Home and at Work* (Manchester: EOC).

Hepple, B. (1984) *Equal Pay and the Industrial Tribunals* (London: Sweet and Maxwell).

(1995) 'Social Values and European Law', *Current Legal Problems* 48, 2: 39–61.

(2002) 'Enforcement: The Law and Politics of Cooperation and Compliance', in B. Hepple (ed.), *Social and Labour Rights in a Global Context: International and Comparative Perspectives* (Cambridge: Cambridge University Press), 238–57.

Hewlett, B. (1991) *Intimate Fathers: The Nature and Content of Aka Pygmy Paternal Infant Care* (Michigan: University of Michigan Press).

Hobson, B. and Morgan, D. (2002) 'Introduction: Making Men into Fathers' in B. Hobson (ed.), *Making Men into Fathers: Men, Masculinities and the Social Politics of Fatherhood* (Cambridge: Cambridge University Press), 1–21.

IRS Employment Review (2004a) Issue 804, July 2004. IRS. See http://www.irser.co.uk/

(2004b) Issue 798, April 2004 IRS. See http://www.irser.co.uk/

Jarman, J. (1992) *Which Way Forward? Conceptual Issues from the Current Proposals To Amend the British Equal Pay Act.* Sociological Research Group Working Papers 8. University of Cambridge.

Kymlicka, W. (1990) *Contemporary Political Philosophy* (Oxford: Clarendon Press).

Labour Party (2005) *Labour Party Manifesto* (London: Labour Party).

Malinowski, B. (1927) *The Father in Primitive Psychology* (London: Kegan Paul).

Mead, M. (1935) *Sex and Temperament in Three Primitive Societies* (New York: Morrow).

Meehan, E. (1985) *Rights at Work: Campaigns and Policy in Britain and the United States* (Basingstoke: Macmillan).

Nagel, T. (1991) *Equality and Partiality* (Oxford: Oxford University Press).

Neathey, F., Dench, S., and Thomson, L. March (2003) Monitoring Progress towards Pay Equality: EOC Research Discussion Series. EOC. Manchester.

O'Brien, M. and Shemilt, I. (2003), *Working Fathers: Earning and Caring*, Research and Discussion Series (Manchester: Equal Opportunities Commission).

ONS (2005a) *The Demographic Characteristics of the Oldest Old in the United Kingdom.* Population Trends 120. Summer 2005 (London: ONS).

(2005b) 'Labour Market, More Lone Parents Working' at www.statistics.gov.uk as of 21 November 2005.

Pittmann, F. (1993) *Man Enough: Fathers, Sons, and the Search for Masculinity* (New York: Berkeley Publishing Co.).

Posner, R. (1992) *Economic Analysis of Law*, 4th ed (London: Little, Brown and Company.

Rubenstein, M. (1984) *Equal Pay for Work of Equal Value* (London: Macmillan).

(2004) 'Equal Value Procedures To Be Improved'. *Equal Opportunities Review* 121, July 2004 (London: LexisNexis Butterworths).

(2005) 'Amending the Sex Discrimination Act'. *Equal Opportunities Review*, 140, April 2005 (London: LexisNexis Butterworths).

Index